226.3
Pea

4.99

GOSPEL

JESUS OF NAZARETH

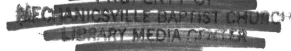
Serendipity House / P.O. Box 1012 / Littleton, CO 80160

TOLL FREE 1-800-525-9563 / www.serendipityhouse.com

02 03 04 05 06 / **201 series • CHG** / 10 9 8 7 6 5

1824

PROJECT ENGINEER:
Lyman Coleman

WRITING TEAM:
Richard Peace, Lyman Coleman, Andrew Sloan, Cathy Tardif

PRODUCTION TEAM:
Christopher Werner, Sharon Penington, Erika Tiepel

COVER PHOTO:
credit to come

CORE VALUES

Community: The purpose of this curriculum is to build community within the body of believers around Jesus Christ.

Group Process: To build community, the curriculum must be designed to take a group through a step-by-step process of sharing your story with one another.

Interactive Bible Study: To share your "story," the approach to Scripture in the curriculum needs to be open-ended and right brain—to "level the playing field" and encourage everyone to share.

Developmental Stages: To provide a healthy program in the life cycle of a group, the curriculum needs to offer courses on three levels of commitment: (1) Beginner Stage—low-level entry, high structure, to level the playing field; (2) Growth Stage—deeper Bible study, flexible structure, to encourage group accountability; (3) Discipleship Stage—in-depth Bible study, open structure, to move the group into high gear.

Target Audiences: To build community throughout the culture of the church, the curriculum needs to be flexible, adaptable and transferable into the structure of the average church.

ACKNOWLEDGMENTS

To Zondervan Bible Publishers
for permission to use
the NIV text,
The Holy Bible, New International Bible Society.
© 1973, 1978, 1984 by International Bible Society.
Used by permission of Zondervan Bible Publishers.

Questions & Answers

STAGE

1. What stage in the life cycle of a small group is this course designed for?

Turn to the first page of the center section of this book. There you will see that this 201 course is designed for the second stage of a small group. In the Serendipity "Game Plan" for the multiplication of small groups, your group is in the Growth Stage.

GOALS

2. What are the goals of a 201 study course?

As shown on the second page of the center section (page M2), the focus in this second stage is equally balanced between Spiritual Formation, Group Building, and Mission / Multiplication.

BIBLE STUDY

3. What is the approach to Bible Study in this course?

Take a look at page M3 of the center section. The objective in a 201 course is to discover what a book of the Bible, or a series of related Scripture passages, has to say to our lives today. We will study each passage seriously, but with a strong emphasis on practical application to daily living.

FOUR-STAGE LIFE CYCLE OF A GROUP

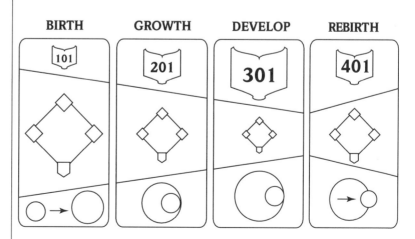

GROUP BUILDING

4. What is the meaning of the baseball diamond on pages M2 and M3 in relation to Group Building?

Every Serendipity course includes group building. First base is where we share our own stories; second base means affirming one another's stories; third base is sharing our personal needs; and home plate is deeply caring for each others' needs. In this 201 course we will continue "checking in" with each other and holding each other accountable to live the Christian life.

MISSION / MULTIPLICATION

5. What is the mission of a 201 group?

The mission of this 201 Covenant group is to discover the future leaders for starting a new group. (See graph on the previous page.) During this course, you will be challenged to identify three people and let this team use the Bible Study time to practice their skills. The center section will give you more details.

THE EMPTY CHAIR

6. How do we fill "the empty chair"?

First, pull up an empty chair during the group's prayer time and ask God to bring a new person to the group to fill it. Second, have everyone make a prospect list of people they could invite and keep this list on their refrigerator until they have contacted all those on their list.

AGENDA

7. What is the agenda for our group meetings?

A three-part agenda is found at the beginning of each session. Following the agenda and the recommended amount of time will keep your group on track and will keep the three goals of Spiritual Formation, Group Building, and Mission / Multiplication in balance.

SUBGROUPING

If you have nine or more people at a meeting, Serendipity recommends you divide into groups of 4–6 for the Bible Study. Count off around the group: "one, two, one, two, etc."—and have the "ones" move quickly to another room for the Bible Study. Ask one person to be the leader and follow the directions for the Bible Study time. After 30 minutes, the Group Leader will call "Time" and ask all subgroups to come together for the Caring Time.

ICE-BREAKERS

8. ***How do we decide what ice-breakers to use to begin the meetings?***

   Page M7 of the center section contains an index of ice-breakers in four categories: (1) those for getting acquainted in the first session or when a new person comes to a meeting; (2) those for the middle sessions to help you report in to your group; (3) those for the latter sessions to affirm each other and assign roles in preparation for starting a new group in the future; and (4) those for evaluating and reflecting in the final session.

GROUP COVENANT

9. ***What is a group covenant?***

   A group covenant is a "contract" that spells out your expectations and the ground rules for your group. It's very important that your group discuss these issues—preferably as part of the first session (also see page M32 in the center section).

GROUND RULES

10. ***What are the ground rules for the group?*** (Check those you agree upon.)

   ❐ PRIORITY: While you are in the course, you give the group meetings priority.

   ❐ PARTICIPATION: Everyone participates and no one dominates.

   ❐ RESPECT: Everyone is given the right to their own opinion and all questions are encouraged and respected.

   ❐ CONFIDENTIALITY: Anything that is said in the meeting is never repeated outside the meeting.

   ❐ EMPTY CHAIR: The group stays open to new people at every meeting.

   ❐ SUPPORT: Permission is given to call upon each other in time of need—even in the middle of the night.

   ❐ ADVICE GIVING: Unsolicited advice is not allowed.

   ❐ MISSION: We agree to do everything in our power to start a new group as our mission (see center section).

Introduction to Mark

The Gospel of Mark is, according to William Barclay, "the most important book in the world." He says this, of course, because Mark is the first written account of Jesus' life and ministry. To be sure, Jesus is mentioned in documents that predate Mark. Paul's epistles contain a number of such references. But in Mark's Gospel we find for the first time an account that focuses on Jesus: who he was and what he did.

Author

The author of this Gospel is nowhere named. However, there is a strong and unbroken tradition dating from early in the second century that Mark wrote this Gospel. That a Gospel was said to be written by someone who was not an apostle is remarkable (since generally those books written by apostles were accepted as authoritative) and is strong proof in itself that he wrote it. Many hold that Mark was the apostle Peter's secretary, and that this Gospel reflects Peter's point of view. Writing around A.D. 140 (or even earlier), Bishop Papias said: "Mark, having become the interpreter of Peter, wrote down accurately all that he remembered of the things said and done by our Lord, but not however in order." And indeed, when one compares the sermons of Peter in the book of Acts with the way the Gospel unfolds, there is great similarity. Furthermore, it is evident that Mark worked with Peter in Rome and that Peter felt a warm affection for him. Peter calls him "my son Mark" (1 Peter 5:13).

Who then is Mark? His full name was John Mark. He was a Jewish Christian. His mother's name was Mary and she was evidently well-to-do. The disciples used her home in Jerusalem as a meeting place in the days following Jesus' death and resurrection. After his miraculous escape from prison, the first place Peter went was to the home of Mary (Acts 12:12–17). As a young man, Mark was immersed in the life of the newly forming church.

When Paul and Barnabas went on their first missionary journey, John Mark went with them. Barnabas was Mark's cousin (Col. 4:10). Mark unaccountably left the party at Perga when they started inland to Asia. No reason is given for his departure, though it has been variously conjectured that he left because they were about to start on a notoriously dangerous road and he was afraid; or that he left because he chafed under Paul's domination of his kinsman Barnabas. Chrysostom, the early church father, said that Mark went home because he missed his mother! In any case, this led to a sharp disagreement between Paul and Barnabas when Barnabas wanted to take Mark along on the second missionary journey. As a result, Paul and Barnabas split up. Barnabas took Mark with him to Cyprus, while Paul teamed up with Silas (Acts 15:36–41). Later on, however, Paul and Mark were reconciled so that when Paul was in prison in Rome Mark was with him. Paul also sent him on a mission to Asia Minor (Col. 4:10; Philem. 24). During his final imprisonment, Mark is one of the people Paul wants with him (2 Tim. 4:11). Also, in his final letter to Timothy, Paul comments how helpful Mark has been to him in ministry.

Thus Mark was in an ideal position to write the first account of our Lord's life. As a young man, he may well have been an eyewitness of the final days of Jesus' life. He witnessed the founding of the first church in Jerusalem. He also worked with the two key leaders of first-century Christianity: Peter and Paul. From Peter he would have heard firsthand accounts about Jesus)\. From Paul he would have gained an appreciation for the Old Testament roots of Christianity and a sense of the significance of Jesus' life and death. Mark was evidently a very bright man (judging from the quality of his manuscript) who then took all this material and, under the guidance of the Holy Spirit, produced the first account of Jesus' life told in this new form of literature. Barclay may well be right that this is "the most important book in the world."

The Primacy of Mark

Did Mark write the first Gospel? For most of the history of the church, it was assumed that Matthew's Gospel was written first (hence the order of the four Gospels in our Bibles). However, based on the research of scholars early in the 20th century, it now seems more likely that Mark wrote first and that Luke and Matthew copied large chunks of his work. It is clear that there is a literary connection between the three Synoptic Gospels (Matthew, Mark and Luke) since they share so much common material. For example, even the parenthetical phrase in the story of the healing of the paralytic—"He said to the paralytic"—is in the identical place in all three accounts (see Matt. 9:6, Mark 2:10, and Luke 5:24). All but 24 verses of Mark appear in the other two Synoptics. To put this another way: there are 105 sections in Mark, and all but four occur in Matthew or Luke. In fact, Matthew uses nearly 90% of the sections in Mark (93 of the 105), including not just the same stories but 51% of Mark's very words.

The problem comes in explaining the nature of this connection. This is a complex question, but the best guess is that Matthew and Luke used what Mark wrote, polished up the language, and then added new material on the teaching of Jesus.

Date and Audience

When it comes to ancient manuscripts, it is difficult to pinpoint exactly when they were written. However, it is almost certain that Mark wrote his Gospel sometime between A.D. 50 and 70. It is clear from the text that he wrote to Greek-speaking readers who were not familiar with Jewish customs (see 7:3–4; 12:18; and 14:12 for examples of how Mark explains Jewish customs). Beyond this, we do not know for sure who his audience is or why he wrote, since he does not tell us in his Gospel.

One good guess is that Mark was writing to Christians living in Rome following the disastrous fire in that city in A.D. 64. This is what William Lane contends in his excellent commentary on Mark. And it does seem as if Mark was in Rome with Peter at the time of the crisis under Nero (see 1 Peter 5:13).

Lane points out that for a long time Christians were fairly anonymous in the Roman Empire. When and if they were noticed, it was assumed that they were just another exotic religious sect, of which there were many in the first century. They were often thought to be a splinter group within Judaism. But all this changed after Nero burned down Rome. Despite the generous aid he gave to the victims of the fire and the widespread urban renewal that followed the fire (in which he widened the roads, put in parks and rebuilt the city with fireproof construction materials), Nero continued to be blamed for the fire. Suetonius, the Roman historian, wrote that Nero "set fire to the city so openly that several former consuls did not venture to lay hands on his chamberlains although they caught them on their estates with tow and firebands."

To quell this criticism Nero needed a scapegoat, and the Christians were chosen for this dubious honor. As Lane says, Nero introduced the church to martyrdom. Tacitus wrote about the events in that day:

> Neither human resources, nor imperial munificence, nor appeasement of the gods, eliminated sinister suspicions that the fire had been instigated. To suppress this rumor, Nero fabricated scapegoats—and punished with every refinement the notoriously depraved Christians (as they were popularly called). ... First, Nero had self-acknowledged Christians arrested. Then, on their information, large numbers of others were condemned—not so much for incendiarism as for their anti-social tendencies. Their deaths were made farcical. Dressed in wild animals' skins, they were torn to pieces by dogs, or crucified, or made into torches to be ignited after dark as substitutes for daylight. Nero provided his Gardens for the spectacle. ... Despite their guilt as Christians, and the ruthless punishment it deserved, the victims were pitied. For it was felt that they were being sacrificed to one man's brutality rather than to the national interest.

If this was indeed the motivation for the writing of this Gospel, then what Mark has done is to put together the story of our Lord so as to guide and comfort the dying Christians. And indeed one finds in this Gospel many parallels between what the Christians in Rome were going through and what happened in the life of our Lord. He too suffered. He too had wilderness experiences. He too was misunderstood, betrayed, misused by officialdom, and finally killed. But—and this is the hope that Mark brings—his death was not in vain. In fact, his death was what his life was all about. It was by his death that his ministry was successfully completed. That his death had a purpose in God's scheme of things must have brought great comfort to the martyrs in Rome.

Themes

Certainly the death of Jesus is one of the central themes in this Gospel. In fact, Mark's Gospel has been called "a passion-narrative with an extended introduction." Of the 16 chapters, over one-third focus on the last week of Jesus' life and the events surrounding the Crucifixion. Furthermore, right from the beginning of the Gospel, the coming death of Jesus is present like a bass note throbbing beneath the action.

In fact, as the Gospel unfolds it becomes evident that who Jesus is will not become clear until his crucifixion. This is one reason why Jesus keeps silencing the demons who know him. People would misunderstand unless they knew he came to die. Even the Twelve do not understand fully who Jesus is prior to his death.

This leads to a second theme within this Gospel: Jesus as the teacher of the Twelve. We watch as the Lord calls the Twelve to join his band and then gradually reveals to them who he is. At first they don't understand. They see him as just a better-than-average rabbi: a teacher with unusual gifts to teach, heal, and cast out demons. Then they realize that his powers extend far beyond those of a rabbi. He has power over the elements, over evil, over disease, and even over death itself. It dawns on them that he is the Messiah. But even then they do not understand what kind of Messiah he is.

They are thinking of the Messiah as a conquering hero who will oust Rome and set up his kingdom in Jerusalem. Jesus must teach them that instead he has come to suffer and die. They never understand this—at least, not until he does indeed die and rise again. So, in Mark we see Jesus as the skilled teacher who must overcome the cultural bias and personal ambitions of the Twelve in order that they will come to see him for who he truly is.

A third theme in the book emerges from the first two. Mark is all about what it means to be a disciple of Jesus. It is not what the Twelve expected—all glory and triumph. To follow the one who came as a Suffering Servant who gave himself for others is to take up one's cross as the Lord did. There is a profound view of the Christian life in this Gospel.

Literary Focus

Mark created a new style of literature. This is the first example of a "Gospel"; i.e., a historical narrative of the life of Jesus with theological intention. A Gospel is not a biography, in that it omits much of what we have come to expect in that type of writing. There is no mention in Mark of the childhood of Jesus, of what he looked like, of who his friends were, of what events shaped his early imagination, etc. Instead, Mark plunges straightway into the adult life of Jesus. In fact, he only deals with the last three years of his life. Even within that narrow focus, Mark is highly selective. He focuses primarily on one event: the death of Jesus. The story of Jesus' final week occupies over one-third of the story.

Each Gospel writer has his own vantage point. Matthew wrote to a Jewish audience and told the story of King Jesus, the son of David, who came as the long-expected Messiah. Luke wrote about the Son of Man who came to seek and save the needy and the outcasts. John wrote about Jesus, the divine Son of God. Mark, however, focuses on Jesus the Suffering Servant who died for the sake of others. Mark wrote to Gentile Christians who themselves were suffering and dying and to whom it would be a great encouragement to remember that their Lord, in whose name they are dying, walked the same path as they.

Style

Mark's style of writing is distinctive. He uses short, punchy sentences often linked together by the word "and." His verbs are active and his pace is rapid. Yet, despite the way he hurries through the material, his account is rich in vivid eyewitness detail. For example, when Mark tells about the blessing of the children, he alone points out that Jesus first took the children into his arms (Mark 10:13–16).

An interesting thing that Mark does is to sandwich a story in between the beginning and the end of another story. For example, the first time he does this is in 3:20–35. He begins by talking about the concerns that Jesus' family had and their decision "take charge of him." In between this decision and their arrival at his place of ministry, Mark relates the story of how the teachers of the Law concluded that Jesus was possessed by Beelzebub. The section ends with Jesus' family outside the house asking for him. Mark interposes two stories when they interconnect and interpret each other.

Central to the Gospel as a literary genre is what Lightfoot calls the "little stories" that make up the account. Rather than a running narrative, a Gospel is a series of stories about Jesus pieced together by each author. Sometimes the same stories are used in different ways in different Gospels. These little stories (or "pericopes") are, of course, what the Christian community memorized and retold to one other. Out of the great pool of stories about Jesus, Mark selects certain ones and puts them in a particular order that will communicate what he wants to say about Jesus.

Outline

In Mark's Gospel there is a very careful and deliberate ordering of the stories. The result is a skillfully crafted outline. In fact, Mark has told the story of Jesus in a highly skilled and remarkably sophisticated way. This cannot have been easy given the material he had to use. Mark could not sit down and start from scratch to tell Jesus' story. Rather, he had to use the stories everyone knew in the way they knew them. He could not alter them. He was merely the chronicler of the tradition, not the creator of it. The church would not have used his work if it contained spurious tales or if he had mistold stories. No, Mark's creativity under the guidance of the Holy Spirit came at the level of choosing which stories to set next to each other. As you read through the Gospel, be alert to the significance of the sequence of stories as they unfold.

Mark does not put his stories in chronological order as we might expect, given the way history is written today (though overall there is a rough chronology to the story). Instead, he groups his stories thematically. Mark uses several organizing principles simultaneously. For one thing, it is clear that he has structured his story *geographically*. Jesus' ministry begins up north in Galilee and then he moves down to Jerusalem, where he is finally killed. Mark also structures the story in terms of *Jesus' unfolding ministry:* preparation, proclamation, and completion. There is also an unfolding vision of *who Jesus is.* In broad terms, the first half of the book focuses on the discovery of Jesus as the Messiah, and the second half on the discovery of Jesus as the Son of God. In terms of the *disciples' growing awareness,* they move from experiencing Jesus as an exceptional rabbi, to seeing him as a man of power, and then as the healer of hardened hearts. After Caesarea Philippi and their realization that he is the Messiah, they next know him as a teacher. In Jerusalem during the final week of his life, they come to realize that he is the Son of God.

THREE-PART AGENDA

ICE-BREAKER
15 Minutes

BIBLE STUDY
30 Minutes

CARING TIME
15–45 Minutes

 LEADER: Be sure to read pages 3–5 in the front of this book, and go over the ground rules on page 5 with the group in this first session. See page M7 in the center section for a good ice-breaker. Have your group look at pages M1–M5 in the center section and fill out the team roster on page M5.

TO BEGIN THE BIBLE STUDY TIME
(Choose 1 or 2)

1. What is the strangest thing you have ever eaten?

2. What desert area have you ever seen or visited?

3. When you were a kid, who kept you on the "straight and narrow path" and made sure you didn't get out of line?

READ SCRIPTURE & DISCUSS
(If you don't have time for all the questions in this section, conclude the Bible Study [30 min.] by answering question #7.)

1. Who is the wildest preacher you have ever heard? How did you respond to their message?

2. Many people came from Judea and Jerusalem to listen to John and get baptized. What qualities of a preacher or church (or small group) would bring you all the way into the "desert region" in order to get involved?

3. Why is John the Baptist so important to the story of Jesus? How well do you think he fulfilled Isaiah's prophecy (vv. 2–3)?

John the Baptist Prepares the Way

1 **The beginning of the gospel about Jesus Christ, the Son of God.**

²**It is written in Isaiah the prophet:**

> **"I will send my messenger ahead of you,**
> **who will prepare your way"—**
> ³**"a voice of one calling in the desert,**
> **Prepare the way for the Lord,**
> **make straight paths for him.' "**

⁴**And so John came, baptizing in the desert region and preaching a baptism of repentance for the forgiveness of sins.** ⁵**The whole Judean countryside and all the people of Jerusalem went out to him. Confessing their sins, they were baptized by him in the Jordan River.** ⁶**John wore clothing made of camel's hair, with a leather belt around his waist, and he ate locusts and wild honey.** ⁷**And this was his message: "After me will come one more powerful than I, the thongs of whose sandals I am not worthy to stoop down and untie.** ⁸**I baptize you with water, but he will baptize you with the Holy Spirit."**

The Baptism and Temptation of Jesus

⁹**At that time Jesus came from Nazareth in Galilee and was baptized by John in the Jordan.** ¹⁰**As Jesus was coming up out of the water, he saw heaven being torn open and the Spirit descending on him like a dove.** ¹¹**And a voice came from heaven: "You are my Son, whom I love; with you I am well pleased."**

¹²**At once the Spirit sent him out into the desert,** ¹³**and he was in the desert forty days, being tempted by Satan. He was with the wild animals, and angels attended him.**

4. What purpose do you see in Jesus' baptism and in his temptation (see notes on vv. 9 and 13)? How would these events prepare him for his public ministry?

5. John the Baptist prepared "the way for the Lord." Who prepared the way for the Lord in your life?

6. As Jesus came out of the water when he was baptized, what did the voice from heaven say? What would you like to hear God say to you?

7. What brought you to this study and what are you hoping to get out of it?

CARING TIME

1. Has your group agreed on its group covenant and ground rules (see page 5 in the front of this book)?

2. Have you filled out your team roster (see page M5 in the center section)? Like any winning team, every position needs to be covered.

3. Who is someone you would like to invite to this group for next week?

Share prayer requests and close in prayer. Be sure to pray for "the empty chair" (p. 4).

Notes—Mark 1:1–13

Summary. This short prologue (which probably actually extends to verse 15) is rich in theological insight regarding the person and work of Jesus. In a few brief sentences, Mark's use of imagery and quotes from the Old Testament evokes a dramatic picture of Jesus as the one who fulfills the Old Testament hope for the coming reign of God ushered in by the Messiah.

1:1 *gospel.* Literally, "good news." At this time, this word was used to describe the birth of a new king or to announce a great military victory. This context made it an especially appropriate word to describe the story of Jesus.

the Son of God. In the Old Testament this term was used to describe angels and divine figures (Dan. 3:25), as well as Israel's kings (Ps. 2:7), as figures who exercised a God-like authority over the people. In a Christian context, the phrase came to identify Jesus' divine nature as the One who fully bears all the characteristics of God.

> *The essence of repentance is a change in the way one thinks and lives so as to come into line with God's ways: it is a moral U-turn in which one turns from sin to pursue God.*

1:2–3 The Jews expected that an Elijah-like figure would precede the Messiah and announce his coming (see Mal. 3:1,4:5; Mark 9:4). In typical rabbinic fashion, Mark has combined several Old Testament texts—Mal. 3:1 (v. 2) and Isa. 40:3 (v. 3)—by which he shows that John's coming was foretold, that this "messenger" would pave the way for the Lord, and thus that Jesus was, indeed, the long-promised Messiah.

1:3 *make straight paths for him.* When a king or a royal figure was planning to visit or pass through a town, a messenger would be sent on ahead of the royal entourage so that the towns along the way could get things ready for his coming, literally straightening and smoothing the roads. In this context, making straight paths for the Lord implies repentance from sin (Mark 1:15).

1:4 *And so John came.* The promised messenger turns out to be John the Baptist, who spread the message of radical repentance and preparation.

baptizing. When Gentiles converted to Judaism they were required to bathe in a river as part of the ceremony. This signified that—in a symbolic way— their sins had been washed away. It was highly unusual, however, for *Jews* to submit to such a rite, and the fact that they did signals, perhaps, the desperation they felt at that point in history.

the desert region. This was the term used for a particular area in Israel located in the lower Jordan Valley between central Judea and the Dead Sea. This region was some 10 to 15 miles wide and extended for nearly 60 miles. It was a desolate and blistering-hot place, consisting of jagged limestone precipices and sparse vegetation. It was not a nice place to live!

a baptism of repentance. Their washing with water represented the removal of their sins. However, this was not meant simply as a ritual to be observed but as a sign of a change of heart and action. The essence of repentance is a change in the way one thinks and lives so as to come into line with God's ways: it is a moral U-turn in which one turns from sin to pursue God.

forgiveness of sins. Sin is a moral debt owed to God for violating God's will and nature. The ultimate need for humanity is to experience divine forgiveness for its attitude and lifestyle of rebellion.

1:5 *The whole Judean countryside.* Mark uses a hyperbole (literally, "all the Judean country") to show John's enormous popularity. Israel had been without a prophet for more than 300 years, and John certainly looked and talked like a prophet.

all the people of Jerusalem. It was a difficult 20-mile trip from Jerusalem to where John was baptizing, and yet the crowds came.

the Jordan River. John's ministry of baptism had a special meaning in this particular river which had an important place in Israel's history. After the exodus from Egypt, it was the miraculous crossing of this river that brought the people of Israel into the land God had promised them (Josh. 3). John's ministry in the Jordan River was a call for the people to once again come into the wilderness and cross over the river in order to experience the fulfillment of God's promise regarding the Messiah.

> *Sin is a moral debt owed to God for violating God's will and nature. The ultimate need for humanity is to experience divine forgiveness for its attitude and lifestyle of rebellion.*

1:6 *camel's hair / leather belt.* This description of John's clothes, parallel to that found in 2 Kings 1:8 which describes what the prophet Elijah wore, is meant to identify John as the prophet who came in the spirit and power of Elijah.

locusts and wild honey. The locusts he ate could be either an insect (Lev. 11:22–23) or a kind of bean from the locust tree. Honey could refer either to what bees produce or to the sap of a certain tree. In either case, this was the food eaten by the poorest of people.

1:7 Although John was recognized as an especially important prophet, his emphasis was that the one to come after him was so far superior to him that John could not be considered worthy to perform even the humblest of tasks in his service.

1:8 *baptize you ... with the Holy Spirit.* This dramatic promise summed up all the hopes the people of Israel had for their future. For the first-century Jew, this statement would not have referred to some type of personal spiritual experience, but to that time when God, through pouring out his Spirit upon the people as a whole, would establish a wondrously new social order in which oppression was vanquished and justice, peace, fullness and freedom would characterize the life of the nation (Isa. 32:15–20; 44:3–5). It was the time when God's reign would break into history for all the world to see. This day would occur when the Messiah came. It was this expectation that moved people to respond so powerfully to John's message.

1:9 *At that time Jesus came.* In the midst of this supercharged atmosphere—one foretold by Old Testament prophets (vv. 2–3), prepared by a New Testament prophet (vv. 4,6–7), and witnessed by the expectant crowds (v. 5)—Jesus starts his ministry. The subsequent drama of his baptism and temptation (vv. 9–13) brings in to this already impressive scene a supernatural host—God the Father, God the Holy Spirit and, of course, God the Son (v. 11), as well as angels and Satan himself (v. 13). As the next figure on the scene after John (v. 4), Mark makes it clear that Jesus is the one John anticipated.

baptized. By allowing himself to be baptized, Jesus identified with the people of Israel and with their sin (though he himself was without sin—1 Peter 2:22), prefiguring his death for sin a few years hence.

1:10 *heaven being torn open and the Spirit descending on him like a dove.* This is the divine confirmation of Jesus' ministry as the bearer of the Spirit sent by God (Isa. 61:1–3).

1:11 *a voice.* These words from God are directed to Jesus, not to the crowds. They are an unqualified affirmation of him as he is about to launch his ministry. In the days ahead it will be Jesus' task to make known to Israel who he is.

1:12 *the Spirit sent him.* The same Spirit who had come to Jesus in such affirming power now sends him forth to this time of testing.

desert. Literally, "wilderness." Jesus, like Israel after the Exodus, likewise must undergo a period of testing to affirm his loyalty to God.

1:13 *forty days ... tempted.* After Israel was delivered from Egypt, the people spent 40 years in the wilderness during which time they rebelled against God and failed to trust in his promises (Num. 14:26–35). Mark alludes to this experience to indicate how Jesus likewise was tested for 40 days, but came through without rebelling. Thus, he was uniquely prepared to carry on God's will in a way Israel as a nation never did.

wild animals. For the Christians to whom this letter was written (who were facing wild beasts in the Roman Coliseum), it must have been comforting to know that Jesus had also faced such beasts and was sustained by angels.

13

2 Jesus' Ministry—Mark 1:14–45

THREE-PART AGENDA

ICE-BREAKER
15 Minutes

BIBLE STUDY
30 Minutes

CARING TIME
15–45 Minutes

 LEADER: If there's a new person in your group in this session, start with an ice-breaker (see page M7 in the center section). Then begin the session with a word of prayer. If you have more than nine in your group, see the box about the "Subgrouping" on page 4. Count off around the group: "one, two, one, two, etc."—and have the "ones" move quickly to another room for the Bible Study.

TO BEGIN THE BIBLE STUDY TIME
(Choose 1 or 2)

1. Where did you go the first time you went away from home? How did you feel?

2. What is the worst illness or injury you've ever had?

3. What is the most amazing thing you've ever witnessed?

READ SCRIPTURE & DISCUSS
(If you don't have time for all the questions in this section, conclude the Bible Study [30 min.] by answering question #7.)

1. What is the best thing that has happened to you lately?

2. Why did the disciples decide to follow Jesus? What is it about Jesus that would make you follow him?

3. What is most striking to you about the encounter between Jesus and the evil spirit (vv. 21–28)?

The Calling of the First Disciples

¹⁴After John was put in prison, Jesus went into Galilee, proclaiming the good news of God. ¹⁵"The time has come," *he said. "The kingdom of God is near. Repent and believe the good news!"*

¹⁶As Jesus walked beside the Sea of Galilee, he saw Simon and his brother Andrew casting a net into the lake, for they were fishermen. ¹⁷"Come, follow me," Jesus said, "and I will make you fishers of men." ¹⁸At once they left their nets and followed him.

¹⁹When he had gone a little farther, he saw James son of Zebedee and his brother John in a boat, preparing their nets. ²⁰Without delay he called them, and they left their father Zebedee in the boat with the hired men and followed him.

Jesus Drives Out an Evil Spirit

²¹They went to Capernaum, and when the Sabbath came, Jesus went into the synagogue and began to teach. ²²The people were amazed at his teaching, because he taught them as one who had authority, not as the teachers of the law. ²³Just then a man in their synagogue who was possessed by an evil[a] spirit cried out, ²⁴"What do you want with us, Jesus of Nazareth? Have you come to destroy us? I know who you are—the Holy One of God!"

²⁵"Be quiet!" said Jesus sternly. "Come out of him!" ²⁶The evil spirit shook the man violently and came out of him with a shriek.

²⁷The people were all so amazed that they asked each other, "What is this? A new teaching—and with authority! He even gives orders to evil spirits and they obey him." ²⁸News about him spread quickly over the whole region of Galilee.

4. After a hectic day of helping others, Jesus needed some time to be alone and pray (v. 35). What do you think he prayed for? What do you do when you need to get away and be with God?

5. According to verses 38–39, how did Jesus view his mission?

6. Despite what Jesus told the leper he healed (vv. 43–44), what did this man do and with what result? What would you have done if you had been in this man's shoes?

7. Jesus healed many people of destructive beliefs and physical ailments. What would Jesus have to "cast out" of your life in order to help you live more fully for God?

CARING TIME

(Choose 1 or 2 of these questions before closing in prayer. Be sure to pray for the empty chair.)

1. How comfortable do you feel sharing your struggles with this group?

2. Who is someone you could invite to this group?

3. How can the group help you in prayer this week?

Jesus Heals Many

29As soon as they left the synagogue, they went with James and John to the home of Simon and Andrew. 30Simon's mother-in-law was in bed with a fever, and they told Jesus about her. 31So he went to her, took her hand and helped her up. The fever left her and she began to wait on them.

32That evening after sunset the people brought to Jesus all the sick and demon-possessed. 33The whole town gathered at the door, 34and Jesus healed many who had various diseases. He also drove out many demons, but he would not let the demons speak because they knew who he was.

Jesus Prays in a Solitary Place

35Very early in the morning, while it was still dark, Jesus got up, left the house and went off to a solitary place, where he prayed. 36Simon and his companions went to look for him, 37and when they found him, they exclaimed: "Everyone is looking for you!"

38Jesus replied, "Let us go somewhere else—to the nearby villages—so I can preach there also. That is why I have come." 39So he traveled throughout Galilee, preaching in their synagogues and driving out demons.

A Man With Leprosy

40A man with leprosy b came to him and begged him on his knees, "If you are willing, you can make me clean."

41Filled with compassion, Jesus reached out his hand and touched the man. "I am willing," he said. "Be clean!" 42Immediately the leprosy left him and he was cured.

43Jesus sent him away at once with a strong warning: 44"See that you don't tell this to anyone. But go, show yourself to the priest and offer the sacrifices that Moses commanded for your cleansing, as a testimony to them." 45Instead he went out and began to talk freely, spreading the news. As a result, Jesus could no longer enter a town openly but stayed outside in lonely places. Yet the people still came to him from everywhere.

a23 Greek *unclean,* also in verses 26 and 27
b40 The Greek word was used for various diseases affecting the skin—not necessarily leprosy.

Notes—Mark 1:14–45

Summary. In his first major unit (1:14–4:34), Mark presents a series of stories that show Jesus primarily in his role as a teacher. At this point, this is the category by which the people (including his disciples) understand who he is. This unit also records the various responses Jesus encounters to his teaching. The crowds in general are amazed and flock to him (1:21–45), but he soon encounters the opposition of the religious leaders (2:1–3:6). Mark 3:7–35 shows four major responses to Jesus, while the parables in chapter 4 serve as a reflection upon the meaning of those responses.

1:14–15 His preparation complete, Jesus begins his ministry. These are transition verses in which Mark defines the nature of Jesus' ministry and summarizes his message.

1:14 *After John was put in prison.* There is a gap of perhaps a year between the incidents recorded in Mark 1:9–13 and those recorded here. The story of John's imprisonment is told in Mark 6:17–29.

Galilee. This was the northern province of Palestine. It was small, some 25 by 35 miles in size, with a population in the time of Jesus of approximately 350,000 (100,000 of whom were Jews). Galilee was a rich farming and fishing region. Its Jewish population was considered rebellious in spirit, and lax when it came to religious matters. Those living in Jerusalem considered Galilee a cultural backwater populated by unsophisticated, uneducated country folk who spoke with an accent.

1:15 *The time has come.* That event—long expected and desired—had now come to pass in Israel. It was the fullness of time and the Messiah had entered history.

kingdom of God. The Jews regarded themselves as God's special people. He alone was their King. Yet they were under the domination of Rome. Caesar functioned as their king. Still, they were confident that one day the Messiah would rescue them. They fantasized that he would be a bloody warrior-king with invincible power who would lead Israel to a military victory and then establish Jerusalem as the capital of the world. It will take Jesus' whole ministry to show that he is not this sort of Messiah. In the end, it took his death and resurrection before even his disciples saw that he had quite a different sort of kingdom in mind.

> *While repentance is a turning away from sin to pursue God, to believe means to entrust oneself to God, counting on God to be true to his promises.*

believe. While repentance is a turning away from sin to pursue God, to believe means to entrust oneself to God, counting on God to be true to his promises. The object of belief here is the "good news" that in Jesus the kingdom of God has arrived. "The rest of the Gospel ... consists of illustrations of the way in which the deeds and words and character of Jesus himself brought this sovereignty of God to bear on his people. Wherever he was, there people found themselves confronted with the 'kingdom of God' " (Moule).

1:17 Jesus calls these men in terms they could understand. In asking them to "follow" him, he was inviting them to join his band of disciples. Simon and Andrew would have been familiar with rabbis who had small groups of followers. In telling them he would make them "fishers of men," he defined their task using a metaphor they understood: they would be seeking converts to his teaching.

1:18 *At once they left.* According to verse 14, Jesus had been preaching in Galilee. These fishermen probably had the chance to hear his message prior to their call. Still, what they did was an act of great faith and courage. In the first century you lived where you were born, you stayed in your family cluster, and you took up your father's occupation. This was a decisive leaving of the old ways in order to follow Jesus.

1:20 *the hired men.* James and John came from a middle-class family. Their father Zebedee had men working for him and a boat with which to trawl the lake for fish. (See Luke 5:3,10, where it appears that Simon also had a boat.)

1:21–28 With his four newly chosen disciples present, Jesus' first public act of ministry recorded by Mark occurs in a synagogue. Here, with God's chosen people assembled, Jesus makes his presence known by the quality of his teaching and by his extraordinary power over the demonic.

1:21 Capernaum. A town on the north end of the Sea of Galilee, three miles west of the Jordan River. It was a center of the fishing industry and the site of a custom's post.

synagogue. In first-century Israel, the temple in Jerusalem was the sole site for sacrifices and was attended by numerous priests and other officials. In contrast, there were synagogues in each population center which people attended each week for worship and instruction. Synagogues were run by lay committees with no professional clergy. Anyone could speak as long as he had permission from the leaders.

1:22 the teachers of the law. These were the scribes, men charged with the responsibility of interpreting and applying God's law to the people. They had developed an extensive tradition of interpretation which defined what it meant to keep the Law in all manner of circumstances. Their teaching was a matter of affirming and conserving Jewish tradition through reciting what earlier rabbis had taught. In contrast, Jesus' teaching had a fresh, direct, penetrating quality about it.

1:23 an evil spirit. Malignant, supernatural beings, able to harm and even possess people. These were Satan's legions. In overcoming this evil spirit, Jesus demonstrated his power over Satan. This is the first encounter in what would be an ongoing battle.

1:24 What do you want with us. At first the evil spirit is defiant and resistant.

I know who you are. By identifying Jesus, first using his human name and then his divine title, the demon hoped to gain mastery over Jesus. It was believed that knowledge of a person's true identity (or secret name) gave one power over that person. It does not work with Jesus however!

the Holy One of God. The evil spirit recognizes Jesus for who he is—the divine Son of God. In contrast, it will be quite some time before anyone, even the disciples, understands this.

1:25–26 Jesus' word of authority over the spirit is irresistible.

1:25 Be quiet! In the beginning stages of his ministry, Jesus did not want his identity or power spo-ken about publicly, probably because people would have misunderstood the meaning of his ministry. Before Jesus could allow himself to be identified, he had to make sure that people knew that he was not the militaristic, nationalistic Messiah people imagined was coming. In contrast, his messiahship would be marked by service, suffering and, ultimately, death on behalf of his people.

1:27 Mark notes the two things about Jesus that caught the attention of the people: the quality of his teaching and the power of his actions.

amazed. A word used repeatedly in Mark to describe the response of the people to Jesus: here to his word of power, and previously (in v. 22) to his word of instruction. Their amazement, however, contains not only joy but some alarm (even fear). Who is this man who possesses such unsuspected power? Still, such an action would have been interpreted only as confirmation that he was indeed a powerful teacher. Some exceptional rabbis were credited with having the power to exorcize demons and heal the sick.

1:28 News about him spread. People witnessed amazing power and heard extraordinary teaching, so it is not at all surprising that they told everyone they met what happened in the synagogue.

1:29–31 In contrast to his public display of power in the synagogue, Jesus' next act of healing is quiet and private.

1:31 took her hand. A detail that only an eyewitness such as Peter (Mark's apparent source) would know about.

The fever left her. This was a real, immediate cure. She suffered none of the weakness that normally follows when a fever breaks.

wait on them. In a Jewish home, unless a family was wealthy enough to have servants, the women would prepare and serve the meal. Understandably, Peter's mother-in-law would have been anxious to have everything in order, since her son-in-law was bringing home such an important guest.

1:32 after sunset. Since healing was forbidden on the Sabbath, they came only after the sun set, signalling the end of the Sabbath.

1:34 *drove out many demons.* First-century exorcists used elaborate incantations, special spells and magic apparatus to cast out demons, in contrast to Jesus, whose word alone sufficed.

would not let the demons speak. See note on verse 25.

1:35 *he prayed.* In the midst of great success, Jesus is quick to acknowledge his dependence on God as the source of his power.

1:36 In contrast to Jesus who sought the Father's will, Peter was simply following the will of the people. It seemed natural to him to stay around where Jesus was so appreciated!

1:38 With this verse Mark ends his account of an incredibly busy day in the life of Jesus.

so I can preach there also. Jesus is determined to carry on his central mission, which is proclaiming ("preaching") the kingdom of God (see vv. 14–15).

Let us go. Thus Jesus begins his preaching tour of Galilee. His was to be an itinerant ministry.

1:40–45 Mark ends the first chapter with an account of a powerful healing. Jesus once again does battle with the power of evil. Leprosy is a particularly apt illustration of the nature of Satan's work. It brings with it progressive disintegration—both physical and psychological.

1:40 *leprosy.* No disease was dreaded more than leprosy, since it brought not only physical disfigurement but social banishment.

came to him. What the leper did was forbidden by law. The leper should have sought to avoid drawing near Jesus so as not to render him religiously unclean. The rabbis taught that if a leper passed by a clean man, the clean man would not become unclean. However, if the leper stopped, then the clean man would become unclean.

1:41 *Filled with compassion.* Human suffering evoked a deep, affective response from Jesus. He was not afraid of strong emotions.

touched. Actually touching a leper was unimaginable to most first-century people. Not only did one risk contracting the disease, but such contact made the well person ritually impure and thus unable to participate in the religious life of the community. The effect of Jesus' touch on this leper must have been overwhelming.

> *Human suffering evoked a deep, affective response from Jesus. He was not afraid of strong emotions.*

1:42 *Immediately.* This is a favorite word for Mark. In this context it shows the immediacy and efficacy of Jesus' word. It is reminiscent of the word of God in creation as seen in Genesis 1 in which "And God said ..." is immediately followed by "And it was so."

1:44 *offer the sacrifices.* In Leviticus 14:1–32 the ritual is outlined whereby a leper is declared "clean." Such certification was vital to a leper: it was that person's way back into normal contact with human society.

1:45 *talk freely.* Jesus' plea was to no avail. The leper's joy could not be contained. He told everyone how he came to be healed.

lonely places. Mark began this cycle of stories with Jesus emerging from the wilderness in order to start his ministry. This section ends with him back in a place of isolation, driven there by the disobedience of the leper (understandable though it may be) and thus hindered in his Galilean ministry.

the people still came to him. This is the point which Mark wants to make in this opening description of Jesus' ministry: Jesus is immensely popular with the common people. In his next section (2:1–3:6), Mark will show that, in contrast, he was not at all popular with the religious leaders.

3 Healing a Paralytic—Mark 2:1–17

THREE-PART AGENDA

ICE-BREAKER
15 Minutes

BIBLE STUDY
30 Minutes

CARING TIME
15–45 Minutes

> **LEADER:** If there's a new person in your group in this session, start with an ice-breaker (see page M7 in the center section). Then begin the session with a word of prayer. If you're following the 13-week study plan, allow 60 minutes for the Bible Study time, as you are covering questions from two sessions. Follow the usual agenda for the Ice-Breaker and Caring Time, choosing those questions from either session.

TO BEGIN THE BIBLE STUDY TIME
(Choose 1 or 2)

1. What was a memorable prank you pulled off with your friends in high school or college?

2. For what "sold-out" event (concert, ballgame, etc.) have you been able to get tickets? How?

3. Who knows you so well they can "read your mind"?

READ SCRIPTURE & DISCUSS
(If you don't have time for all the questions in this section, conclude the Bible Study [30 min.] by answering question #7.)

1. In a big emergency, what four friends would you call first?

2. How would you feel if you were the paralytic when your friends decided to help you "drop in on Jesus"?

3. Why did Jesus say to the paralytic, "Son, your sins are forgiven" (v. 15)? With what results?

Jesus Heals a Paralytic

2 *A few days later, when Jesus again entered Capernaum, the people heard that he had come home. ²So many gathered that there was no room left, not even outside the door, and he preached the word to them. ³Some men came, bringing to him a paralytic, carried by four of them. ⁴Since they could not get him to Jesus because of the crowd, they made an opening in the roof above Jesus and, after digging through it, lowered the mat the paralyzed man was lying on. ⁵When Jesus saw their faith, he said to the paralytic, "Son, your sins are forgiven."*

⁶Now some teachers of the law were sitting there, thinking to themselves, ⁷"Why does this fellow talk like that? He's blaspheming! Who can forgive sins but God alone?"

⁸Immediately Jesus knew in his spirit that this was what they were thinking in their hearts, and he said to them, "Why are you thinking these things? ⁹Which is easier: to say to the paralytic, 'Your sins are forgiven,' or to say, 'Get up, take your mat and walk'? ¹⁰But that you may know that the Son of Man has authority on earth to forgive sins ...." He said to the paralytic, ¹¹"I tell you, get up, take your mat and go home." ¹²He got up, took his mat and walked out in full view of them all. This amazed everyone and they praised God, saying, "We have never seen anything like this!"

The Calling of Levi

¹³Once again Jesus went out beside the lake. A large crowd came to him, and he began to teach them. ¹⁴As he walked along, he saw Levi son of Alphaeus sitting at the tax collector's booth. "Follow me," Jesus told him, and Levi got up and followed him.

¹⁵While Jesus was having dinner at Levi's house, many tax collectors and "sinners" were eating with him and his disciples, for there were many who followed him. ¹⁶When the teachers of the law who were Pharisees saw him eating with the "sinners" and tax collectors, they asked his disciples: "Why does he eat with tax collectors and 'sinners'?"

¹⁷On hearing this, Jesus said to them, "It is not the healthy who need a doctor, but the sick. I have not come to call the righteous, but sinners."

4. Why did the teachers of the Law get so upset (see notes on v. 7)?

5. In what way have you experienced Jesus' words, "Your sins have been forgiven," in your life?

6. How do you think Levi felt to have a popular teacher eating at his table? When have you ever felt like Levi—a sinner who was happy to have a friend named Jesus?

7. How can you (and your group) reach out to those whom others consider "unacceptable"?

CARING TIME

(Choose 1 or 2 of these questions before closing in prayer. Be sure to pray for the empty chair.)

1. Does your group have a person for every position on the team roster (see page M5 in the center section)?

2. If you were to describe your last week in terms of weather, what was it like: Sunny? Cold? Rainy? Stormy? Other? What is the forecast for the coming week?

3. How can the group pray for you?

2:1–12 It was Jesus' ability to heal people that drew large crowds to him. This is not at all surprising in a day and age in which there were no hospitals, no reliable doctors, no antibiotics, and only rudimentary procedures and drugs. The life span was short. Illness was the enemy. Parents lived in dread of childhood diseases that wiped out their families. Thus when Jesus appeared and actually cured a wide range of diseases, the people were overjoyed. Paralysis was a common ailment in the Middle East. Sometimes the inability to use a limb was congenital. However, people were mostly crippled as the result of an accident or because of a disease such as polio. Clearly, here Jesus heals organic damage to the man's spine. While this story deals with healing and with faith, this is not its central point. The point of the story is the revelation by Jesus of who he is: the Son of Man who, like God, has the power to forgive sin.

2:1 *A few days later.* Each of the five incidents in 2:1–3:6 is introduced by some sort of indefinite time measure (see also 2:13,18,23; 3:1), indicating that these incidents probably did not happen in sequence, one right after the other. Mark's interest was not chronology. Instead, by grouping stories together around various themes he hopes to reveal to his readers who Jesus is.

home. Capernaum served as Jesus' base for his travels in Galilee, quite possibly Peter and Andrew's house (Mark 1:29,32–33).

2:3 *Some men.* Apparently the paralytic had not been healed on Jesus' previous visit. His friends do not want to let this new opportunity pass.

a paralytic. Any chronic disease or ailment was thought of as a punishment for sin. A paralytic was totally dependent on begging or upon family members to meet his or her needs.

2:4 *an opening in the roof.* The roof of a typical Palestinian house was flat (it was often used for sleeping) and was reached by an outside ladder or stairway. It was constructed of earth and brushwood that was packed between wooden beams set about three feet apart. The roof was easily opened up (and could be easily repaired). A rather large opening would have been required to lower a man on a mat. While this was going on, with the noise and falling dirt, all attention inside would have been diverted from Jesus' sermon to the ever-growing hole.

mat. The bed of a poor person.

2:5 *faith.* This is the first time in Mark that this word is used. It increasingly becomes the quality Jesus looks for in those to whom he ministers.

your sins are forgiven. The friends, the man, and the crowd expected a healing: sin was a whole new issue that had not yet been raised by Jesus. This was a deliberate action on Jesus' part to force the religious authorities who were present to grapple with the issue of his identity.

2:6 *teachers of the law.* Literally, "scribes," religious lawyers who interpreted Jewish law. Originally, it was their job to make copies of the Old Testament. Because of their familiarity with Scripture, people consulted them about points of law and hence their role evolved into that of teacher of the Law.

2:7 *this fellow.* Used as a term of contempt.

blaspheming. Blasphemy is "contempt for God," and under Jewish law its penalty is death (see Lev. 24:16). The teachers of the Law believed that illness was the direct result of sin (e.g., John 9:2), so that the sick could not recover until their sin had been forgiven by God. They also knew that God alone could offer forgiveness. Hence they are distressed that Jesus has said to the paralytic, "Your sins are forgiven." This was to claim in quite explicit terms that he was divine and this was, in their eyes, the vilest blasphemy.

2:8 Jesus knows what they are thinking—whether by their body language, by his knowledge of how they would react, or by his divine insight.

2:9 *Which is easier.* Jesus responds to their question (v. 7) in typical rabbinic fashion: he asks them a question. The answer to his question is obvious. It is far easier to say, "Your sins are forgiven," than it is to heal the man right then and there. There is no way to verify whether sins have been forgiven, but it is obvious whether a lame man walks or not.

2:10 *But that you may know.* If Jesus is able to heal the paralytic, in terms of their own theology (which linked forgiveness and healing) the scribes would have to admit that he had, indeed, forgiven the man's sins. For the scribes, in other words, the visible healing verified the invisible forgiveness. If they were consistent, the teachers of the Law would now have to admit that Jesus was God (or at least a representative of God), because it is they who said, "Who can forgive sins but God alone?" (v. 7).

2:12 The onlookers draw no conclusions about Jesus' identity from this event, but, as in the previous scenes, are simply awed by Jesus' power.

This amazed everyone. Mark's miracle stories often end with an observation of the amazement on the part of those who witnessed the event. The "everyone" would not seem to include the teachers of the Law, who from this time on became more and more resistant to Jesus.

2:13–17 This second conflict story, which builds upon the issue of Jesus' relationship with sin raised in the story of the paralytic, centers around Jesus' association with people considered to be religiously undesirable.

2:14 *Levi.* Elsewhere he is identified as Matthew (Matt. 9:9), the disciple who eventually wrote one of the Gospels. In his role as a tax collector, Matthew would have been hated by both the religious establishment and the common people. The taxation of Israel by Rome was a volatile political issue. Israel resented Roman domination, and the tax system was set up in such a way so as to almost guarantee abuse. There were no set rates which the public could count upon. Instead, tax collectors paid Rome an annual fee for the right to operate a tax station (such as at a toll road or at a harbor where fishermen brought fish to sell) but were then allowed to collect whatever they could get away with from the people, backed up by the full authority of Rome. Once they collected the amount for the annual fee, the rest was theirs to keep. Jews in this business were seen as traitors to Israel, financially profiting through exploiting their own people by cooperating with the oppressor. Tax collectors were considered as vile as robbers or murderers. For Jesus to associate with Levi and his friends would raise the same objections most church people today would feel if they knew their pastor was associating closely with Mafia figures.

2:15 *having dinner.* To share a meal with another was a significant event, implying acceptance of that person. In this way, Jesus extends his forgiveness (see v. 5) to those who were outside orthodox religious life.

tax collectors. See note on verse 14.

"sinners." A slang phrase for those who failed to observe religious practices. These were generally the common people who had to work for a living and thus did not have enough time to keep all the ritual laws (e.g., they did not wash their hands in a special, complicated way before a meal).

2:16 *Pharisees.* This was a small, strict sect of Jews who devoted themselves to observing the traditions of the rabbis as a means of gaining God's favor. Seeing themselves as the truly righteous in Israel, they tended as a whole to look down upon other Jews who could not follow their practices.

Why does he eat. This is the second question asked of Jesus (see verse 9). They could not understand how a truly religious person could eat with rabble who might serve food not prepared according to ritual, on dishes that were ritually (though not literally) unclean.

2:17 Jesus responds by way of a metaphor laced with irony. At first glance, the Pharisees would perhaps have considered this a reasonable explanation of his behavior: he came to heal those who were sick—which to them meant the "sinners" with whom he ate. In later reflection they might come to wonder if perhaps Jesus considered them the sick ones. Jesus' response puts a twist on a proverb that was used to describe the mission of a holy person. The Pharisees would see their role in a similar way. They were to teach the people the ways of God. They did so by separating themselves from the common people in order to set an example of religious and ceremonial holiness that others might be moved to follow. Holiness to them was defined as conforming to ritual law and tradition. In contrast, Jesus defined holiness as a way of relating to God and others, and chose to befriend "sinners" in their present circumstances.

4 Jesus Questioned—Mark 2:18–3:6

THREE-PART AGENDA

ICE-BREAKER
15 Minutes

BIBLE STUDY
30 Minutes

CARING TIME
15–45 Minutes

> *LEADER: Remember to choose an appropriate ice-breaker if you have a new person at the meeting (see page M7 in the center section), and then begin with a prayer. As the leader, you may want to choose question #2 in the Caring Time to facilitate the group in handling accountability issues.*

TO BEGIN THE BIBLE STUDY TIME
(Choose 1 or 2)

1. What is the longest you have gone without eating?

2. What is your favorite thing to do on a Sunday?

3. When you were a teenager, which of your parents' rules did you break the most?

READ SCRIPTURE & DISCUSS
(If you don't have time for all the questions in this section, conclude the Bible Study [30 min.] by answering question #7.)

1. What food would you miss the most if you fasted for several days?

2. What do you see as the purpose of fasting today? In what situations you face might fasting be helpful?

3. How is Jesus and his teaching like the unshrunk cloth and new wine (2:21–22)? How has (or should) Jesus' "new wine" burst some of your "old wineskins"—your religious rituals and ruts?

Jesus Questioned About Fasting

¹⁸Now John's disciples and the Pharisees were fasting. Some people came and asked Jesus, "How is it that John's disciples and the disciples of the Pharisees are fasting, but yours are not?"

¹⁹Jesus answered, "How can the guests of the bridegroom fast while he is with them? They cannot, so long as they have him with them. ²⁰But the time will come when the bridegroom will be taken from them, and on that day they will fast.

²¹"No one sews a patch of unshrunk cloth on an old garment. If he does, the new piece will pull away from the old, making the tear worse. ²²And no one pours new wine into old wineskins. If he does, the wine will burst the skins, and both the wine and the wineskins will be ruined. No, he pours new wine into new wineskins."

Lord of the Sabbath

²³One Sabbath Jesus was going through the grainfields, and as his disciples walked along, they began to pick some heads of grain. ²⁴The Pharisees said to him, "Look, why are they doing what is unlawful on the Sabbath?"

²⁵He answered, "Have you never read what David did when he and his companions were hungry and in need? ²⁶In the days of Abiathar the high priest, he entered the house of God and ate the consecrated bread, which is lawful only for priests to eat. And he also gave some to his companions."

²⁷Then he said to them, "The Sabbath was made for man, not man for the Sabbath. ²⁸So the Son of Man is Lord even of the Sabbath."

3 *Another time he went into the synagogue, and a man with a shriveled hand was there. ²Some of them were looking for a reason to accuse Jesus, so they watched him closely to see if he would heal him on the Sabbath. ³Jesus said to the man with the shriveled hand, "Stand up in front of everyone."*

⁴Then Jesus asked them, "Which is lawful on the Sabbath: to do good or to do evil, to save life or to kill?" But they remained silent.

⁵He looked around at them in anger and, deeply distressed at their stubborn hearts, said to the man, "Stretch out your hand." He stretched it out, and his hand was completely restored. ⁶Then the Pharisees went out and began to plot with the Herodians how they might kill Jesus.

4. In the stories in 2:23–3:5, what are the two kinds of "work" the Pharisees accuse Jesus of doing in violation of the Sabbath?

5. Why did the Pharisees want to kill Jesus? Who would you say are the modern-day Pharisees?

6. The Pharisees taught a Sabbath which had priority over human needs. When have you felt like church rules and regulations were more important than you?

7. What can you and this group do to make your church a place that is more concerned with people's needs than with rules and regulations?

CARING TIME

(Choose 1 or 2 of these questions before closing in prayer. Be sure to pray for the empty chair.)

1. How are you doing at inviting others to this group?

2. Is there an area in your life for which you would like to ask this group to help hold you accountable?

3. How can this group pray for you in the coming week?

Summary. The entire section from 2:1–3:6 is one that tells the story of the growth of the opposition to Jesus. These last three conflict stories (2:18–22; 2:23–28; 3:1–6) deal with Jesus' violation of two important aspects of rabbinical law and practice: fasting and Sabbath keeping. While there were many Jewish sects which differed on a variety of points, all Jewish sects regularly practiced fasting and believed the Sabbath was an inviolable institution. It was Jesus' seemingly casual attitude toward these two deeply honored religious traditions that angered the religious leaders.

2:18 the Pharisees. Members of a small (about 6,000 members at the time of Herod) but powerful religious sect whose prime concern was knowing and keeping the Old Testament Law in all its detail.

fasting. The Pharisees did not eat from 6 a.m. to 6 p.m. on Mondays and Thursdays as an act of piety.

2:19–20 For the very poor there were few events to break the monotony and tedium of their lives. Marriage was one such occasion. Rather than go on a honeymoon, a Jewish couple stayed with their friends for a week-long feast during which everyone was released from all religious obligations, including fasting.

2:19 bridegroom. In the Old Testament, God was often referred to as Israel's bridegroom, another subtle indication of Jesus' divine identity.

2:20 will be taken from them. An ominous note predicting Jesus' death. That would be an appropriate time for fasting as a genuine expression of his disciples' grief for sin and desire for God's mercy.

2:21–22 Jesus uses two more mini–parables to make his point. His new way is not compatible with the old way of the Pharisees, any more than one can sew new cloth on old and not have it pull apart. Nor can one put new wine in an old, dry wineskin and not have the young, vigorous wine burst out.

2:22 new wine. New wine is still fermenting. Hence, no one would have poured it into a leather container which was old, dry and crusty. New wine required new skins which were supple and flexible, able to expand as the wine fermented. Otherwise, the fermenting wine would burst the skin, ruining the skin and spilling the wine.

2:23–28 In this fourth encounter of conflict, Jesus not only goes against deeply held traditions about what constitutes work on the Sabbath, he also makes the claim to have the right to have precedence over all such laws. The issue in this story and the next is Sabbath prohibitions.

2:23 Sabbath. The seventh day of the week (Saturday), which begins Friday at sunset and ends Saturday at sunset. The Fourth Commandment is to rest from all labor on the Sabbath (Ex. 20:8–11). While the intent of the Law was to encourage personal restoration, protect people from oppressive working conditions, and encourage people to look forward to that time when they would indeed be able to rest in security and safety because of God's presence with them, by the first century scores of regulations had evolved which defined what could and could not be done on the Sabbath. These regulations overshadowed the intent of the Law, becoming only another form of oppression. For example, in this case the regulations would insist these men go hungry rather than glean a few ears of grain for food.

pick some heads of grain. It was permissible for hungry travelers to pluck and eat grain from a field (Deut. 23:25). The issue is not stealing. What the Pharisees objected to was the "work" this involved. Reaping was one of the 39 categories of work forbidden on the Sabbath.

2:24 unlawful. The "law" they cite refers to those customs and regulations (both written and oral) that the Pharisees zealously guarded. Jesus did not take issue with Exodus 34:21, which required rest on the Sabbath (even during harvest), but with the rigid interpretation given it.

2:26 In the days of Abiathar. In fact, it was Abiathar's father, Ahimelech, who was high priest when this incident occurred (see 1 Sam. 21:1–6). This may be a scribal error, though it is probably just a reference to a general section of Scripture.

ate the consecrated bread. David did what was unlawful (Ex. 25:30; Num. 4:7), providing a precedent that human need can supersede religious law.

2:27 So many Sabbath laws had evolved that the Sabbath had become a burden, not a blessing. Jesus seeks to restore the original meaning of the

Sabbath. This is one of the few verses found only in Mark.

2:28 *Son of Man.* This is Jesus' favorite title for himself. In the Aramaic that Jesus spoke it would not have been a title at all, but simply a common expression meaning "a man." But it was also true that this phrase was used as a messianic title in Daniel 7 and in the apocryphal book of Enoch (written around 70 B.C.). So by using this rather colorless, vague title to characterize himself (which nonetheless had messianic connotations), Jesus would be able to define it in his own way and say, "This is the kind of Messiah I am."

3:1–6 In the final incident in these five confrontation stories (2:1–3:6), the religious leaders come to a conclusion about Jesus: he is dangerous, and so must die.

3:1 *Another time.* The time reference is ambiguous. These stories are told together because of the common theme of opposition to Jesus, not because they necessarily happened right after each other.

3:2 *they watched him closely.* By this time the religious leaders no longer questioned Jesus. Now they simply watched to see if his actions betrayed a disregard for the Law so they might accuse him.

if he would heal him on the Sabbath. The issue is not healing, but whether Jesus would do so on the Sabbath in defiance of the oral tradition, which allowed healing only if there was danger to life. Jesus could have waited until the next day to heal this long-paralyzed hand. These Pharisees fail to see the need of the man, focusing only on the mandates of their tradition.

3:3 *Stand up in front of everyone.* As with the paralytic, Jesus once again takes a deliberate action to force the confrontation with his questioners. He did not shy away from their accusations, but took action to expose the foolishness of the charges of his opponents.

3:4 *Jesus asked them.* Jesus began this series of confrontations with a question (2:8–9) and ends it with another. The religious leaders may have been investigating Jesus, but Jesus was also getting to know their hearts. Jesus' implication is that refusing to heal this man just because it was the Sabbath was actually to commit evil, since a real human need would be allowed to go unmet.

they remained silent. Their silence reflected their refusal to reconsider their position.

3:5 *anger / deeply distressed.* Jesus felt strongly about the injustice of a system that sacrificed the genuine needs of people for religious traditions that had nothing to do with God.

stubborn hearts. Just as the religious leaders have come to a conclusion about him (see 3:6), he has come to understand them. Their problem is that their hearts (the center of their beings) have calcified. The Greek word translated "stubborn" is also used to describe a gall stone or a tooth. Later Jesus will indicate that the disciples have the same problem (Mark 6:52; 8:17).

Stretch out your hand. Just as he deliberately declared the paralytic's sins forgiven (knowing that this was blasphemy to the teachers of the Law), here he deliberately heals on the Sabbath (knowing that this too was anathema to his critics).

3:6 *Herodians.* A political group made up of influential Jewish sympathizers of King Herod. They were normally despised by the Pharisees, who considered them traitors (for working with Rome) and irreligious (unclean as a result of their association with Gentiles). However, the Pharisees had no power to kill Jesus. Only the civil authority can do this, and hence the collaboration.

how they might kill Jesus. Mark makes use of irony here. The Pharisees believed Jesus violated the Sabbath by healing on that day, but failed to see that they themselves were violating the Sabbath law by plotting how to kill him on that day!

5 Followers & Family—Mark 3:7–35

THREE-PART AGENDA

ICE-BREAKER
15 Minutes

BIBLE STUDY
30 Minutes

CARING TIME
15–45 Minutes

> *LEADER: Remember to choose an appro-priate ice-breaker if you have a new person at the meeting (see page M7 in the center section), and then begin with a prayer. If you have more than nine in your group, divide into subgroups of 4–6 for the Bible Study (see the box about the "Subgrouping" on page 4).*

TO BEGIN THE BIBLE STUDY TIME
(Choose 1 or 2)

1. What nicknames have you had?

2. What is the largest crowd you have ever been in: A sporting event? A parade? A political rally? Times Square on New Year's Eve?

3. What is something you have done that made your family or friends wonder how sane you were?

READ SCRIPTURE & DISCUSS
(If you don't have time for all the questions in this section, con-clude the Bible Study [30 min.] by answering question #7.)

1. When have you felt that there was no place you could go to escape the demands on you?

2. What do you think the crowds were looking for in Jesus? What do you think he was looking for in them?

3. What surprises you most about Jesus' choice of apostles (see note on vv. 16–19)?

Crowds Follow Jesus

7Jesus withdrew with his disciples to the lake, and a large crowd from Galilee followed. 8When they heard all he was doing, many people came to him from Judea, Jerusalem, Idumea, and the regions across the Jordan and around Tyre and Sidon. 9Because of the crowd he told his disciples to have a small boat ready for him, to keep the people from crowding him. 10For he had healed many, so that those with diseases were pushing forward to touch him. 11Whenever the evil spirits saw him, they fell down before him and cried out, "You are the Son of God." 12But he gave them strict orders not to tell who he was.

The Appointing of the Twelve Apostles

13Jesus went up on a mountainside and called to him those he wanted, and they came to him. 14He appointed twelve—designating them apostles—that they might be with him and that he might send them out to preach 15and to have authority to drive out demons. 16These are the twelve he appointed: Simon (to whom he gave the name Peter); 17James son of Zebedee and his brother John (to them he gave the name Boanerges, which means Sons of Thunder); 18Andrew, Philip, Bartholomew, Matthew, Thomas, James son of Alphaeus, Thaddaeus, Simon the Zealot 19and Judas Iscariot, who betrayed him.

Jesus and Beelzebub

20Then Jesus entered a house, and again a crowd gathered, so that he and his disciples were not even able to eat. 21When his family heard about this, they went to take charge of him, for they said, "He is out of his mind."

22And the teachers of the law who came down from Jerusalem said, "He is possessed by Beelzebub! By the prince of demons he is driving out demons."

23So Jesus called them and spoke to them in parables: "How can Satan drive out Satan? 24If a kingdom is divided against itself, that kingdom cannot stand. 25If a house is divided against itself, that house cannot stand. 26And if Satan opposes himself and is divided, he cannot stand; his end has come. 27In fact, no one can enter a strong man's house and carry off his possessions unless he first ties up the strong man. Then he can rob his house. 28I tell you the

4. If you were Jesus, what would be the hardest for you to handle: People's constant demands (v. 20)? Your family thinking you were crazy (v. 21)? The religious leaders thinking you were demon-possessed (v. 22)?

5. What would you say to someone who is afraid they have "blasphemed against the Holy Spirit" (see note on vv. 28–29)?

6. Have you ever experienced a conflict between what God wanted for you and what your family expected of you? What happened?

7. Which relationship do you need to work on the most—your relationship with Christ, your biological family, or your spiritual family? How will you do so?

CARING TIME

(Choose 1 or 2 of these questions before closing in prayer. Be sure to pray for the empty chair.)

1. Share with the group a challenge you are facing this week.

2. Is there a spiritual struggle or victory from this last week you would like to share?

3. How can the group help you in prayer this week?

> *truth, all the sins and blasphemies of men will be forgiven them. ²⁹But whoever blasphemes against the Holy Spirit will never be forgiven; he is guilty of an eternal sin."*
>
> *³⁰He said this because they were saying, "He has an evil spirit."*
>
> Jesus' Mother and Brothers
>
> *³¹Then Jesus' mother and brothers arrived. Standing outside, they sent someone in to call him. ³²A crowd was sitting around him, and they told him, "Your mother and brothers are outside looking for you."*
>
> *³³"Who are my mother and my brothers?" he asked.*
>
> *³⁴Then he looked at those seated in a circle around him and said, "Here are my mother and my brothers! ³⁵Whoever does God's will is my brother and sister and mother."*

Notes—Mark 3:7–35

Summary. In 1:16–45 Mark described the enthusiasm with which the crowds greeted Jesus. In 2:1–3:6 he described, in contrast, the hostility the religious leaders had toward Jesus. In this passage he further differentiates the reactions to Jesus. Two groups are for him: the crowds (vv. 7–12) and the disciples (vv. 13–19). Two groups are against him: his family (vv. 20–21, 31–35) and the teachers of the Law (vv. 22–30).

3:7–12 In a day when there was little effective medicine, the crowds flock to Jesus because he was a successful healer and because he had the power to cast out demons (see Mark 1:27–28).

3:7–8 They came from near (Galilee) and far, from the north (Tyre and Sidon), the south (Judea and Idumea), and the east (the region across the Jordan was called Perea). (To the west was the Mediterranean Sea.) They came from Jewish and from Gentile regions. They came from the country regions (Galilee) and from the heart of the nation (Jerusalem).

3:9 The lake provided a barrier against the crowds as well as a natural amplifier for his voice.

3:11–12 Once again the evil spirits correctly identify him ("the Son of God"). They name him because in ancient times it was thought that knowing a person's true name gave you the ability to control that person. But in a vindication of this title, Jesus exerts power over these evil forces and silences them, lest they stir up the crowds to follow him as the Messiah who will lead them in revolt against Rome.

3:13–19 In contrast to the crowds who came to have their needs met, Jesus selected ("called to him," "appointed," or "designated") 12 to be his disciples.

3:14 *twelve.* There were 12 tribes in Israel. Jesus and his disciples will inaugurate the new Israel.

apostles. Ambassadors commissioned to go out in his name.

3:16–19 Peter's name heads each list of the apostles; Judas is always last. There are two (possibly three) sets of brothers and several sets of friends. Some of these men are strong-willed and impetuous (e.g., the Sons of Thunder, who want to consume a village with fire in Luke 9:51–56); some are so invisible they are known only from the lists (e.g. Thaddaeus). There are two natural enemies: the pro–government tax collector Matthew (Levi) and the anti–government guerrilla Simon the Zealot.

3:20–21,31–35 For the first time, Jesus' family is heard from, though in a surprising role. Whether out of good motives (they are concerned that he is not able to take care of himself with the crowds constantly pressing him, v. 20) or out of misunderstanding (he is acting strange, v. 21), his family wants to stop Jesus' ministry.

3:21 *they went.* They undertook the 30-mile journey from Nazareth to Capernaum.

take charge of him. Take him home by force (see 6:17, where the same word is translated "arrested").

out of his mind. Literally, "he is beside himself." His family concludes that he is suffering from some sort of ecstatic, religiously induced mental illness.

3:22–30 Sandwiched into the story of his family is this account of how the teachers of the Law explain Jesus' power. This is the first of several occasions in which Mark places a story between the beginning and the end of another story. In this way the two stories amplify and explain one another.

3:22 *came down from Jerusalem.* To go from Jerusalem in the south to Galilee in the north, you descend (because Jerusalem stood at an elevation of 2,400 feet above sea level, while the Sea of Galilee was 600 feet below sea level).

He is possessed by Beelzebub. Beelzebub is probably a slang expression for a demon-prince, meaning something like "The Lord of Dung." To be possessed by this demon is to be controlled and empowered by him, which is how the teachers of the Law explained Jesus' miracles. They cannot deny his healing and exorcism, and since they know they are God's representatives (and Jesus is not one of them), the only other source of such power is Satan. The charge that Jesus is a sorcerer was found frequently in Jewish literature until the modern age.

3:23–27 Jesus begins by pointing out the flaw in their argument: the power of Satan cannot be used to undo the power of Satan. Then by means of three brief parables he drives home his point. A kingdom (or even a house) that wars against itself will fall. Furthermore, he has used his power to bind Satan

("the strong man"), as demonstrated by the fact that he is undoing Satan's works every time he heals or casts out a demon.

3:28–29 Jesus ends by stating that all manner of sin will be forgiven ("all the sins and blasphemies of men"). However, in order for forgiveness to be given it must be requested. And the teachers of the Law are so blind (their hearts are stubborn, 3:5) that they do not notice the blasphemy in their calling Jesus (who is God's Son) a tool of Satan (who is the prince of demons). Thus it would never occur to them to ask for forgiveness. To blaspheme against the Holy Spirit is to resist the Spirit's convicting work and thus not to see the sin, and so fail to ask for forgiveness. Anxiety about whether one has committed "an eternal sin" is the very demonstration that one is still open to the convicting work of the Spirit. Jesus warns his critics not to be guilty of the very thing they accused him of in the story of the paralytic (2:7)!

> *Anxiety about whether one has committed "an eternal sin" is the very demonstration that one is still open to the convicting work of the Spirit.*

3:30 The way the Greek is phrased here indicates that the teachers of the Law had a callous and fixed attitude of mind.

3:31–32 The family's assessment that Jesus is "out of his mind" is a milder version of the claim by the teachers of the Law that "he is possessed by Beelzebub." At this point the family arrives to "take charge" of Jesus (this is not a friendly visit). They find him surrounded by the crowd (v. 32). Not wanting to confront him in that setting, they send someone to call him out.

3:33 Jesus' question is rhetorical. He does not expect an answer.

3:34–35 Jesus gives a new definition of family. Kinship is not a matter of heredity, it is a matter of spirit; i.e., doing God's will (which his natural family is not doing by trying to stop his ministry). Eventually his family will move from doubt to faith (see John 19:25–27; Acts 1:14; 1 Cor. 15:7).

31

6 Parable of the Sower—Mark 4:1–20

THREE-PART AGENDA

ICE-BREAKER
15 Minutes

BIBLE STUDY
30 Minutes

CARING TIME
15–45 Minutes

> **LEADER:** Check page M7 in the center section for a good ice-breaker, particularly if you have a new person at this meeting. Is your group working well together—with everyone "fielding their position" as shown on the team roster on page M5?

TO BEGIN THE BIBLE STUDY TIME
(Choose 1 or 2)

1. How "green" is your thumb? Who do you know that can make anything grow?

2. If you were a farmer, what would you enjoy doing the most?

3. What has been your biggest worry lately?

READ SCRIPTURE & DISCUSS
(If you don't have time for all the questions in this section, conclude the Bible Study [30 min.] by answering question #7.)

1. When do you recall someone planting the "seed" of the Gospel in your life?

2. According to Jesus, why does God's Word not take root at all in some people (v. 15)? What causes the plants in the second type of soil to wither (vv. 16–17)? What three things choked off the third plants (vv. 18–19)?

3. What do you think Jesus means by the spectacular harvest produced by the good soil (v. 20): New converts? Good deeds? Godly character qualities?

The Parable of the Sower

4 *Again Jesus began to teach by the lake. The crowd that gathered around him was so large that he got into a boat and sat in it out on the lake, while all the people were along the shore at the water's edge. ²He taught them many things by parables, and in his teaching said: ³"Listen! A farmer went out to sow his seed. ⁴As he was scattering the seed, some fell along the path, and the birds came and ate it up. ⁵Some fell on rocky places, where it did not have much soil. It sprang up quickly, because the soil was shallow. ⁶But when the sun came up, the plants were scorched, and they withered because they had no root. ⁷Other seed fell among thorns, which grew up and choked the plants, so that they did not bear grain. ⁸Still other seed fell on good soil. It came up, grew and produced a crop, multiplying thirty, sixty, or even a hundred times."*

⁹Then Jesus said, "He who has ears to hear, let him hear."

¹⁰When he was alone, the Twelve and the others around him asked him about the parables. ¹¹He told them, "The secret of the kingdom of God has been given to you. But to those on the outside everything is said in parables ¹²so that,

> *" 'they may be ever seeing but never perceiving,*
> *and ever hearing but never understanding;*
> *otherwise they might turn and be forgiven!'*ᵃ *"*

¹³Then Jesus said to them, "Don't you understand this parable? How then will you understand any parable? ¹⁴The farmer sows the word. ¹⁵Some people are like seed along the path, where the word is sown. As soon as they hear it, Satan comes and takes away the word that was sown in them. ¹⁶Others, like seed sown on rocky places, hear the word and at once receive it with joy. ¹⁷But since they have no root, they last only a short time. When trouble or persecution comes because of the word, they quickly fall away. ¹⁸Still others, like seed sown among thorns, hear the word; ¹⁹but the worries of this life, the deceitfulness of wealth and the desires for other things come in and choke the word, making it unfruitful. ²⁰Others, like seed sown on good soil, hear the word, accept it, and produce a crop—thirty, sixty or even a hundred times what was sown."

ᵃ12 Isaiah 6:9,10

4. How satisfied are you with the time and energy you give to hearing and acting on God's Word?

5. Which of the four kinds of soil best describes the condition of your heart right now?

6. How can "the worries of this life, the deceitfulness of wealth and the desires for other things" hinder your ability to produce a bountiful crop?

7. What can you do to develop stronger spiritual roots?

CARING TIME

(Choose 1 or 2 of these questions before closing in prayer. Be sure to pray for the empty chair.)

1. Are all the players on the team roster fulfilling the assignments of their position? (Look at the roster again on page M5 of the center section.)

2. What is something you feel God may be calling you to do?

3. How can the group pray for you this week?

Summary. The emphasis in the so-called Parable of the Sower is really on the soils. The parable clearly is intended to be a comment upon the four types of responses to Jesus seen in chapter 3, in which the Pharisees accuse him of being demon-possessed (3:22), the crowd seeks him out as a miracle worker to be enjoyed for their purposes (3:7–11), his family, concerned that things are getting out of hand, thinks he is mad (3:21), and the disciples sit at his feet to listen and practice his teaching (3:34–35). The parable also foreshadows the types of responses that are to come later on in Mark's Gospel.

4:1 *The crowd.* The scene is similar to that described in 3:7–9. This crowd was probably also drawn to Jesus in hopes of seeking healing and exorcism. However, this time Jesus takes refuge in the boat in order to be able to speak to the people.

4:2 *parables.* Parables are comparisons that draw upon common experience in order to teach about the realities of God's kingdom. These metaphors or analogies are often presented in story form; they draw upon the known to explain the unknown. They are often strange or vivid, forcing the hearer to think about their meaning.

4:3 *Listen!* Pay attention! There is more to this story than appears at first. Jesus uses this word to warn the hearers that they must think about this or they will get it wrong.

sow his seed. Farmers would throw seed into the soil by a broadcast method. In Palestine, farmers sowed their seeds first, scattering them by hand, and then they plowed.

4:4 *the path.* The soil of the pathways was so packed down that seed could not penetrate the soil and so germinate. The birds came along and ate up this seed which just sat on the surface of the ground.

4:5 *rocky places.* Some soil covered a limestone base a few inches beneath the surface. Seed that fell here would germinate but it would not last, since a proper root system could not develop.

4:7 *thorns.* In other places, there were the roots of weeds. When the seed grew up, so did the weeds, which invariably stunted the growth of the good

seed. Although it lived, such seed would not bear fruit.

4:8 *good soil.* However, some of the seed did fall where it could germinate, grow and produce a crop.

thirty, sixty, or even a hundred times. The good soil yielded a spectacular crop. The normal yield for a Palestinian field is seven and a half times what is sown, while 10 times is an especially good harvest. This is where the emphasis in the parable lies: not with the unproductive soil, but with the miracle crop. This is what would have arrested the attention of Jesus' hearers.

4:9 Jesus urges his hearers to ponder his parable. Part of a parable's power lies in the fact that people must reflect on it in order to understand it. The question is: What topic does this story from ordinary life provide insight into?

let him hear. The concept of spiritual deafness is an important theme in this Gospel. The crowds are deaf to the meaning of Jesus' words as are the teachers of the Law and even the disciples. Jesus heals a deaf man in Mark 7:32, and this act for Mark is symbolic of the healing that must go on for all people (in this case, the Twelve) in order for them to understand who Jesus really is (see Mark 4:12,23; 7:31–37; 8:18; 9:14–29).

4:10 The subject of Jesus' parable about the soils is not yet clear even to the disciples! Nor in fact will Jesus' teaching become fully clear to the disciples right up to his death. It is not easy for them (and others) to break through their assumptions about how God acts to see who Jesus really is and what the kingdom is actually all about.

4:11–12 At first reading, this quotation from Isaiah 6:9–10 may appear to be saying that parables are designed to obscure the truth. In fact, this simply states (with some irony) what is a fact: some understand and some do not. The teachers of the Law, for example, see Jesus' miracles and hear Jesus' teaching and yet they ascribe his power to Satan (Mark 3:22). They see but do not perceive.

4:11 *The secret.* A secret in the New Testament is something which was previously unknown but has now been revealed to all who will hear. The secret given the disciples is the kingdom of God has come.

the kingdom of God. How God establishes his reign in human affairs is what Jesus' parables in this section are all about. This is the interpretive key (see Mark 1:14–15).

> *In order to be forgiven, people must repent (turn). In order to repent, they must understand their true situation.*

has been given to you. Not even the disciples who have been given "the secret" perceive fully what is going on (v. 13). So, to be "given the secret" must mean something like "called to follow Jesus." It is as the disciples follow Jesus that they will come to understand more fully what he means.

those on the outside. The point is not that God calls some and excludes others. Rather, those who are on the outside are simply those who fail to pursue the kingdom. The secret is open to all who, like the disciples, ask.

4:12 *ever seeing / ever hearing.* This quote is from Isaiah 6:9–10, in which God called the prophet to speak his word even though Israel would not listen. Although they saw God's messenger and heard his word, they refused to heed his message.

might turn and be forgiven. In order to be forgiven, people must repent (turn). In order to repent, they must understand their true situation.

4:13–20 This is the only parable that Jesus explains in Mark. This fact, coupled with its length (20 verses when most stories occupy 10 verses or less), indicates how important this parable is for Mark. By it, he helps the reader understand the four types of responses to Jesus seen thus far in the Gospel. In this parable, it becomes clear that only one response (that of the Twelve) will bear fruit for the kingdom.

4:14 The seed is the message of God's kingdom.

4:15 Some, like the teachers of the Law, are so hardened (like the soil on the paths between plots) that the seed of the Word never penetrates. It is snatched away by Satan before it can germinate.

Satan. The teachers of the Law have charged Jesus with being dominated by Satan when, in fact, it turns out that they are the ones under his influence!

4:16–17 Others, like the crowds, are superficially attracted to Jesus. They like what he can give them, but their commitment is not deep (see Mark 3:7–12). They will fall away as soon as there is any hint of persecution.

4:16 *receive it with joy.* Indeed, the common people flocked to Jesus once they saw what he could do (see Mark 1:16–45; 3:7–12).

4:18–19 Still others, like his family, allow the wrong concerns to squeeze out the newly growing plant (see Mark 3:20–21,31–35; 6:1–6).

4:19 *the deceitfulness of wealth and the desires for other things.* Being a disciple of Christ requires wholehearted loyalty to him. While money and the "other things" in view here are not evil in themselves, the disciple is warned not to allow anything else to take priority over hearing and practicing the words of Jesus.

making it unfruitful. The weeds do not kill the plant, but they do prevent it from bringing forth fruit.

4:20 But in the end, some, like the Twelve, will reproduce abundantly (see Mark 3:13–19). These are people who respond to Jesus' word by consistently putting it into practice.

a crop. The crop in view here is a life full of the qualities of discipleship, such as righteousness, love, joy, peace, goodness, etc. (Gal. 5:22–23; Phil. 1:11).

thirty, sixty or even a hundred times. In this parable there are three types of unproductive soil (hard, rocky, weed-filled) and three types of productive soil (that bearing 30-, 60-, and 100-fold). Or looked at another way, there are only two kinds of soil: unproductive and productive.

> *But in the end, some, like the Twelve, will reproduce abundantly. These are people who respond to Jesus' word by consistently putting it into practice.*

35

7 Jesus' Parables—Mark 4:21–41

THREE-PART AGENDA

ICE-BREAKER
15 Minutes

BIBLE STUDY
30 Minutes

CARING TIME
15–45 Minutes

> **LEADER:** *If there's a new person in this session, start with an ice-breaker from the center section (see page M7). Remember to stick closely to the three-part agenda and the time allowed for each segment. Is your group praying for the empty chair?*

TO BEGIN THE BIBLE STUDY TIME
(Choose 1 or 2)

1. What is the worst storm you can remember?

2. How sound of a sleeper are you? What does it take to wake you up?

3. What kind of light best describes you (desk lamp, night-light, torch, candle, etc.)?

READ SCRIPTURE & DISCUSS
(If you don't have time for all the questions in this section, conclude the Bible Study [30 min.] by answering question #7.)

1. On a scale from 1 (rock bottom) to 10 (sky high), what is the stress level in your life at the moment?

2. In what ways do you boldly "let your light shine"? In what ways is it difficult for you to let your light shine for Christ?

3. In verses 26–29, what part (if any) do people play in the growth of God's kingdom? Does this cause you to rest more or work more?

A Lamp on a Stand

²¹He said to them, "Do you bring in a lamp to put it under a bowl or a bed? Instead, don't you put it on its stand? ²²For whatever is hidden is meant to be disclosed, and whatever is concealed is meant to be brought out into the open. ²³If anyone has ears to hear, let him hear."

²⁴"Consider carefully what you hear," he continued. "With the measure you use, it will be measured to you— and even more. ²⁵Whoever has will be given more; whoever does not have, even what he has will be taken from him."

The Parable of the Growing Seed

²⁶He also said, "This is what the kingdom of God is like. A man scatters seed on the ground. ²⁷Night and day, whether he sleeps or gets up, the seed sprouts and grows, though he does not know how. ²⁸All by itself the soil produces grain—first the stalk, then the head, then the full kernel in the head. ²⁹As soon as the grain is ripe, he puts the sickle to it, because the harvest has come."

The Parable of the Mustard Seed

³⁰Again he said, "What shall we say the kingdom of God is like, or what parable shall we use to describe it? ³¹It is like a mustard seed, which is the smallest seed you plant in the ground. ³²Yet when planted, it grows and becomes the largest of all garden plants, with such big branches that the birds of the air can perch in its shade."

³³With many similar parables Jesus spoke the word to them, as much as they could understand. ³⁴He did not say anything to them without using a parable. But when he was alone with his own disciples, he explained everything.

Jesus Calms the Storm

³⁵That day when evening came, he said to his disciples, "Let us go over to the other side." ³⁶Leaving the crowd behind, they took him along, just as he was, in the boat. There were also other boats with him. ³⁷A furious squall came up, and the waves broke over the boat, so that it was nearly swamped. ³⁸Jesus was in the stern, sleeping on a cushion. The disciples woke him and said to him, "Teacher, don't you care if we drown?"

4. What does the Parable of the Mustard Seed (vv. 30–32) teach about God's kingdom? What evidence of growth have you seen in your spiritual life in the last year?

5. How did the disciples' fear during the storm (vv. 35–41) differ from their fear afterward? What was Jesus teaching them about himself?

6. What do you do when Jesus seems asleep during your difficult times?

7. What is the worst personal "storm" you have faced in your life? What helped you get through it?

CARING TIME
(Choose 1 or 2 of these questions before closing in prayer. Be sure to pray for the empty chair.)

1. What is something for which you are particularly thankful?

2. How has this group been an encouragement to you?

3. How can the group support you in prayer this week?

> ³⁹*He got up, rebuked the wind and said to the waves, "Quiet! Be still!" Then the wind died down and it was completely calm.*
> ⁴⁰*He said to his disciples, "Why are you so afraid? Do you still have no faith?"*
> ⁴¹*They were terrified and asked each other, "Who is this? Even the wind and the waves obey him!"*

Notes—Mark 4:21–41

4:21–32 These parables are used by Matthew and Luke in quite different ways in their Gospels (see Matt. 5:14–16; 10:26; 7:2; 25:29; Luke 8:16–18; 6:38; 19:26). The parables teach that the kingdom of God (like Jesus' messiahship) will have a hidden period, but one day it will be revealed for what it really is.

4:21–23 This parable is a comment on the secrecy motif introduced in Mark 4:11. The kingdom of God is not meant to be hidden but to be revealed.

4:21 *lamp.* A pottery vessel filled with olive oil.

bowl. A basket which could hold about one peck.

bed. The couch people reclined on while eating.

4:24–25 Again in verse 24, the hearers are warned to listen carefully (see 4:9,23). Then they are told a riddle that emphasizes that there are consequences to how they hear Jesus. Those who do not hear nor heed his words will miss out on God's kingdom, while those who grasp what is happening will grow in their understanding of the emerging kingdom. The measure by which they measured Jesus' words will bring them either more understanding or leave them with no understanding.

4:26–29 This is the only parable unique to Mark. It shows how the seed falling into the good soil (the fourth kind in the Parable of the Sower—4:8,20) grows into abundant fruit. Such an insignificant act as sowing seed yields, in the fullness of time, an incredible harvest.

4:30–32 The final parable contrasts the insignificance of a tiny mustard seed with the luxurious plant it becomes. So, too, the seeming insignificance of Jesus' ministry: he was a freelance rabbi with 12 largely non-descript disciples. Yet one day his work will blossom into the magnificent kingdom of God.

4:31 *mustard seed.* The mustard tree was known for having the smallest seed. Along the Lake of Galilee, mustard shrubs grew to eight or 10 feet. The shade they provided, along with the tasty black seeds, attracted flocks of birds.

4:33 *as much as they could understand.* This reinforces the fact that the intention was not to veil his message by means of parables, but to reveal it. The problem was the understanding level of his hearers. Hence the repeated urging in this section to listen carefully.

4:35–41 Mark begins a new section that continues through 5:43. In 1:14–4:34, he explored various responses to Jesus. Despite differing reactions to Jesus, everyone seemed to regard him as a rabbi: He taught with authority (e.g., 1:27), he healed effectively (e.g., 1:34), and he cast out demons easily (e.g., 1:39). In other words, he did what other rabbis did (or tried to do), except that he was exceptionally good at it. In these four stories, a whole new side of Jesus is revealed: Mark unveils the awesome *power* of Jesus. The disciples see that he has authority over the very elements (4:35–41); over the most extreme case of possession by evil (5:1–20); over long-term, seemingly incurable disease (5:24–34); and even over death itself (5:21–24,36–43). No rabbi had *this* kind of power. Whoever Jesus was, he went beyond normal categories.

4:35 *That day.* This story comes at the end of a day of teaching by the lake (see 4:1).

> *The command to be still is God's command to the tumult of people and nature which attempt to rise up against his power. This command to silence presses God's peace into the strife that fights against God and his ways.*

when evening came. The voyage begins as the sun is setting.

4:36 *There were also other boats with him.* Although these boats do not play any other role in the story, their mention, as well as that of other details not found in the parallel accounts (Matt. 8:23–27; Luke 8:22–25), indicate an eyewitness testimony of the event.

4:37 *A furious squall.* The Sea of Galilee was a deep, freshwater lake, 13 miles long and eight miles wide at its widest point. It was pear-shaped and ringed by mountains, though open at its north and south ends. Fierce winds blew into this bowl-shaped lake, creating savage and unpredictable storms.

4:38 *sleeping.* In the Old Testament, sleeping peacefully is a sign of trust in the power of God (e.g., Ps. 4:8). The fact that Jesus was asleep during a storm is also a sign of his exhaustion from a day of teaching.

on a cushion. This was probably a cushion used for the rowers to sit upon.

Teacher. This is who they understood Jesus to be: a rabbi.

don't you care if we drown? This is a rebuke. Jesus' ability to sleep in the midst of the storm was not seen as a sign of his trust in God but as a sign of his callousness toward the plight of the disciples. They wake Jesus up so that he can help them bail out the boat since it was about to be swamped (v.

37). As their later response indicates (v. 41), they had no expectation that he would have any power over the storm.

4:39 Instead of bailing, Jesus commands the wind and the waves to be still and so they are. He has power over the very elements—in the same way that God does (see Ps. 65:7; 106:9). This was something no ordinary rabbi could do.

Be still! This is literally, "Be muzzled!" as if the storm were some wild beast needing to be subdued. The command to be still is God's command to the tumult of people and nature which attempt to rise up against his power. This command to silence presses God's peace into the strife that fights against God and his ways.

4:40 *afraid.* This was a situation which provoked a lot of fear in the disciples. Some of the disciples were fishermen who knew how serious their peril was. However, once Jesus displays his power, their fear of the storm turns into fear of Jesus. The disciples were totally unprepared for this action.

Do you still have no faith? Faith here is "faith in God's helping power present and active in Jesus" (Cranfield). Although Jesus had not yet performed any miracle of this nature, the disciples "should by this time have learned something of the secret of the kingdom of God, which is the secret that the kingdom is come in the person and work of Jesus" (Cranfield). This miracle would force the disciples to reconsider all they had heard and seen from Jesus: What had he said or done that should lead them to expect he could act like this?

4:41 *terrified.* Terror replaced fear. This is what is felt in the presence of an unknown force or power, such as a demon, angel or ghost or some other strange, supernatural experience would inspire.

Who is this? This is the key question in Mark's Gospel. The congregation in the synagogue wondered about this (1:27). The religious leaders asked this question (2:7; 3:22). Now his disciples discover that they do not understand who he is. Only the readers of the Gospel (1:1), God (1:11), and the demons (1:24,34) know his true identity. The rest of Mark describes how the disciples overcome their culturally conditioned assumptions and discover Jesus' true nature.

8 Demon-Possessed Man—Mark 5:1–20

THREE-PART AGENDA

ICE-BREAKER
15 Minutes

BIBLE STUDY
30 Minutes

CARING TIME
15–45 Minutes

> *LEADER: If there's a new person in this session, start with an ice-breaker from the center section (see page M7). Remember to stick closely to the three-part agenda. Allow yourself 60 minutes for Bible Study if you're following the 13-week plan.*

TO BEGIN THE BIBLE STUDY TIME
(Choose 1 or 2)

1. What's the *worst* place you've ever lived?

2. How accident prone were you as a kid?

3. What is the scariest place you've ever been in?

READ SCRIPTURE & DISCUSS
(If you don't have time for all the questions in this section, conclude the Bible Study [30 min.] by answering question #7.)

1. What is the most dramatic transformation you have seen Jesus Christ work in someone's life?

2. How do you think the demon-possessed man felt about meeting Jesus: Hopeful? Fearful? Too tired to care? Wanting mercy? Other?

3. In the interplay between the demon and Jesus in verses 9–13, what do you learn about demons?

4. Contrast what result Jesus had on the man versus what the demons did to the pigs. What does this tell you about Jesus? About demons?

The Healing of a Demon-possessed Man

5 *They went across the lake to the region of the Gerasenes. ²When Jesus got out of the boat, a man with an evil spirit came from the tombs to meet him. ³This man lived in the tombs, and no one could bind him any more, not even with a chain. ⁴For he had often been chained hand and foot, but he tore the chains apart and broke the irons on his feet. No one was strong enough to subdue him. ⁵Night and day among the tombs and in the hills he would cry out and cut himself with stones.*

⁶When he saw Jesus from a distance, he ran and fell on his knees in front of him. ⁷He shouted at the top of his voice, "What do you want with me, Jesus, Son of the Most High God? Swear to God that you won't torture me!" ⁸For Jesus had said to him, "Come out of this man, you evil spirit!"

⁹Then Jesus asked him, "What is your name?"

"My name is Legion," he replied, "for we are many." ¹⁰And he begged Jesus again and again not to send them out of the area.

¹¹A large herd of pigs was feeding on the nearby hillside. ¹²The demons begged Jesus, "Send us among the pigs; allow us to go into them." ¹³He gave them permission, and the evil spirits came out and went into the pigs. The herd, about two thousand in number, rushed down the steep bank into the lake and were drowned.

¹⁴Those tending the pigs ran off and reported this in the town and countryside, and the people went out to see what had happened. ¹⁵When they came to Jesus, they saw the man who had been possessed by the legion of demons, sitting there, dressed and in his right mind; and they were afraid. ¹⁶Those who had seen it told the people what had happened to the demon-possessed man—and told about the pigs as well. ¹⁷Then the people began to plead with Jesus to leave their region.

¹⁸As Jesus was getting into the boat, the man who had been demon-possessed begged to go with him. ¹⁹Jesus did not let him, but said, "Go home to your family and tell them how much the Lord has done for you, and how he has had mercy on you." ²⁰So the man went away and began to tell in the Decapolis how much Jesus had done for him. And all the people were amazed.

5. Why were the people afraid when they saw the man who had been possessed "sitting there, dressed and in his right mind" (v. 15)? Why did they ask Jesus to leave?

6. In contrast to earlier stories, why did Jesus tell this man to share with others what happened to him (see note on v. 19)?

7. Who can you tell this week "how much the Lord has done for you" (v. 19)?

CARING TIME
(Choose 1 or 2 of these questions before closing in prayer. Be sure to pray for the empty chair.)

1. It's "gut check" time. How's it going in your spiritual life *really*?

2. Who is someone you could invite to join this group?

3. How can this group help you in prayer this week?

Notes—Mark 5:1–20

Summary. Both the Gospels of Mark and Matthew (which has a briefer account of this story—Matthew 8:28–34) include this story with a group of other stories of Jesus' power which illustrate his authority over all kinds of realms, natural and supernatural. By doing so, the authors accomplish two goals: (1) readers uncertain of Jesus' identity are continually stretched to see him as divine, and (2) those who follow Jesus are encouraged by these reminders that nothing is outside the scope of his authority. While Matthew mentions two demoniacs, the point of both stories is to accent Jesus' authority over seemingly overwhelming, powerful supernatural forces of evil. The demoniac is ravished by not one but thousands of demons. Once again Jesus demonstrates his power by casting out this combined force of demons and healing a man whose body and personality had been overwhelmed by their evil possession.

5:1 *They went across the lake.* Jesus and his disciples were in a boat on the Sea of Galilee. This incident takes place after Jesus calms the fierce storm that threatened to swamp their boat (Mark 4:35–41). Given the fact that Jesus and the Twelve left the Galilee side of the lake "when evening came" (4:35), by the time they arrive at the other side it is probably dark.

the region of the Gerasenes. The precise location of their landing is not clear. However, it is on the other side of the lake from Capernaum, in Gentile territory, probably near the lower end of the Sea of Galilee.

5:2 *Jesus got out of the boat.* No mention is made of the disciples in this story. Given what they had been through on the lake (and the fact that they landed in a Gentile region at night in a graveyard with a nightmare-like figure howling at them), it is not surprising that only Jesus got out of the boat to face this terror.

a man with an evil spirit. There was widespread belief that demons could enter and take control of a person's body, speaking and acting through that person. First-century people lived in dread of demons (see note on 1:23 in Session 2). They avoided places, like cemeteries, where demons were thought to dwell. The demons were understood to be Satan's legions. In overcoming them, Jesus was demonstrating his power over Satan and his work.

tombs. The ragged limestone cliffs with their caves and depressions provided a natural burial site. The demoniac occupied the place of the dead, indicating the nature of the evil that was at work in him.

5:3–5 The man was a living terror: naked, physically so powerful he could not be subdued, cut up and perhaps bleeding, crying out in the tombs.

5:6–9 The demons recognize Jesus as a threat. By naming him, they are probably relying on ancient magical practices in the hope of gaining mastery over Jesus. It was believed that knowledge of a person's true identity (or secret name) gave one power over that person. Since the demons named Jesus, supposedly they would have Jesus in their power. All the while Jesus is commanding the demons to leave the man (v. 8). Finally, Jesus compels the demons to reveal their name (v. 9).

5:6 *fell on his knees.* Thus the demons acknowledge Jesus' power over them. Likewise, in verse 7 they request that he not torture them, again acknowledging his superior power.

5:7 *Son of the Most High God.* The disciples ask who Jesus is (see 4:41); the demon-filled man, with supernatural insight, points out Jesus' divine nature (see 1:11). Interestingly, this is how God was often referred to by Gentiles (see Gen. 14:17–24; Ps. 97:9; Dan. 4:17).

Swear to God that you won't torture me! It is not clear what they feared. According to Jewish apocalyptic literature, the torment of demons was to take place at the time of the final judgment. Jesus' presence signals to them the beginning of the end times.

5:8 Jesus' power is acknowledged by the reluctant obedience they give to this command.

5:9 *Legion.* The name for a company of 6,000 Roman soldiers. The man was occupied not by one, but by a huge number of demons. This name also conveys the sense of warfare that is going on between Jesus and Satan. The Roman legions were the first-century world's most fierce fighting force. As such it is an apt name for the kind of overwhelmingly powerful possession by evil that had occurred. Even in this ultimate situation, Jesus demonstrates his power over evil. It cannot stand against him, even in its most virulent form.

5:10 Again, it is not clear what they feared. Perhaps they feared being banished to hell. Contrary to popular thought, hell is not the realm where Satan and his demons are in charge. The New Testament pictures it as the place of their torment. According to Jude 6, Christ would bind such disobedient spirits until the Day of Judgment. Nor is it clear that being allowed to enter the pigs—who were quickly drowned—was all that more desirable.

5:11 *pigs.* This was a Gentile herd, since no Jew would raise pigs (Lev. 11:1–8). This was probably a herd made up of pigs owned by various people in town.

5:12 *Send us among the pigs.* Rather than having Jesus condemn them to hell, the demons begged to be allowed to inhabit the bodies of the pigs. To Jewish readers especially, this would stress the unclean, corrupt nature of the demons.

5:13 *rushed down the steep bank.* The stampede of the herd gave evidence that the demons had, indeed, been driven out of the man. Their mad, suicidal rush into the lake illustrates the demons' ultimate intention for the man as well. The story demonstrates the destructive, murderous effect of evil spirits in contrast to the healing and peace offered by Jesus.

5:14–17 The whole incident is reported to the townspeople, who arrive in mass and find not only the drowned pigs but the healed demoniac.

5:15 *they were afraid.* It might be expected that they would rejoice that this man who had terrorized them (and whom they could no longer restrain) was now healed. But instead they are fearful of Jesus, who had the power to overcome the demons and destroy their town herd.

5:17 *the people began to plead with Jesus to leave.* They want no part of one who in their eyes would appear to be a powerful magician—one who regarded a single madman to be worth more than their whole town herd.

5:18–20 The focus shifts from the frightened townfolk to the grateful ex-demoniac. He wants to join Jesus' band, but is instead commanded to return home and share his story of God's mercy.

5:19 *tell.* In contrast to what Jesus said to the leper: "See that you don't tell this to anyone" (Mark 1:44), he wants this man to share the story of his healing. The difference is that the leper was Jewish and his story might cause people to think that the Messiah had come before they knew what kind of Messiah Jesus was. Gentiles, however, did not have such messianic expectations. Interestingly, what the ex-demoniac could tell them was limited. He could explain what he was like before he met Jesus, what had happened to him when he encountered Jesus, and what little he knew about Jesus. This first Gentile witness to Jesus had no theological training; he simply had an amazing story to tell by which God's nature would be revealed.

5:20 *Decapolis.* A league of 10 Gentile cities patterned after the Greek way of life. This is the first of several ventures by Jesus into Gentile areas, demonstrating what Mark later points out (13:10; 14:9), that the Gospel is to be preached to all nations.

9 Powerful Healings—Mark 5:21–43

THREE-PART AGENDA

ICE-BREAKER
15 Minutes

BIBLE STUDY
30 Minutes

CARING TIME
15–45 Minutes

> *LEADER: Check page M7 in the center section for a good ice-breaker, particularly if you have a new person at this meeting. In the Caring Time, is everyone sharing and are prayer requests being followed up?*

TO BEGIN THE BIBLE STUDY TIME
(Choose 1 or 2)

1. What is your remedy for stopping a bloody nose?

2. Who is the best doctor you've ever had? What's the longest time you've spent in the hospital?

3. Whose voice or touch can you recognize in an instant—even in a crowded room?

READ SCRIPTURE & DISCUSS
(If you don't have time for all the questions in this section, conclude the Bible Study [30 min.] by answering question #7.)

1. What's the longest you've had to suffer with a physical ailment?

2. Of all the people pressing for Jesus' attention, two get through to him in this story. Why?

3. What obstacles did Jairus and the bleeding woman have to overcome to reach out to Jesus for help (see notes on v. 22 and v. 25)?

4. After the woman was healed, why was it important to Jesus that she be identified?

A Dead Girl and a Sick Woman

21When Jesus had again crossed over by boat to the other side of the lake, a large crowd gathered around him while he was by the lake. 22Then one of the synagogue rulers, named Jairus, came there. Seeing Jesus, he fell at his feet 23and pleaded earnestly with him, "My little daughter is dying. Please come and put your hands on her so that she will be healed and live." 24So Jesus went with him.

A large crowd followed and pressed around him. 25And a woman was there who had been subject to bleeding for twelve years. 26She had suffered a great deal under the care of many doctors and had spent all she had, yet instead of getting better she grew worse. 27When she heard about Jesus, she came up behind him in the crowd and touched his cloak, 28because she thought, "If I just touch his clothes, I will be healed." 29Immediately her bleeding stopped and she felt in her body that she was freed from her suffering.

30At once Jesus realized that power had gone out from him. He turned around in the crowd and asked, "Who touched my clothes?"

31"You see the people crowding against you," his disciples answered, "and yet you can ask, 'Who touched me?' "

32But Jesus kept looking around to see who had done it. 33Then the woman, knowing what had happened to her, came and fell at his feet and, trembling with fear, told him the whole truth. 34He said to her, "Daughter, your faith has healed you. Go in peace and be freed from your suffering."

35While Jesus was still speaking, some men came from the house of Jairus, the synagogue ruler. "Your daughter is dead," they said. "Why bother the teacher any more?"

36Ignoring what they said, Jesus told the synagogue ruler, "Don't be afraid; just believe."

37He did not let anyone follow him except Peter, James and John the brother of James. 38When they came to the home of the synagogue ruler, Jesus saw a commotion, with people crying and wailing loudly. 39He went in and said to them, "Why all this commotion and wailing? The child is not dead but asleep." 40But they laughed at him.

After he put them all out, he took the child's father and mother and the disciples who were with him, and went in where the child was. 41He took her by the hand and said to

5. What factors were involved in the healing of the woman?

6. When do you remember being the most desperate for God's intervention? How did you "reach out" to Jesus?

7. Where in your life do you need to reach out in faith to Jesus now?

CARING TIME

(Choose 1 or 2 of these questions before closing in prayer. Be sure to pray for the empty chair.)

1. Share something God taught you during a period of hardship.

2. What issue in your life has needed quiet prayer this week, but you never got around to it?

3. In what specific way can the group pray for you this week?

her, "Talitha koum!" (which means, "Little girl, I say to you, get up!"). ⁴²Immediately the girl stood up and walked around (she was twelve years old). At this they were completely astonished. ⁴³He gave strict orders not to let anyone know about this, and told them to give her something to eat.

Notes—Mark 5:21–43

Summary. Mark tells two more "power" stories to emphasize Jesus' absolute and universal authority over all forces that oppress humanity. Just as the Gentile demoniac would have been considered ceremonially "unclean" by the Jews, so this woman with the interminable menstrual flow and the dead girl would be viewed as "unclean" people to be avoided by those who wished to maintain their purity before God. The two stories are interwoven, signifying that they are to be understood in relation to each other. Both deal with females who were second-class citizens in the first-century scheme of things; both women are ceremonially unclean; both are confronted by desperate situations which lead to death; and both women are healed by faith through Jesus' touch. Despite these similarities, there is a stark contrast in the two stories as well: Jairus is a respected leader in the community, a man with religious authority. In contrast, the other character is an impoverished woman others would shun. Yet both realize that Jesus is the answer to their desperate need. These two stories relate to the two in 4:35–5:20 in that all the stories deal with the threat (or reality) of death, all are situations beyond human control, and all accent Jesus' authority in ways that were totally unexpected.

5:21 *the other side of the lake.* Jesus is once again in Jewish territory.

5:22 *synagogue rulers.* The temple in Jerusalem was the sole place for sacrifice, and was attended by many priests and officials. In contrast, synagogues were found in each town. People met there every Sabbath for worship and instruction. Synagogues were run by a committee of lay people (the rulers).

he fell at his feet. In light of the "official" position of the religious leadership against Jesus, it could not have been easy for Jairus, this leader in the community, to humble himself before Jesus in this way. But his concern for his daughter outweighs his pride.

5:23 *put your hands on her.* The laying on of hands was a common practice used for ordination, for blessing, in the sacrificial ritual, and for healing.

5:25 *a woman was there.* She should not have been there in the crowd. Because of the nature of her illness, she was considered "unclean." If people touched her, they too would become "unclean" and have to undergo a lengthy ritual of purification before being allowed to participate in the religious and social life of the community again.

subject to bleeding. Probably hemorrhaging from the womb. In any case, any such bleeding rendered her ritually impure (see Lev. 15:25–30), thus cutting her off from contact with other people, including her husband. As a result, she has to seek out Jesus in this surreptitious way.

5:26 When Luke the physician told this story (Luke 8:42–48), he left out this verse with its rather scathing condemnation of doctors!

the care of many doctors. Typical cures would have included such things as carrying the ash of an ostrich egg in a certain cloth, or drinking wine mixed with rubber, alum and garden crocuses.

5:28 *If I just touch his clothes, I will be healed.* Jesus' reputation as a healer had obviously preceded him. Yet the woman's perception of Jesus at this point was probably tinged with superstitious notions about how even the garments of a healer possessed power. There is no attempt on her part to establish genuine contact with Jesus: she simply wants to brush up against him so that she can be brought in contact with his power. Nonetheless, by this action the woman showed that she had "ears to hear" (Mark 4:9) and had faith that Jesus could indeed heal her.

5:29 *Immediately.* This is a prominent word throughout Mark's Gospel. It emphasizes the irresistible power inherent in Jesus' person. The same word is translated in verse 30 as "at once."

5:30 *power.* The mysterious power of God. For the first time, Mark identifies clearly what these four stories in 4:35–5:43 are all about.

Who touched my clothes? Jesus desired a relationship with those he helped. He was not an impersonal power source.

5:32 *Jesus kept looking around.* Jesus insists that the person who touched him identify herself. Her healing will not be complete without this, since her illness had not only physical but social consequences. Jesus makes it publicly known that she has been healed so that she can once again have a normal relational life (see also Mark 1:44).

5:33 *trembling with fear.* Fear is a common element in all four power stories (4:40–41; 5:15,36). Not only do the people in the scenes face frightening circumstances, but there is fear of Jesus as everyone is caught off guard by his authority that exceeds all their expectations. This woman may have feared that she had done something wrong; she may have feared that Jesus would shame her in front of everyone; she may have feared that her healing would be revoked.

5:34 *your faith has healed you.* It was her faith that impelled her to reach out to Jesus—the source of healing power. The word Jesus uses to tell her that she is healed comes from the same root as the words "salvation" and "Savior." Spiritual as well as physical healing is in view here.

Go in peace. Jesus did not mean by this, "Be free from worry." This phrase means, "Be complete, be whole." Each of these four incidents portrays an

extreme situation in which there is no hope, and yet each ends in peace as the result of the power of Jesus (see Mark 4:39; 5:15; 5:34; 5:42).

5:35–36 It is reported to Jairus that his daughter has died, so Jesus' help is not needed. Jesus might be able to heal a sick girl, but no one expected that he could do anything about a dead child. Jesus, however, counsels faith in the face of fear. Three different faith responses are seen in the four accounts: the disciples' fear on the lake stifled their faith (Mark 4:40); the townspeople's fear blinded them to Jesus' heralding power (Mark 5:15); the woman and Jairus, however, display faith in spite of fear.

5:37 *Peter, James and John.* These three disciples become a sort of inner circle around Jesus (see Mark 9:2; 13:3; 14:33).

5:38 *people crying and wailing loudly.* These were in all likelihood professional mourners. Even the poorest person was required to hire not less than two flutes and one wailing woman to mourn a death. They are a sign that all felt the child was dead.

5:39 *The child is not dead but asleep.* This is said to reassure the father. The presence of the mourners, the report of the messengers, the laughter that greeted this statement all say the same thing: the child was truly dead. Jesus uses this same expression in reference to Lazarus (John 11:11–15).

5:41 *Talitha koum!* This is Aramaic, the language of Palestine. It means, literally, "Arise, lamb" and emphasizes Jesus' compassion. Mark translates this phrase for the benefit of his Gentile readers.

5:42 *Immediately.* Once again, this is shown to be a genuine miracle. She is made fully alive and is able to walk and eat. Jesus has actually done the impossible. He has raised a person from the dead in this ultimate demonstration of his power.

5:43 *strict orders not to let anyone know about this.* Jesus' statement that she is asleep, not dead (v. 39), makes it possible for her parents to obey his request. At this point in his ministry, if word got out that Jesus could raise people from the dead, it would cause the populace to make the wrong assumptions about him ("He is the Messiah who will lead us to victory over the Romans"), and thus frustrate his true ministry.

10 Jesus' Reputation—Mark 6:1–29

THREE-PART AGENDA

ICE-BREAKER
15 Minutes

BIBLE STUDY
30 Minutes

CARING TIME
15–45 Minutes

> **LEADER: Check page M7 in the center section for a good ice-breaker, particularly if you have a new person at this meeting. Is your group working well together—with everyone "fielding their position" as shown on the team roster on page M5?**

TO BEGIN THE BIBLE STUDY TIME
(Choose 1 or 2)

1. What childhood escapade of yours do you hear about most often when you're together with family?

2. Where would you like to go on your next vacation?

3. If you were granted one wish for your next birthday, what would it be?

READ SCRIPTURE & DISCUSS
(If you don't have time for all the questions in this section, conclude the Bible Study [30 min.] by answering question #7.)

1. Where did you grow up? What did you like best—and least—about your hometown?

2. What kind of response did Jesus get when he went to his hometown of Nazareth? How do you handle insults and put-downs?

3. What three tasks that characterized Jesus' ministry did he send the disciples to do (vv. 12–13)? Where does Jesus want to send you?

A Prophet Without Honor

6 *Jesus left there and went to his hometown, accompanied by his disciples. ²When the Sabbath came, he began to teach in the synagogue, and many who heard him were amazed.*

"Where did this man get these things?" they asked. "What's this wisdom that has been given him, that he even does miracles! ³Isn't this the carpenter? Isn't this Mary's son and the brother of James, Joseph,ª Judas and Simon? Aren't his sisters here with us?" And they took offense at him.

⁴Jesus said to them, "Only in his hometown, among his relatives and in his own house is a prophet without honor." ⁵He could not do any miracles there, except lay his hands on a few sick people and heal them. ⁶And he was amazed at their lack of faith.

Jesus Sends Out the Twelve

Then Jesus went around teaching from village to village. ⁷Calling the Twelve to him, he sent them out two by two and gave them authority over evilᵇ spirits.

⁸These were his instructions: "Take nothing for the journey except a staff—no bread, no bag, no money in your belts. ⁹Wear sandals but not an extra tunic. ¹⁰Whenever you enter a house, stay there until you leave that town. ¹¹And if any place will not welcome you or listen to you, shake the dust off your feet when you leave, as a testimony against them."

¹²They went out and preached that people should repent. ¹³They drove out many demons and anointed many sick people with oil and healed them.

John the Baptist Beheaded

¹⁴King Herod heard about this, for Jesus' name had become well known. Some were saying,ᶜ "John the Baptist has been raised from the dead, and that is why miraculous powers are at work in him."

¹⁵Others said, "He is Elijah."

And still others claimed, "He is a prophet, like one of the prophets of long ago."

¹⁶But when Herod heard this, he said, "John, the man I beheaded, has been raised from the dead!"

4. Why did Herod throw John in prison, and why did Herod's wife want John killed (vv. 17–19)?

5. Of the people involved in the death of John the Baptist, who do you hold most responsible?

6. Would you consider John's ministry a success or a tragedy? How do you measure spiritual success?

7. On a scale of 1 (Jello pudding) to 10 (Rock of Gibralter), how would you rate yourself on standing up for what is morally right?

CARING TIME
(Choose 1 or 2 of these questions before closing in prayer. Be sure to pray for the empty chair.)

1. How is your group functioning in your "team assignments"? (Review the team roster on page M5 in the center section.)

2. If you could compare last week to a circus (clowns, trapeze artist, lion tamer, human cannonball, juggler, dog show, etc.), how would you describe it?

3. What would you like to share with this group for prayer this week?

[17] *For Herod himself had given orders to have John arrested, and he had him bound and put in prison. He did this because of Herodias, his brother Philip's wife, whom he had married.* [18] *For John had been saying to Herod, "It is not lawful for you to have your brother's wife."* [19] *So Herodias nursed a grudge against John and wanted to kill him. But she was not able to,* [20] *because Herod feared John and protected him, knowing him to be a righteous and holy man. When Herod heard John, he was greatly puzzled; yet he liked to listen to him.*

[21] *Finally the opportune time came. On his birthday Herod gave a banquet for his high officials and military commanders and the leading men of Galilee.* [22] *When the daughter of Herodias came in and danced, she pleased Herod and his dinner guests.*

The king said to the girl, "Ask me for anything you want, and I'll give it to you." [23] *And he promised her with an oath, "Whatever you ask I will give you, up to half my kingdom."*

[24] *She went out and said to her mother, "What shall I ask for?"*

"The head of John the Baptist," she answered.

[25] *At once the girl hurried in to the king with the request: "I want you to give me right now the head of John the Baptist on a platter."*

[26] *The king was greatly distressed, but because of his oaths and his dinner guests, he did not want to refuse her.* [27] *So he immediately sent an executioner with orders to bring John's head. The man went, beheaded John in the prison,* [28] *and brought back his head on a platter. He presented it to the girl, and she gave it to her mother.* [29] *On hearing of this, John's disciples came and took his body and laid it in a tomb.*

[a] *3 Greek Joses, a variant of Joseph*
[b] *7 Greek unclean*
[c] *14 Some early manuscripts He was saying*
[d] *20 Some early manuscripts he did many things*

6:1–6 Having demonstrated the great power of Jesus in the previous section, Mark now tells a story in which Jesus is unable to use this power because of the lack of people's faith.

6:1 *his hometown.* Nazareth, which was located in the hill country of Galilee some 20 miles southwest of Capernaum. (See also Luke 4:14–30.)

accompanied by his disciples. This was not a private visit. Jesus arrived as a rabbi with a band of disciples. He then taught in the synagogue as would a rabbi.

6:2 *amazed.* The townspeople responded to what Jesus said in the same way as had others before them (see 1:22,27; 2:12; 5:20).

Where did this man get these things? The townspeople do not deny Jesus' wisdom nor his power to do miracles. But they are puzzled as to the origin of such abilities.

6:3 The tone of these questions implies that these people are wondering, "Who does this illegitimate working-class kid think he is?" They fail to acknowledge him even as a rabbi worth listening to.

carpenter. The Greek word refers to a general craftsman who works not only in wood but also in stone and metal. This word usually referred to skilled workers who traveled throughout the countryside working at their trade.

Mary's son. A man was never described as the son of his mother (even if she was a widow) except as an insult. The townsfolk probably heard rumors of Jesus' unusual birth and took him to be illegitimate rather than virgin-born.

brother / sisters. Mark names four brothers and indicates that Jesus had sisters too.

they took offense at him. They could not get past his humble and familiar origins—therefore, they couldn't give credence to who he really was.

6:4 This was a proverbial saying Jesus applied to himself indicating that typically an influential person finds it hardest to earn the respect of those who already assume they know all about him or her.

among his relatives and in his own house. Jesus' family continues to oppose his ministry (see also 3:20–21).

a prophet. Jesus uses this term for himself. It is an accurate description, though not a complete one (see 6:14–16; 8:27–30).

6:5 The emphasis is not on Jesus' inability to do miracles (Mark has amply demonstrated that he has the power to do so), but on the hostile environment that stifles that power. To be healed, a person must have at least enough faith to come to Jesus and ask for healing.

6:6 *amazed.* Now it is Jesus' turn to be amazed. The townspeople were amazed at his teaching (v. 1), but they could not get over their assumptions about him. They fault him for being ordinary ("with brothers and sisters like us"), for acting like a rabbi ("only a common laborer"), and for the supposed scandal of his birth ("Mary's son"). So they do not ask for healing. This amazes Jesus.

6:7–13 In contrast to the negative response to his power by his relatives and childhood friends, Mark shows the positive response of his disciples, who accept the challenge to go out on their own and minister in the same way as Jesus has ministered (teaching, healing, exorcism).

6:7 *he sent them out.* To go out on a ministry tour is not the idea or plan of the Twelve. Jesus does the sending.

two by two. He did not send them alone—perhaps as a protection against robbers; perhaps because two witnesses have more credibility than one (see Deut. 17:6); perhaps so that they will support one another as they learn to minister. The parallel accounts in Matthew and Luke indicate that their mission was to announce and demonstrate the fact that God's kingdom was now at hand (Mark 1:15).

gave them authority. He empowers them to do battle with evil. It is in his name and power that they minister.

6:8–9 These are not universal prohibitions (see Luke 22:35–36).

6:8 *instructions.* These instructions cause the Twelve to pare down to the bare minimum. They take only the clothes on their backs and a staff, the tool of a shepherd, a point which will be underscored in the story of the feeding of the five thousand (6:30–44). By faith they must trust that God will provide the rest of their needs as they go about his work. These instructions reflect the urgency of the task upon which the Twelve have been sent.

no bag. The reference is (probably) to a begging bag commonly used by wandering priests to collect funds.

6:9 *extra tunic.* That would be used as a blanket during the chilly nights.

6:10 They are not to dishonor their host by accepting better accommodations.

6:11 Hospitality for travelers was a sacred duty. Villages not offering it were judged by the prophetic action that Jesus here commands. This is similar to what pious Jews did when they left a Gentile region and returned to Israel. They shook off the dust of the lands through which they had just traveled so as to disassociate themselves from the coming judgment against the Gentiles.

6:12–13 The Twelve performed each of the tasks that characterized Jesus' ministry: preaching repentance (1:15), casting out demons (1:27), and healing the sick (1:34).

6:14–29 In a parenthetical flashback, Mark describes how John the Baptist died at the hands of Herod. This account, sandwiched between the sending out of the Twelve (vv. 7–13) and their return (v. 30) foreshadows the type of response those who are faithful to God can expect to receive from the powerful people of the world. This account also contrasts the relative powerlessness of Herod (despite the fact that he had all the trappings of political power) to the great power of Jesus (who had no official status at all). Two kings and two kingdoms are contrasted in the story of Herod's party and that of Jesus' feeding of the five thousand (6:30–44).

6:14–16 The issue once again is: Who is Jesus? (See also 1:27, 2:7; 4:41.) Three answers are proposed. He is John the Baptist come back from the dead (the answer Herod opts for in his guilt); he is Elijah (the forerunner of the Messiah); or he is a new prophet.

6:14 *King Herod.* Herod Antipas was the ruler of the Roman provinces of Galilee and Perea from 4 B.C. to A.D. 39. He was the son of Herod the Great, the Jewish ruler who ordered the slaughter of the babies at the time of Jesus' birth. Herod Antipas was, as Matthew 14:1 says, a "tetrarch"—the ruler of a fourth of a region. Therefore, he was not, in fact, the "king." When he went to Rome some years later to request this title, his power was taken away and he was banished. Herod is pretending to be king when, in fact, the real King of Israel (Jesus) is largely unrecognized.

John the Baptist has been raised from the dead. Obviously, only people personally unfamiliar with the background of Jesus would have assumed this since Jesus and John were contemporaries. However, the fact that Jesus' ministry did not begin until after John's death led some people to assume that only a holy person who had come back from death could possibly have such powers.

6:15 *Elijah.* The Jews felt that when Elijah returned, as foretold in Malachi 3:1 and 4:5–6, their deliverance from Rome was near.

a prophet. Others did not credit Jesus with being the final prophet, but felt he was one of the long line of prophets associated with Israel's past.

6:16 "In Jewish thinking resurrection is the prelude to judgment, and the terror of judgment may be caught in Herod's statement, 'John, the man I beheaded, has been raised from the dead' " (Lane). Herod fears God's judgment upon him is drawing near.

6:17–29 This is a flashback within the flashback as Herod recalls how he came to kill John.

6:18 *It is not lawful.* According to Leviticus 18:16 and 20:21, it was not lawful for a man to marry his brother's wife while that brother was still alive. Herod, a Jew himself, scandalized his people by divorcing the Nabatean Princess Aretas to marry Herodias, who was his niece (the daughter of his half-brother) and his sister-in-law (the wife of a different brother). More than personal resentment against John's accusation was probably involved. In the account of John's execution written by the Jewish historian Josephus, fear of a political uprising is given as the motive for Herod's imprisonment of John. Herod's fears of this prospect may well have been grounded in the fact that his dismissal of his former wife in favor of Herodias had incensed both the neighboring Nabateans as well as the Jews in his own province. John was seen as an agitator stirring up trouble by his bold accusations.

6:20 Herod serves as an example of someone who is like the thorny soil (4:18–19). He is attracted to what John says, but his concern for power prevents him from heeding John's call to repentance.

6:21 *the opportune time.* Herodias was plotting a way to kill John (v. 19) because of his criticism of her marriage.

a banquet. The sparseness of the lifestyle of the Twelve (vv. 8–11) would have contrasted greatly with the opulence of Herod's birthday party. The men in attendance would have been wealthy landowners, those in high government positions, and military officials. The terms used are those used to describe the official court in Rome, probably an ironic reminder that Herod, though only a tetrarch, modeled his court on the royal example. He is a pretend king.

6:22 *the daughter of Herodias.* Herodias' teenage daughter (from her first marriage), whose name is Salome (according to the historian Josephus).

danced. For a princess to dance publicly before an audience of drunken men was considered most shameful. Her dance was undoubtedly highly sensual (although there is no historical evidence that it involved the seven veils mentioned in dramatized versions of this event).

his dinner guests. These are the leading men of the nation (v. 21). They contrast with the common folk among whom the ministry of the Twelve took place (vv. 12–13) and who will later be in attendance at the "banquet" Jesus hosts (6:30–44).

Ask me for anything you want. This was a foolhardy promise, a boastful display of power gone bad. Herodias succeeds in manipulating Herod by exploiting his lust, his drunkenness, and his tendency to show off. This is the opportunity she has been waiting for (see vv. 19–20).

6:25 *the head of John the Baptist on a platter.* This was a gruesome act: serving John's head on a platter as if it were another course in the banquet.

6:26 Once again, Herod is shown to be like the thorny soil. While distressed at the request, his concern for "other things" (4:19) led him to go ahead with Herodias' plan. He does so in order that he not look weak before the other men at the party, however the fact that he was manipulated into this position reveals his actual powerlessness and lack of true authority.

6:27 There are two passion stories in Mark. The death of John the Baptist is the first. It sets the stage for the second: the passion and death of Jesus, the telling of which is Mark's main intention for his Gospel.

11 Two Miracles—Mark 6:30–56

THREE-PART AGENDA

ICE-BREAKER
15 Minutes

BIBLE STUDY
30 Minutes

CARING TIME
15–45 Minutes

LEADER: Have you started working with your group about your mission—for instance, by having them review page M3 in the center section? If you have a new person at the meeting, remember to do an appropriate ice-breaker from the center section.

TO BEGIN THE BIBLE STUDY TIME
(Choose 1 or 2)

1. What's the most people you've ever had over for a meal?

2. Describe your first experience swimming, water-skiing, surfing or ice-skating.

3. Where do you like to go "to get away from it all"?

READ SCRIPTURE & DISCUSS
(If you don't have time for all the questions in this section, conclude the Bible Study [30 min.] by answering question #7.)

1. When has a vacation you've taken not gone according to plan?

2. The disciples thought they were getting a break (v. 31), but they ended up serving. If you were one of the disciples, how would you have felt?

3. What is the difference between the way Jesus looked on the crowd and the way the disciples viewed them?

4. What is the closest you have come to experiencing "compassion fatigue"—the stress and distress of constantly trying to respond to overwhelming human needs?

Jesus Feeds the Five Thousand

³⁰*The apostles gathered around Jesus and reported to him all they had done and taught. ³¹Then, because so many people were coming and going that they did not even have a chance to eat, he said to them, "Come with me by yourselves to a quiet place and get some rest."*

³²*So they went away by themselves in a boat to a solitary place. ³³But many who saw them leaving recognized them and ran on foot from all the towns and got there ahead of them. ³⁴When Jesus landed and saw a large crowd, he had compassion on them, because they were like sheep without a shepherd. So he began teaching them many things.*

³⁵*By this time it was late in the day, so his disciples came to him. "This is a remote place," they said, "and it's already very late. ³⁶Send the people away so they can go to the surrounding countryside and villages and buy themselves something to eat."*

³⁷*But he answered, "You give them something to eat."*

*They said to him, "That would take eight months of a man's wages*ᵃ*! Are we to go and spend that much on bread and give it to them to eat?"*

³⁸*"How many loaves do you have?" he asked. "Go and see."*

When they found out, they said, "Five—and two fish."

³⁹*Then Jesus directed them to have all the people sit down in groups on the green grass. ⁴⁰So they sat down in groups of hundreds and fifties. ⁴¹Taking the five loaves and the two fish and looking up to heaven, he gave thanks and broke the loaves. Then he gave them to his disciples to set before the people. He also divided the two fish among them all. ⁴²They all ate and were satisfied, ⁴³and the disciples picked up twelve basketfuls of broken pieces of bread and fish. ⁴⁴The number of the men who had eaten was five thousand.*

Jesus Walks on the Water

⁴⁵*Immediately Jesus made his disciples get into the boat and go on ahead of him to Bethsaida, while he dismissed the crowd. ⁴⁶After leaving them, he went up on a mountainside to pray.*

⁴⁷*When evening came, the boat was in the middle of the lake, and he was alone on land. ⁴⁸He saw the disciples*

5. How do the disciples respond when Jesus walks on water?

6. What would you do if you saw Jesus walking on a lake? What miracle would you like Jesus to do in your life?

7. In what situation in your life do you need to hear Jesus' words, "Don't be afraid" (v. 50)?

CARING TIME
(Choose 1 or 2 of these questions before closing in prayer. Be sure to pray for the empty chair.)

1. What is your dream for the future mission of this group?

2. How are you doing with spending personal time in prayer and Bible Study?

3. How can this group help you in prayer?

straining at the oars, because the wind was against them. About the fourth watch of the night he went out to them, walking on the lake. He was about to pass by them, ⁴⁹but when they saw him walking on the lake, they thought he was a ghost. They cried out, ⁵⁰because they all saw him and were terrified.

Immediately he spoke to them and said, "Take courage! It is I. Don't be afraid." ⁵¹Then he climbed into the boat with them, and the wind died down. They were completely amazed, ⁵²for they had not understood about the loaves; their hearts were hardened.

⁵³When they had crossed over, they landed at Gennesaret and anchored there. ⁵⁴As soon as they got out of the boat, people recognized Jesus. ⁵⁵They ran throughout that whole region and carried the sick on mats to wherever they heard he was. ⁵⁶And wherever he went—into villages, towns or countryside—they placed the sick in the marketplaces. They begged him to let them touch even the edge of his cloak, and all who touched him were healed.

ᵃ37 Greek *take two hundred denarii*

Notes—Mark 6:30-56

Summary. Mark begins his third major section. In the first section (1:14–4:34), the disciples (and others) view Jesus as an exceptionally gifted teacher. In section two (4:35–6:29), Jesus is shown to be a prophet of amazing power. In section three (6:30–8:30), he is discovered to be the Messiah (8:27–30). Thus, the disciples' understanding of Jesus continues to unfold. In this section there are two parallel cycles of stories. The point is made in both cycles that it will take a miracle from Jesus to heal the hardened hearts of the Twelve so that they can see who he really is—or at least understand as much as they can prior to his death and resurrection. Cycle one (6:30–7:37) begins with the feeding of the five thousand and ends with the healing of a deaf and mute man. Cycle two (8:1–26) begins with the feeding of the four thousand and ends with the

healing of a blind man. In both cycles, the reader is shown the inability of the disciples to understand what is happening. It is as if they are deaf, dumb and blind. As a foil for their hardness of heart, both cycles contain a comment on the hardness of heart on the part of the Pharisees. In both cycles of stories, the crowds who witness these amazing events likewise fail to understand who Jesus really is.

6:30–44 In this story, Mark begins to reveal who Jesus really is. Mark does not do this directly; he does it symbolically. The fact that there are two feeding stories in Mark point in this direction. One feeding story is all that would have been necessary if the point Mark wants to make is that Jesus can perform such a miracle. Furthermore, the two stories differ in the symbols they contain. The feeding

56

of the five thousand is filled with symbols that point to Jesus' role in Israel. The feeding of the four thousand is filled with symbols that point to his role with the Gentiles.

Here in the feeding of the five thousand the symbols allude to Moses and David. Jesus is seen to be the new Moses and the new David. Thus, he is revealed to be the long-expected, now returning King of Israel, the Messiah. That the disciples come to understand the meaning of these symbolic elements is demonstrated by Peter's declaration in Mark 8:29 that they know that Jesus is the Messiah. No other information has been presented to the Twelve that would lead them to this conclusion apart from seeing Jesus function as the new Moses and new David in the two feeding stories.

6:30 The Twelve return from their mission and report to the Lord what took place in their attempt at independent ministry.

apostles. This is the only time this term is used in Mark. Here it is not so much a title as a description of what they have just done. An apostle is "one who is sent," and they have just completed the missionary work the Lord sent them out to do (6:7).

6:31 get some rest. It is Jesus who insists on rest—even though the crowds are there with all their needs and the opportunity for ministry is great (see also 1:35).

6:32–44 The feeding of the five thousand is the only miracle described in all four Gospels. Mark's main intention in telling this story is to paint for the reader a powerful picture of Jesus' divine identity.

6:33 ran on foot. The crowds are now wise to this tactic of simply sailing off across the lake and leaving them standing on the shore (see 4:35–36). So they follow on foot. The distances would not have been great (the lake was only eight miles at its widest). They could probably see where they were sailing to. As they run around the lake after Jesus, they gather more and more people.

6:34 a large crowd. It took a while for Jesus to arrive (perhaps there was a headwind or no wind that day).

sheep without a shepherd. Without a shepherd, sheep are hopelessly lost. They have no way to defend themselves and will probably starve. This

was an apt metaphor for the condition of the crowd. By and large they had been abandoned by the religious leaders. This phrase is taken from the Old Testament. It is found in Moses' prayer that God send someone to lead the people of Israel after he dies (Num. 27:17). It is also used in reference to David (Ezek. 34). This is the first of several allusions to Moses and David.

> *Without a shepherd, sheep are hopelessly lost. They have no way to defend themselves and will probably starve.*

6:35–36 The disciples recognize that they have a problem on their hands. How are they going to feed the enormous crowd that has gathered?

6:35 a remote place. This is the third reference to a wilderness area (see also vv. 31–32). This is another allusion to Moses, who fed the people in the wilderness. Jesus clearly makes this connection to himself in John 6:26–51.

6:36 Send the people away. This is the disciples' solution! "Let the people buy what they need in the nearby towns." This is not a reasonable suggestion if the situation is viewed in ordinary terms, for there are too many people for the supplies available in the local villages.

6:37 You give them something to eat. But Jesus has quite a different solution in mind! The response of the disciples indicates they had no clue as to how Jesus expected them to do this. Jesus' statement, and the entire scene, is similar to that found in 2 Kings 4:42–44. In that situation Elisha, a great prophet of the Lord, miraculously provided food for 100 people from 20 loaves of bread. Once again, Jesus is connected to an Old Testament hero through whom God worked.

eight months of a man's wages. Once again, as in the storm on the lake (4:37–38), the disciples do not expect Jesus to solve the problem in a miraculous way. The only way they can see to feed the crowd is to buy lots of food, and they do not feel an expenditure that large is warranted.

Are we to go and spend. This may mean that they did have enough money in their common purse to do this, but were reluctant to spend it this way. Or this may be just a rhetorical question. Their exasperation with Jesus is evident (see 4:38). Mark notes not only Jesus' emotional state (v. 34), but also that of the disciples.

6:39 groups on the green grass. A lovely, descriptive touch which could only come from an eyewitness. The people sat in groups in their bright red and yellow robes on the green grass, looking like a flower garden spread out across the hills. (The word translated "groups" was used to describe a Greek garden.) It was spring (mid-April), since this was the only time the grass was green.

6:40 The division of people into these groups parallels what Moses did (see Ex. 18:21).

6:41 five loaves. Small round cakes made of wheat or barley.

two fish. Probably smoked or pickled fish that was used as a sauce for the bread.

gave thanks. A common Jewish blessing at meals was "Blessed art thou, O Lord our God, king of the universe, who bringest forth bread from the earth" (Mann).

gave thanks / broke / gave. There are overtones here of the Last Supper (Mark 14:22) and the church's practice of the Eucharist (1 Cor. 11:23–24). This feeding, like the Eucharist, foreshadows the feeding of all God's people at the messianic banquet.

6:42 satisfied. Miraculously, the five loaves and two fish fed everyone not meagerly but abundantly, so that they were filled.

6:43 twelve. The number of the tribes of Israel, reinforcing the idea that what Jesus is doing here has prophetic significance as a demonstration that Jesus provides nourishment for all God's people (see note on 8:19 in Session 13).

basketfuls. Small wicker containers carried by all Jews. Each disciple returned with his full. The word used for basket describes a distinctly Jewish type of basket.

broken pieces. The Law required that the scraps of a meal be collected.

bread. Bread and eating are recurring themes in these two cycles of stories (see 6:31,36–37,42–43; 7:3–4,27–28; 8:1–4,8,14,16–17).

6:44 men. Literally, "males" (see Matt. 14:21). When all the women and children are taken into account, this was a huge crowd.

6:45–52 Matthew, Mark and John all follow the story of the feeding of the five thousand with this scene. In Mark's version, the disciples are simply overwhelmed at Jesus' power; they do not yet grasp its significance (vv. 51–52). Likewise, Mark wants to force his readers to grapple themselves with the meaning of Jesus' actions.

6:45 The reason for Jesus' abrupt dismissal of the disciples and the crowd is explained in the Gospel of John (John 6:14–15). Apparently the crowd wanted to make Jesus the king by force. The disciples are sent away, perhaps, to keep them from catching this false messianic fever.

Bethsaida. Literally, "house of the fisher." This is a village on the northern shore of the Sea of Galilee, several miles east of Capernaum. This was the birthplace of Philip, Andrew and Peter.

> *In the midst of great success and popular acclaim, once again Jesus goes off to pray. He is quick to acknowledge his dependence on God as the source of his power.*

6:46 he went ... to pray. In the midst of great success and popular acclaim, once again Jesus goes off to pray. He is quick to acknowledge his dependence on God as the source of his power. Mark recounts three occasions on which Jesus prays on his own. He did so after the initial enthusiastic response to his healing and exorcism in Galilee (1:35); he prays in the Garden of Gethsemane prior to his arrest (14:32–42), and he prays here after the crowds want to proclaim him king. On each occasion, it is dark and Jesus is alone.

6:48 *the wind was against them.* Once again (see also 4:37), the elements work against the disciples. This time the problem is not a storm, but a strong headwind that would make rowing very difficult.

the fourth watch. This was the way Roman soldiers told time. The fourth watch ran from 3 a.m. to 6 a.m. Assuming the disciples set out to sea in the late afternoon, they had been struggling at the oars for probably seven or more hours.

walking on the lake. It has already been established that Jesus is Lord over the wind and the water (4:39,41). This sort of power points to the fact that he is more than just the successor to Moses and David. In the Old Testament, it is God who treads on the water (see Job 9:8; Ps. 77:19).

He was about to pass by them. This could be translated: "for he intended to pass their way," presumably to reveal his presence and remind them of his power in the midst of their distress. Or perhaps Mark's intention is to recall Moses once again and the incident in which God revealed himself to Moses by "passing by" him on Mount Sinai (Ex. 33:19–23). This would fit in with previous allusions and amplify the sense that this incident revealed Jesus' divine nature (see notes on v. 50).

6:49 *a ghost.* The sea, especially at night, was thought to be a dwelling place for demons. Hence the response of the disciples.

6:50 *terrified.* Once before on this lake they were terrified by an event they did not expect and did not understand, namely the calming of the sea by Jesus (4:41). This is the terror of experiencing something that defies all categories of understanding.

It is I. Literally, "I am." This phrase can just be a simple declaration by Jesus that he is the "ghost" they are afraid of. However, in the Old Testament this is a phrase used by God to describe himself. (See especially Ex. 3:1–14, where in the burning bush, God reveals himself by this name to Moses.) This phrase was used by Jesus in his debate with the Jews in which he claims deity (see John 8:58). In

the context of Jesus' ongoing revelation of himself to the disciples, this is a telling phrase. Jesus is not just a new Moses or the new king in the line of David. He is the Son of God. Like the feeding of the five thousand, this miracle was intended to be a sign of his divine identity.

6:52 *they had not understood about the loaves.* The disciples had not seen in the multiplication of the loaves what that incident revealed about who Jesus is. They had not understood that he came from God, that he came as the successor to Moses and David, and that he was their true King (i.e., the Messiah). That the feeding of the five thousand was a crucial event in Jesus' self-revelation is seen in the space Mark devotes to recounting this event (it is, uncharacteristically, longer than that in Matthew or Luke), and by the fact that Mark recounts two feedings, not just one. This was an important (though enigmatic) act of self-revelation on the part of Jesus, and Mark wants to make sure his readers get the point, even though the disciples apparently do not.

their hearts were hardened. This is the problem. Like the Pharisees in the synagogue (see note on 3:5 in Session 4), the disciples' hearts are like calcified stone (in Greek the same word is used in both texts). In order for the disciples to recognize who Jesus really is, it will take a miracle to open their hearts to new understanding. In these two cycles of stories, Mark shows Jesus twice performing just such a miracle (7:31–37; 8:22–26), and the response at Caesarea Philippi (8:27–30) demonstrates that he has indeed done this very thing for the disciples. Here in chapter 6, Mark has given three examples of people who misunderstood who Jesus is, and therefore who failed to respond properly to him. The first example is the people in his hometown (6:1–6); the second is Herod (6:14–16); and the third is, surprisingly, the disciples.

6:53 *Gennesaret.* The wind having frustrated their plan to go north, they instead cross the lake to a thickly populated, fertile plain some four miles southwest of Capernaum. There, crowds again flock to him as a healer.

12 Clean & Unclean—Mark 7:1–37

THREE-PART AGENDA

ICE-BREAKER
15 Minutes

BIBLE STUDY
30 Minutes

CARING TIME
15–45 Minutes

> **Leader: If you haven't already, now is the time, to begin the process of identifying an Apprentice / Leader to start a new small group (see page M6 in the center section). Check the list of ice-breakers on page M7, especially if you have a new person in this session.**

TO BEGIN THE BIBLE STUDY TIME
(Choose 1 or 2)

1. What is the messiest food that you enjoy the most (fried chicken, cotton candy, sloppy joes, tacos, etc.)?

2. Growing up, how clean did you keep your room?

3. If you were deaf, what sound would you miss hearing the most? If you were unable to speak, what would you miss saying?

READ SCRIPTURE & DISCUSS
(If you don't have time for all the questions in this section, conclude the Bible Study [30 min.] by answering question #7.)

1. When have you had to take a stand on an issue: With family? With friends? With church policy? Other?

2. What is the issue debated by the Pharisees and Jesus (v. 15)? Given this debate, how would each define what it means to be spiritual?

3. How does Jesus' idea of unclean differ from that of the Pharisees?

Clean and Unclean

7 *The Pharisees and some of the teachers of the law who had come from Jerusalem gathered around Jesus and ²saw some of his disciples eating food with hands that were "unclean," that is, unwashed. ³(The Pharisees and all the Jews do not eat unless they give their hands a ceremonial washing, holding to the tradition of the elders. ⁴When they come from the marketplace they do not eat unless they wash. And they observe many other traditions, such as the washing of cups, pitchers and kettles.)*

⁵So the Pharisees and teachers of the law asked Jesus, "Why don't your disciples live according to the tradition of the elders instead of eating their food with 'unclean' hands?"

⁶He replied, "Isaiah was right when he prophesied about you hypocrites; as it is written:

" 'These people honor me with their lips,
but their hearts are far from me.
⁷They worship me in vain;
their teachings are but rules taught by men.'

⁸You have let go of the commands of God and are holding on to the traditions of men."

⁹And he said to them: "You have a fine way of setting aside the commands of God in order to observe your own traditions! ¹⁰For Moses said, 'Honor your father and your mother,' and, 'Anyone who curses his father or mother must be put to death.' ¹¹But you say that if a man says to his father or mother: 'Whatever help you might otherwise have received from me is Corban' (that is, a gift devoted to God), ¹²then you no longer let him do anything for his father or mother. ¹³Thus you nullify the word of God by your tradition that you have handed down. And you do many things like that."

¹⁴Again Jesus called the crowd to him and said, "Listen to me, everyone, and understand this. ¹⁵Nothing outside a man can make him 'unclean' by going into him. Rather, it is what comes out of a man that makes him 'unclean.' "

¹⁷After he had left the crowd and entered the house, his disciples asked him about this parable. ¹⁸"Are you so dull?" he asked. "Don't you see that nothing that enters a man from the outside can make him 'unclean'? ¹⁹For it doesn't go into his heart but into his stomach, and then out of his body." (In saying this, Jesus declared all foods "clean.")

4. Have you ever experienced a conflict between your religious obligations and your obligations to your loved ones? What happened?

5. The Greek woman from Syrian Phoenicia was a religious outsider. Have you ever felt like a religious outsider? What was it like? What can you do to reach out to someone who might feel like they are outside God's love?

6. Jesus listed many things that can come out of someone's heart that indicate uncleanliness (vv. 21–23). Which of these things do you struggle with the most?

7. Jesus helped the man hear and speak. What would you like Jesus to help you say to someone?

CARING TIME
(Choose 1 or 2 of these questions before closing in prayer. Be sure to pray for the empty chair.)

1. Have you started working on your group mission—to choose an Apprentice / Leader from your group to start a new group in the future? (See Mission / Multiplication on page M3.)

2. In what area of your life do you need God's power today?

3. How can the group pray for you?

²⁰*He went on: "What comes out of a man is what makes him 'unclean.'* ²¹*For from within, out of men's hearts, come evil thoughts, sexual immorality, theft, murder, adultery,* ²²*greed, malice, deceit, lewdness, envy, slander, arrogance and folly.* ²³*All these evils come from inside and make a man 'unclean.' "*

The Faith of a Syrophoenician Woman

²⁴*Jesus left that place and went to the vicinity of Tyre. He entered a house and did not want anyone to know it; yet he could not keep his presence secret.* ²⁵*In fact, as soon as she heard about him, a woman whose little daughter was possessed by an evil spirit came and fell at his feet.* ²⁶*The woman was a Greek, born in Syrian Phoenicia. She begged Jesus to drive the demon out of her daughter.*

²⁷*"First let the children eat all they want," he told her, "for it is not right to take the children's bread and toss it to their dogs."*

²⁸*"Yes, Lord," she replied, "but even the dogs under the table eat the children's crumbs."*

²⁹*Then he told her, "For such a reply, you may go; the demon has left your daughter."*

³⁰*She went home and found her child lying on the bed, and the demon gone.*

The Healing of a Deaf and Mute Man

³¹*Then Jesus left the vicinity of Tyre and went through Sidon, down to the Sea of Galilee and into the region of the Decapolis.* ³²*There some people brought to him a man who was deaf and could hardly talk, and they begged him to place his hand on the man.*

³³*After he took him aside, away from the crowd, Jesus put his fingers into the man's ears. Then he spit and touched the man's tongue.* ³⁴*He looked up to heaven and with a deep sigh said to him, "Ephphatha!" (which means, "Be opened!").* ³⁵*At this, the man's ears were opened, his tongue was loosened and he began to speak plainly.*

³⁶*Jesus commanded them not to tell anyone. But the more he did so, the more they kept talking about it.* ³⁷*People were overwhelmed with amazement. "He has done everything well," they said. "He even makes the deaf hear and the mute speak."*

7:1–13 It is not just the disciples' hearts that are hard so that the seed of the Gospel cannot penetrate; so too are the hearts of the Pharisees, as this story shows.

7:1 *from Jerusalem.* This is the second commission of inquiry sent by a worried religious hierarchy (see 3:22).

7:3–4 Mark explains this ritual washing to his Gentile readers.

7:3 *ceremonial washing.* The issue was holiness, not hygiene (germs were unknown in the first century). Before each meal one's hands were washed with special water in a particular way. With fingers pointing upward, at least one and one-half eggshells of water was poured over them, and the fist of one hand was rubbed into the fist of the other. Finally, with fingers pointing downward, more water was poured over the hands and allowed to run off at the fingertips. Originally only priests were required to wash in special ways (Ex. 30:19). Later, such obligations were extended to all who would be holy.

the tradition of the elders. These were the literally thousands of unwritten rules that grew up over time to clarify how the great moral principles of the Old Testament applied in everyday life. A summary of these oral laws was written down in the third century in the Mishnah, a collection of Jewish traditions.

elders. Respected Jewish rabbis whose decisions concerning points of religious law were considered authoritative, and therefore binding.

7:6 *Isaiah.* Both Jesus and the Pharisees accept the authority of the written Word (which makes Jesus' use of it here especially powerful). Their dispute is over the unwritten or oral laws which the Pharisees saw as equally binding—a view which Jesus rejects emphatically.

hypocrites. This is Mark's only use of this term (though he does refer to hypocrisy in 12:15). At this time, this word did not mean a "play-actor" but a person who was overly scrupulous. It was used in reference to those whose religion involved the keeping of certain rules and regulations which caused them to feel that they were holy despite their actual corruption of mind, heart and action. It was

not the Pharisees' lack of inner conviction that Jesus is faulting (they undoubtedly believed that holiness required the observance of the oral traditions), but the fact that in their meticulous observance of the traditions they had lost sight of the true meaning of holiness.

7:9–13 Jesus illustrates how oral tradition has come to nullify written law. The example he uses has to do with the fifth commandment.

7:11 *Corban.* An oath which dedicated an item to God, rendering it thereafter unavailable for normal use. So, a son might declare his property "Corban" with the result that his parents would have no further claim on his support, even though the oath neither required him to transfer his property to the temple nor to cease using it himself until his death. Such oaths were considered unbreakable.

7:12 The point is that by standing on the traditions of the elders such a person was able to circumvent the very clear intention of the Old Testament (the written law) that he take care of his parents.

7:13 *nullify the word of God.* This lies at the heart of Jesus' dispute with the Pharisees. They have elevated their traditions over the revealed Word of God.

7:14–23 Mark now extends his discussion of what is clean and unclean into a new area: abuse of Old Testament commandments. (The previous section dealt with oral traditions.) The issue is the food laws that so circumscribed first-century Jewish life. Large sections of the Old Testament are devoted to the question of food (e.g., Lev. 11; Deut. 14:1–21). Jesus' aim is not to attack these laws, but to challenge the assumption that a person was holy before God simply by keeping them. Furthermore, he makes it clear that consuming certain foods does not make a person unfit to participate in fellowship or worship.

7:15 *make him 'unclean.'* In Greek, this is a verb that means "to render someone impure in a ritual sense." The idea is that those who come into contact with what is taboo are themselves made unclean, and thus are unfit to worship or to come in contact with others. For the Jew, certain animals were unclean (e.g., pigs and snakes), as were dead bodies, lepers, Gentiles, certain cooking bowls, etc. The Old Testament rules concerning what was clean and unclean were expanded into thousands of specific rules in the oral tradition, many of which were complex and seemingly arbitrary at times.

7:18–19 Jesus has already differed with the Pharisees over eating with outcasts (2:15–17), fasting (2:18–22), and keeping the Sabbath (2:23–28). Here he differs at a fourth point: the effect of ritual defilement. In taking on these ritual laws, Jesus is walking in the steps of certain Old Testament prophets (see Isa. 1:10–20; Amos 5:21–27).

7:19 *heart.* A Jewish idiom for the center of an individual's personality; that which guides that person's thoughts and actions (see also 7:6).

out of his body. Literally, "goes into the latrine."

In saying this, Jesus declared all foods "clean." An editorial comment from Mark that was of great significance to his Gentile audience. They are free from Old Testament ceremonial law, he declares. They are not bound by the food (and other) customs of the Jews. As the story of the early church shows, the question of whether Gentiles had to obey Jewish ritual law continued to be a source of debate (see Acts 10; 15:1–29; Rom. 14; Gal. 2).

7:20–23 It is not whether a person eats kosher food that makes them pure or impure. The source of impurity is internal (sin within), not external (observance of ritual patterns).

7:21–22 *evil thoughts.* Evil thoughts precede evil actions.

sexual immorality. A general term encompassing all acts of sexual impurity.

adultery. The breach of marriage vows is singled out for mention from the more general term for sexual misconduct.

greed. The love of having more and more.

malice. Deliberate wickedness.

deceit. Cunning.

slander. Literally, blasphemy.

folly. Moral and spiritual foolishness.

7:24–30 Having declared his opposition to all the unwritten rules and regulations of the Pharisees, Jesus promptly violates one of these traditions by visiting a Gentile home in a Gentile area (Gentiles were considered unclean). Whereas the Pharisees took offense at Jesus and the disciples were uncomprehending, this Gentile woman becomes a model of what a true response of faith entails (v. 28). She, and not Jesus, is really the central character of this story. Jesus' silence and seeming resistance to her serves as a foil to accent her deep faith which perseveres despite difficulties.

7:24 *he could not keep his presence secret.* This may be an allusion to the Parable of the Lamp (4:21–25). The light of Jesus could not be hid.

7:26 *a Greek, born in Syrian Phoenicia.* This woman is described first by her religion, language and culture. She is a Greek-speaking Gentile. Then she is described by her nationality. She came from Phoenicia (modern-day Lebanon), which was administered by Syria.

7:27 This statement was not so much an insult, as it was a proverbial saying illustrating the reason behind Jesus' resistance to responding to the woman. Just as no parent would take away food from his or her children to feed a dog, so it would be incongruous for Israel's Messiah to bless Gentiles before Israel.

First. Jesus' primary mission is to the children of Israel. However, by the use of the word "first," he implies that a mission to the Gentiles was intended from the beginning. Interestingly, when Matthew tells this story to his Jewish readers (Matt. 15:21–28) he omits the "first." For Mark's Gentile audience, however, the insight that they were always included in God's plan was, indeed, good news.

let the children eat. The Israelites were often described as the children of God (see Ex. 4:22; Hos. 11:1).

Leadership Training Supplement

YOU ARE
HERE

BIRTH	GROWTH	DEVELOP	REBIRTH
101	201	301	401

What is the game plan for your group in the 201 stage?

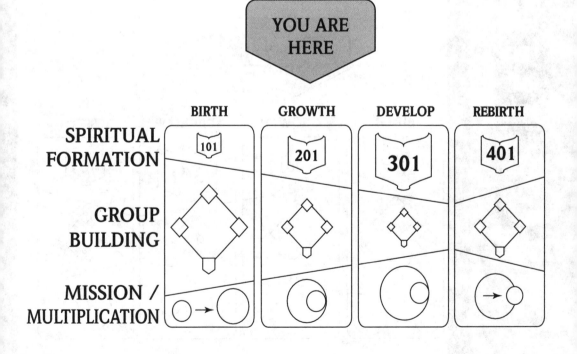

YOU ARE HERE

	BIRTH	GROWTH	DEVELOP	REBIRTH
SPIRITUAL FORMATION	101	201	301	401
GROUP BUILDING				
MISSION / MULTIPLICATION				

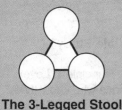

The 3-Legged Stool

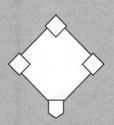

The three essentials in a healthy small group are Bible Study, Group Building and Mission / Multiplication. You need all three to stay balanced—like a 3-legged stool.
- To focus only on Bible Study will lead to scholasticism.
- To focus only on Group Building will lead to narcissism.
- To focus only on Mission will lead to burnout.

You need a game plan for the life cycle of the group where all of these elements are present in a purpose-driven strategy:

Spiritual Formation (Bible Study)

To dig into Scripture as a group.

Group Bible Study is quite different from individual Bible Study. The guided discussion questions are open-ended. And for those with little Bible background, there are reference notes to bring their knowledge level up so they do not feel intimidated. This helps level the playing field.

Group Building

To transform your group into a mission-driven team.

The nine basic needs of a group will be assigned to nine different people. Everyone has a job to fill, and when everyone is doing their job the group will grow spiritually and numerically. When new people enter the group, there is a selection of ICE-BREAKERS to start off the meeting and let the new people get acquainted.

Mission / Multiplication

To identify the Apprentice / Leader for birthing a new group.

In this stage, you will start dreaming about the possibility of starting a new group down the road. The questions at the close of each session will lead you carefully through the dreaming process—to help you discover an Apprentice / Leader who will eventually be the leader of a new group. This is an exciting challenge! (See page M6 for more about Mission / Multiplication.)

Bible Study

What is unique about Serendipity Group Bible Study?

Bible Study for groups is based on six principles. Principle 1: Level the playing field so that everyone can share—those who know the Bible and those who do not know the Bible. Principle 2: Share your spiritual story and let the people in your group get to know you. Principle 3: Ask open-ended questions that have no right or wrong answers. Principle 4: Use the 3-part agenda. Principle 5: Subdivide into smaller subgroups so that everyone can participate. Principle 6: Affirm One Another—"Thanks for sharing."

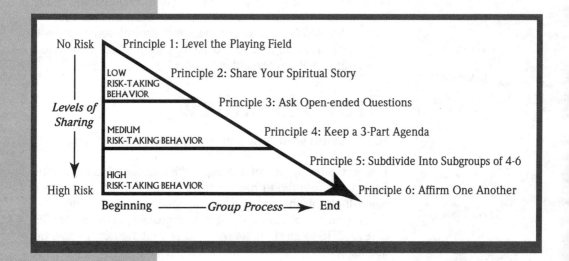

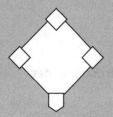

Group Building

What are the jobs that are needed on your team roster?

In the first or second session of this course, you need to fill out the roster on the next page. Then check every few weeks to see that everyone is "playing their position." If you do not have nine people in your group, you can double up on jobs until new people join your group and are assigned a job. The goal is to field a team. Building a team will better prepare you to rebirth a new group when the group becomes pregnant.

Your Small Group Team Roster

Mission Leader
(Left Field)
Keeps group focused on the mission to invite new people and eventually give birth to a new group. This person needs to be passionate and have a long-term perspective.

_____

Host
(Center Field)
Environmental engineer in charge of meeting location. Always on the lookout for moving to a new meeting location where new people will feel the "home field advantage."

_____

Party Leader
(Right Field)
Designates who is going to bring refreshments. Plans a party every month or so where new people are invited to visit and children are welcome.

_____

Caretaker
(Shortstop)
Takes new members under their wing. Makes sure they get acquainted. Always has an extra book, name tags and a list of group members and phone numbers.

_____

Bible Study Leader
(Second Base)
Takes over in the Bible Study time (30 minutes). Follows the agenda. Keeps the group moving. This person must be very time-conscious.

_____

Group Leader
(Pitcher)
Puts ball in play. Team encourager. Motivator. Sees to it that everyone is involved in the team effort.

_____

Caring Time Leader
(Third Base)
Takes over in the Caring Time. Records prayer requests and follows up on any prayer needs during the week. This person is the "heart" of the group.

_____

Worship Leader
(First Base)
Leads the group in singing and prayer when it is appropriate. Also leads the icebreaker to get acquainted, before the opening prayer.

_____

Apprentice / Leader
(Catcher)
The other half of the battery. Observes the infield. Calls "time" to discuss strategy and regroup. Stays focused.

_____

Mission / Multiplication

Where are you in the 4-stage life cycle of your mission?

You can't sit on a one-legged stool—or even a two-legged stool. It takes all three. The same is true of a small group; you need all three legs. A Bible Study and Care Group will eventually fall if it does not have a mission.

The mission goal is to eventually give birth to a new group. In this 201 course, the goals are: 1) to keep inviting new people to join your group and 2) to discover the Apprentice / Leader and leadership core for starting a new group down the road.

When a new person comes to the group, start off the meeting with one of the ice-breakers on the following pages. These ice-breakers are designed to be fun and easy to share, but they have a very important purpose—that is, to let the new person get acquainted with the group and share their spiritual story with the group, and hear the spiritual stories of those in the group.

YOU ARE HERE

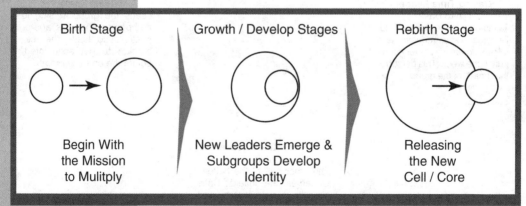

Birth Stage	Growth / Develop Stages	Rebirth Stage
Begin With the Mission to Mulitply	New Leaders Emerge & Subgroups Develop Identity	Releasing the New Cell / Core

Ice-Breakers

I Am Somebody Who ...

Rotate around the group, one person reading the first item, the next person reading the second item, etc. Before answering, let everyone in the group try to GUESS what the answer would be: "Yes" ... "No" ... or "Maybe." After everyone has guessed, explain the answer. Anyone who guessed right gets $10. When every item on the list has been read, the person with the most "money" WINS.

I AM SOMEBODY WHO ...

Y N M

- ❏ ❏ ❏ would go on a blind date
- ❏ ❏ ❏ sings in the shower
- ❏ ❏ ❏ listens to music full blast
- ❏ ❏ ❏ likes to dance
- ❏ ❏ ❏ cries at movies
- ❏ ❏ ❏ stops to smell the flowers
- ❏ ❏ ❏ daydreams a lot
- ❏ ❏ ❏ likes to play practical jokes
- ❏ ❏ ❏ makes a "to do" list
- ❏ ❏ ❏ loves liver
- ❏ ❏ ❏ won't use a portable toilet
- ❏ ❏ ❏ likes thunderstorms
- ❏ ❏ ❏ enjoys romance novels
- ❏ ❏ ❏ loves crossword puzzles
- ❏ ❏ ❏ hates flying
- ❏ ❏ ❏ fixes my own car

Y N M

- ❏ ❏ ❏ would enjoy skydiving
- ❏ ❏ ❏ has a black belt in karate
- ❏ ❏ ❏ watches soap operas
- ❏ ❏ ❏ is afraid of the dark
- ❏ ❏ ❏ goes to bed early
- ❏ ❏ ❏ plays the guitar
- ❏ ❏ ❏ talks to plants
- ❏ ❏ ❏ will ask a stranger for directions
- ❏ ❏ ❏ sleeps until the last second
- ❏ ❏ ❏ likes to travel alone
- ❏ ❏ ❏ reads the financial page
- ❏ ❏ ❏ saves for a rainy day
- ❏ ❏ ❏ lies about my age
- ❏ ❏ ❏ yells at the umpire
- ❏ ❏ ❏ closes my eyes during scary movies

Press Conference

This is a great activity for a new group or when new people are joining an established group. Interview one person with these questions.

1. What is your nickname and how did you get it?

2. Where did you grow up? Where was the "watering hole" in your hometown—where kids got together?

3. What did you do for kicks then? What about now?

4. What was the turning point in your spiritual life?

5. What prompted you to come to this group?

6. What do you want to get out of this group?

Down Memory Lane

Celebrate the childhood memories of the way you were. Choose one or more of the topics listed below and take turns answering the question related to it. If time allows, do another round.

HOME SWEET HOME–What do you remember about your childhood home?

TELEVISION—What was your favorite TV program or radio show?

OLD SCHOOLHOUSE—What were your best and worst subjects in school?

LIBRARY—What did you like to read (and where)?

TELEPHONE—How much time did you spend on the phone each day?

MOVIES—Who was your favorite movie star?

CASH FLOW—What did you do for spending money?

SPORTS—What was your favorite sport or team?

GRANDPA'S HOUSE—Where did your grandparents live? When did you visit them?

POLICE—Did you ever get in trouble with the law?

WEEKENDS—What was the thing to do on Saturday night?

Wallet Scavenger Hunt

With your wallet or purse, use the set of questions below. You get two minutes in silence to go through your possessions and find these items. Then break the silence and "show-and-tell" what you have chosen. For instance, "The thing I have had for the longest time is ... this picture of me when I was a baby."

1.   The thing I have had for the LONGEST TIME in my wallet is ...

2.   The thing that has SENTIMENTAL VALUE is ...

3.   The thing that reminds me of a FUN TIME is ... .

4.   The most REVEALING thing about me in my wallet is ...

The Grand Total

This is a fun ice-breaker that has additional uses. You can use this ice-breaker to divide your group into two subgroups (odds and evens). You can also calculate who has the highest and lowest totals if you need a fun way to select someone to do a particular task, such as bring refreshments or be first to tell their story.

Fill each box with the correct number and then total your score. When everyone is finished, go around the group and explain how you got your total.

☐	X	☐	=	☐
Number of hours you sleep		Number of miles you walk daily		Subtotal

☐	−	☐	=	☐
Number of speeding tickets you've received		Number of times sent to principal's office		Subtotal

☐	÷	☐	=	☐
Number of hours spent watching TV daily		Number of books you read this year for fun		Subtotal

☐	+	☐	=	☐
Number of push-ups you can do		Number of pounds you lost this year		Subtotal

☐

GRAND TOTAL

Find Yourself in the Picture

In this drawing, which child do you identify with—or which one best portrays you right now? Share with your group which child you would choose and why. You can also use this as an affirmation exercise, by assigning each person in your group to a child in the picture.

Four Facts, One Lie

Everyone in the group should answer the following five questions. One of the five answers should be a lie! The rest of the group members can guess which of your answers is a lie.

1. At age 7, my favorite TV show was ...

2. At age 9, my hero was ...

3. At age 11, I wanted to be a ...

4. At age 13, my favorite music was ...

5. Right now, my favorite pastime is ...

Old-Fashioned Auction

Just like an old-fashioned auction, conduct an out loud auction in your group—starting each item at $50. Everybody starts out with $1,000. Select an auctioneer. This person can also get in on the bidding. Remember, start the bidding on each item at $50. Then, write the winning bid in the left column and the winner's name in the right column. Remember, you only have $1,000 to spend for the whole game. AUCTIONEER: Start off by asking, "Who will give me $50 for a 1965 red MG convertible?" ... and keep going until you have a winner. Keep this auction to 10 minutes.

WINNING BID   WINNER

$_____ 1965 red MG convertible in perfect condition   _____

$_____ Winter vacation in Hawaii for two   _____

$_____ Two Super Bowl tickets on the 50-yard line   _____

$_____ One year of no hassles with my kids / parents   _____

$_____ Holy Land tour hosted by my favorite Christian   _____
leader

$_____ Season pass to ski resort of my choice   _____

$_____ Two months off to do anything I want, with pay   _____

$_____ Home theater with surround sound   _____

$_____ Breakfast in bed for one year   _____

$_____ Two front-row tickets at the concert of my choice _____

$_____ Two-week Caribbean cruise with my spouse in   _____
honeymoon suite

$_____ Shopping spree at Saks Fifth Avenue   _____

$_____ Six months of maid service   _____

$_____ All-expense-paid family vacation to Disney World _____

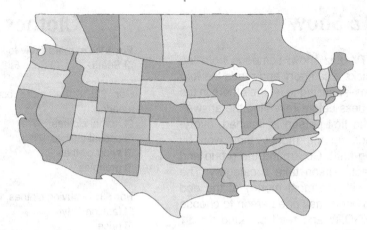

Places in My Life

On the map above, put six dots to indicate these significant places in your journey. Then go around and have each person explain the dots:

- the place where I was born
- the place where I spent most of my life
- the place where I first fell in love
- the place where I went or would like to go on a vacation
- the place where God first became real to me
- the place where I would like to retire

The Four Quaker Questions

This is an old Quaker activity which Serendipity has adapted over the years. Go around the group and share your answers to the questions, everyone answering #1. Then, everyone answers #2, etc. This ice-breaker has been known to take between 30 and 60 minutes for some groups.

1. Where were you living between the ages of 7 and 12, and what were the winters like then?

2. How was your home heated during that time?

3. What was the center of warmth in your life when you were a child? (It could be a place in the house, a time of year, a person, etc.)

4. When did God become a "warm" person to you ... and how did it happen?

KWIZ Show

Like a TV quiz show, someone from the group picks a category and reads the four questions—pausing to let the others in the group guess before revealing the answer. When the first person is finished, everyone adds up the money they won by guessing right. Go around the group and have each person take a category. The person with the most money at the end wins. To begin, ask one person to choose a CATEGORY and read out loud the $1 question. Before answering, let everyone try to GUESS the answer. When everyone has guessed, the person answers the question, and anyone who guessed right puts $1 in the margin, etc. until the first person has read all four questions in the CATEGORY.

Clothes

For $1: I'm more likely to shop at:
❏ Sears ❏ Saks Fifth Avenue

For $2: I feel more comfortable wearing:
❏ formal clothes
❏ casual clothes
❏ sport clothes
❏ grubbies

For $3: In buying clothes, I look for:
❏ fashion / style
❏ price
❏ name brand
❏ quality

For $4: In buying clothes, I usually:
❏ shop all day for a bargain
❏ go to one store, but try on everything
❏ buy the first thing I try on
❏ buy without trying it on

Tastes

For $1: In music, I am closer to:
❏ Bach ❏ Beatles

For $2: In furniture, I prefer:
❏ Early American
❏ French Provincial
❏ Scandinavian—contemporary
❏ Hodgepodge—little of everything

For $3: My favorite choice of reading material is:
❏ science fiction ❏ sports
❏ mystery ❏ romance

For $4: If I had $1,000 to splurge, I would buy:
❏ one original painting
❏ two numbered prints
❏ three reproductions and an easy chair
❏ four cheap imitations, an easy chair and a color TV

Travel

For $1: For travel, I prefer:
❏ excitement ❏ enrichment

For $2: On a vacation, my lifestyle is:
❏ go-go all the time
❏ slow and easy
❏ party every night and sleep in

For $3: In packing for a trip, I include:
❏ toothbrush and change of underwear
❏ light bag and good book
❏ small suitcase and nice outfit
❏ all but the kitchen sink

For $4: If I had money to blow, I would choose:
❏ one glorious night in a luxury hotel
❏ a weekend in a nice hotel
❏ a full week in a cheap motel
❏ two weeks camping in the boondocks

Habits

For $1: I am more likely to squeeze the toothpaste:
❑ in the middle   ❑ from the end

For $2: If I am lost, I will probably:
❑ stop and ask directions
❑ check the map
❑ find the way by driving around

For $3: I read the newspaper starting with the:
❑ front page
❑ funnies
❑ sports
❑ entertainment section

For $4: When I get ready for bed, I put my clothes:
❑ on a hanger in the closet
❑ folded neatly over a chair
❑ into a hamper or clothes basket
❑ on the floor

Shows

For $1: I am more likely to:
❑ go see a first-run movie
❑ rent a video at home

For $2: On TV, my first choice is:
❑ news
❑ sports
❑ sitcoms

For $3: If a show gets too scary, I will usually:
❑ go to the restroom
❑ close my eyes
❑ clutch a friend
❑ love it

For $4: In movies, I prefer:
❑ romantic comedies
❑ serious drama
❑ action films
❑ Disney animation

Food

For $1: I prefer to eat at a:
❑ fast-food restaurant
❑ fancy restaurant

For $2: On the menu, I look for something:
❑ familiar
❑ different
❑ way-out

For $3: When eating chicken, my preference is a:
❑ drumstick
❑ wing
❑ breast
❑ gizzard

For $4: I draw the line when it comes to eating:
❑ frog legs
❑ snails
❑ raw oysters
❑ Rocky Mountain oysters

Work

For $1: I prefer to work at a job that is:
❑ too big to handle
❑ too small to be challenging

For $2: The job I find most unpleasant to do is:
❑ cleaning the house
❑ working in the yard
❑ balancing the checkbook

For $3: In choosing a job, I look for:
❑ salary
❑ security
❑ fulfillment
❑ working conditions

For $4: If I had to choose between these jobs, I would choose:
❑ pickle inspector at processing plant
❑ complaint officer at department store
❑ bedpan changer at hospital
❑ personnel manager in charge of firing

Let Me Tell You About My Day

What was your day like today? Use one of the characters below to help you describe your day to the group. Feel free to elaborate.

GREEK TRAGEDY
It was classic, not a dry eye in the house.

EPISODE OF THREE STOOGES
I was Larry, trapped between Curly and Moe.

SOAP OPERA
I didn't think these things could happen, until it happened to me.

ACTION ADVENTURE
When I rode onto the scene, everybody noticed.

BIBLE EPIC
Cecil B. DeMille couldn't have done it any better.

LATE NIGHT NEWS
It might as well have been broadcast over the airwaves.

BORING LECTURE
The biggest challenge of the day was staying awake.

PROFESSIONAL WRESTLING MATCH
I feel as if Hulk Hogan's been coming after me.

FIREWORKS DISPLAY
It was spectacular.

Music in My Life

Put an *"X"* on the first line below—somewhere between the two extremes—to indicate how you are feeling right now. Share your answers, and then repeat this process down the list. If you feel comfortable, briefly explain your response.

IN MY PERSONAL LIFE, I'M FEELING LIKE ...
Blues in the Night _____ Feeling Groovy

IN MY FAMILY LIFE, I'M FEELING LIKE ...
Stormy Weather _____ The Sound of Music

IN MY EMOTIONAL LIFE, I'M FEELING LIKE ...
The Feeling Is Gone _____ On Eagle's Wings

IN MY WORK, SCHOOL OR CAREER, I'M FEELING LIKE ...
Take This Job and Shove It _____ The Future's So Bright I Gotta Wear Shades

IN MY SPIRITUAL LIFE, I'M FEELING LIKE ...
Sounds of Silence _____ Hallelujah Chorus

My Childhood Table

Try to recall the table where you ate most of your meals as a child, and the people who sat around that table. Use the questions below to describe these significant relationships, and how they helped to shape the person you are today.

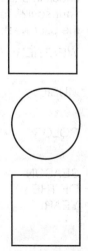

1. What was the shape of the table?
2. Where did you sit?
3. Who else was at the table?
4. If you had to describe each person with a color, what would be the color of (for instance):
   ❏ Your father? (e.g., dark blue, because he was conservative like IBM)
   ❏ Your mother? (e.g., light green, because she reminded me of springtime)
5. If you had to describe the atmosphere at the table with a color, what would you choose? (e.g., bright orange, because it was warm and light)
6. Who was the person at the table who praised you and made you feel special?
7. Who provided the spiritual leadership in your home?

Home Improvement

Take inventory of your own life. Bob Munger, in his booklet *My Heart—Christ's Home*, describes the areas of a person's life as the rooms of a house. Give yourself a grade on each room as follows, then share with the others your best and worst grade.

    ❏ A = excellent   ❏ C = passing, needs a little dusting
    ❏ B = good   ❏ D = passing, but needs a lot of improvement

LIBRARY: This room is in your mind—what you allow to go into it and come out of it. It is the "control room" of the entire house.

DINING ROOM: Appetites, desires; those things your mind and spirit feed on for nourishment.

DRAWING ROOM: This is where you draw close to God—seeking time with him daily, not just in times of distress or need.

WORKSHOP: This room is where your gifts, talents and skills are put to work for God—by the power of the Spirit.

RUMPUS ROOM: The social area of your life; the things you do to amuse yourself and others.

HALL CLOSET: The one secret place that no one knows about, but is a real stumbling block in your walk in the Spirit.

How Is It With Your Soul?

John Wesley, the founder of the Methodist Church, asked his "class meetings" to check in each week at their small group meeting with this question: "How is it with your soul?" To answer this question, choose one of these four allegories to explain the past week in your life:

WEATHER: For example: "This week has been mostly cloudy, with some thunderstorms at midweek. Right now, the weather is a little brighter ..."

MUSIC: For example: "This past week has been like heavy rock music—almost too loud. The sound seems to reverberate off the walls."

COLOR: For example: "This past week has been mostly fall colors—deep orange, flaming red and pumpkin."

SEASON OF THE YEAR: For example: "This past week has been like springtime. New signs of life are beginning to appear on the barren trees, and a few shoots of winter wheat are breaking through the frozen ground."

My Spiritual Journey

The half-finished sentences below are designed to help you share your spiritual story. Ask one person to finish all the sentences. Then move to the next person, etc. If you are short on time, have only one person tell their story in this session.

1. RELIGIOUS BACKGROUND: My spiritual story begins in my home as a child, where the religious training was ...

2. CHURCH: The church that I went to as a child was ...

3. SIGNIFICANT PERSON: The person who had the greatest influence on my spiritual formation was ...

4. PERSONAL ENCOUNTER: The first time God became more than just a name to me was when ...

5. JOURNEY: Since my personal encounter with God, my Christian life might be described as ...

6. PRESENT: On a scale from 1 to 10, I would describe my spiritual energy level right now as a ...

7. NEXT STEP: The thing I need to work on right now in my spiritual life is ...

Bragging Rights

Check your group for bragging rights in these categories.

❏ SPEEDING TICKETS: the person with the most speeding tickets
❏ BROKEN BONES: the person with the most broken bones
❏ STITCHES: the person with the most stitches
❏ SCARS: the person with the longest scar
❏ FISH OR GAME: the person who claims they caught the largest fish or killed the largest animal
❏ STUNTS: the person with the most death-defying story
❏ IRON: the person who can pump the most iron

Personal Habits

Have everyone in your group finish the sentence on the first category by putting an "**X**" somewhere between the two extremes (e.g., on HOUSEWORK ... I would put myself closer to "Where's the floor?"). Repeat this process down the list as time permits.

ON HOUSEWORK, I AM SOMEWHERE BETWEEN:
Eat off the floor_____Where's the floor?

ON COOKING, I AM SOMEWHERE BETWEEN:
Every meal is an act of worship_____Make it fast and hold the frills

ON EXERCISING, I AM SOMEWHERE BETWEEN:
Workout every morning_____Click the remote

ON SHOPPING, I AM SOMEWHERE BETWEEN:
Shop all day for a bargain_____Only the best

ON EATING, I AM SOMEWHERE BETWEEN:
You are what you eat_____Eat, drink and be merry

American Graffiti

If Hollywood made a movie about your life on the night of your high school prom, what would be needed? Let each person in your group have a few minutes to recall these details. If you have more than four or five in your group, ask everyone to choose two or three topics to talk about.

1. LOCATION: Where were you living?
2. WEIGHT: How much did you weigh—soaking wet?
3. PROM: Where was it held?
4. DATE: Who did you go with?
5. CAR / TRANSPORTATION: How did you get there?
   (If you used a car, what was the model, year, color, condition?)
6. ATTIRE: What did you wear?
7. PROGRAM: What was the entertainment?
8. AFTERWARD: What did you do afterward?
9. HIGHLIGHT: What was the highlight of the evening?
10. HOMECOMING: If you could go back and visit your high school, who would you like to see?

Group Orchestra

Read out loud the first item and let everyone nominate the person in your group for this musical instrument in your group orchestra. Then, read aloud the next instrument, and call out another name, etc.

ANGELIC HARP: Soft, gentle, melodious, wooing with heavenly sounds.

OLD-FASHIONED WASHBOARD: Nonconforming, childlike and fun.

PLAYER PIANO: Mischievous, raucous, honky-tonk—delightfully carefree.

KETTLEDRUM: Strong, vibrant, commanding when needed but usually in the background.

PASSIONATE CASTANET: Full of Spanish fervor—intense and always upbeat.

STRADIVARIUS VIOLIN: Priceless, exquisite, soul-piercing—with the touch of the master.

FLUTTERING FLUTE: Tender, lighthearted, wide-ranging and clear as crystal.

SCOTTISH BAGPIPES: Forthright, distinctive and unmistakable.

SQUARE DANCE FIDDLE: Folksy, down-to-earth, toe-tapping—sprightly and full of energy.

ENCHANTING OBOE: Haunting, charming, disarming—even the cobra is harmless with this sound.

MELLOW CELLO: Deep, sonorous, compassionate—adding body and depth to the orchestra.

PIPE ORGAN: Grand, magnificent, rich—versatile and commanding.

HERALDING TRUMPET: Stirring, lively, invigorating—signaling attention and attack.

CLASSICAL GUITAR: Contemplative, profound, thoughtful *and* thought-provoking.

ONE-MAN BAND: Able to do many things well, all at once.

COMB AND TISSUE PAPER: Makeshift, original, uncomplicated—homespun and creative.

SWINGING TROMBONE: Warm, rich—great in solo or background support.

Broadway Show

Imagine for a moment that your group has been chosen to produce a Broadway show, and you have to choose people from your group for all of the jobs for this production. Have someone read out loud the job description for the first job below—PRODUCER. Then, let everyone in your group call out the name of the person in your group who would best fit this job. (You don't have to agree.) Then read the job description for the next job and let everyone nominate another person, etc. You only have 10 minutes for this assignment, so move fast.

PRODUCER: Typical Hollywood business tycoon; extravagant, big-budget, big-production magnate in the Steven Spielberg style.

DIRECTOR: Creative, imaginative brains who coordinates the production and draws the best out of others.

HEROINE: Beautiful, captivating, everybody's heart throb; defenseless when men are around, but nobody's fool.

HERO: Tough, macho, champion of the underdog, knight in shining armor; defender of truth.

COMEDIAN: Childlike, happy-go-lucky, outrageously funny, keeps everyone laughing.

CHARACTER PERSON: Rugged individualist, outrageously different, colorful, adds spice to any surrounding.

FALL GUY: Easy-going, nonchalant character who wins the hearts of everyone by being the "foil" of the heavy characters.

TECHNICAL DIRECTOR: The genius for "sound and lights"; creates the perfect atmosphere.

COMPOSER OF LYRICS: Communicates in music what everybody understands; heavy into feelings, moods, outbursts of energy.

PUBLICITY AGENT: Advertising and public relations expert; knows all the angles, good at one-liners, a flair for "hot" news.

VILLAIN: The "bad guy" who really is the heavy for the plot, forces others to think, challenges traditional values; out to destroy anything artificial or hypocritical.

AUTHOR: Shy, aloof; very much in touch with feelings, sensitive to people, puts into words what others only feel.

STAGEHAND: Supportive, behind-the-scenes person who makes things run smoothly; patient and tolerant.

Wild Predictions

Try to match the people in your group to the crazy forecasts below. (Don't take it too seriously; it's meant to be fun!) Read out loud the first item and ask everyone to call out the name of the person who is most likely to accomplish this feat. Then, read the next item and ask everyone to make a new prediction, etc.

THE PERSON IN OUR GROUP MOST LIKELY TO ...

Make a million selling Beanie Babies over the Internet

Become famous for designing new attire for sumo wrestlers

Replace Vanna White on *Wheel of Fortune*

Appear on *The Tonight Show* to exhibit an acrobatic talent

Move to a desert island

Discover a new use for underarm deodorant

Succeed David Letterman as host of *The Late Show*

Substitute for John Madden as Fox's football color analyst

Appear on the cover of *Muscle & Fitness Magazine*

Become the newest member of the Spice Girls

Work as a bodyguard for Rush Limbaugh at Feminist convention

Write a best-selling novel based on their love life

Be a dance instructor on a cruise ship for wealthy, well-endowed widows

Win the blue ribbon at the state fair for best Rocky Mountain oyster recipe

Land a job as head librarian for Amazon.com

Be the first woman to win the Indianapolis 500

Open the Clouseau Private Detective Agency

Career Placements

Read the list of career choices aloud and quickly choose someone in your group for each job—based upon their unique gifts and talents. Have fun!

SPACE ENVIRONMENTAL ENGINEER: in charge of designing the bathrooms on space shuttles

SCHOOL BUS DRIVER: for junior high kids in New York City (earplugs supplied)

WRITER: of an "advice to the lovelorn" column in Hollywood

SUPERVISOR: of a complaint department for a large automobile dealership and service department

ANIMAL PSYCHIATRIST: for French poodles in a fashionable suburb of Paris

RESEARCH SCIENTIST: studying the fertilization patterns of the dodo bird—now extinct

SAFARI GUIDE: in the heart of Africa—for wealthy widows and eccentric bachelors

LITTLE LEAGUE BASEBALL COACH: in Mudville, Illinois—last year's record was 0 and 12

MANAGER: of your local McDonald's during the holiday rush with 210 teenage employees

LIBRARIAN: for the Walt Disney Hall of Fame memorabilia

CHOREOGRAPHER: for the Dallas Cowboys cheerleaders

NURSE'S AIDE: at a home for retired Sumo wrestlers

SECURITY GUARD: crowd control officer at a rock concert

ORGANIZER: of paperwork for Congress

PUBLIC RELATIONS MANAGER: for Dennis Rodman

BODYGUARD: for Rush Limbaugh on a speaking tour of feminist groups

TOY ASSEMBLY PERSON: for a toy store over the holidays

You and Me, Partner

Think of the people in your group as you read over the list of activities below. If you had to choose someone from your group to be your partner, who would you choose to do these activities with? Jot down each person's name beside the activity. You can use each person's name only once and you have to use everyone's name once—so think it through before you jot down their names. Then, let one person listen to what others chose for them. Then, move to the next person, etc., around your group.

WHO WOULD YOU CHOOSE FOR THE FOLLOWING?

_____ ENDURANCE DANCE CONTEST partner

_____ BOBSLED RACE partner for the Olympics

_____ TRAPEZE ACT partner

_____ MY UNDERSTUDY for my debut in a Broadway musical

_____ BEST MAN or MAID OF HONOR at my wedding

_____ SECRET UNDERCOVER AGENT copartner

_____ BODYGUARD for me when I strike it rich

_____ MOUNTAIN CLIMBING partner in climbing Mt. Everest

_____ ASTRONAUT to fly the space shuttle while I walk in space

_____ SAND CASTLE TOURNAMENT building partner

_____ PIT CREW foreman for entry in Indianapolis 500

_____ AUTHOR for my biography

_____ SURGEON to operate on me for a life-threatening cancer

_____ NEW BUSINESS START-UP partner

_____ TAG-TEAM partner for a professional wrestling match

_____ HEAVY-DUTY PRAYER partner

My Gourmet Group

Here's a chance to pass out some much deserved praise for the people who have made your group something special. Ask one person to sit in silence while the others explain the delicacy they would choose to describe the contribution this person has made to your group. Repeat the process for each member of the group.

CAVIAR: That special touch of class and aristocratic taste that has made the rest of us feel like royalty.

PRIME RIB: Stable, brawny, macho, the generous mainstay of any menu; juicy, mouth-watering "perfect cut" for good nourishment.

IMPORTED CHEESE: Distinctive, tangy, mellow with age; adds depth to any meal.

VINEGAR AND OIL: Tart, witty, dry; a rare combination of healing ointment and pungent spice to add "bite" to the salad.

ARTICHOKE HEARTS: Tender and disarmingly vulnerable; whets the appetite for heartfelt sharing.

FRENCH PASTRY: Tempting, irresistible "creme de la creme" dessert; the connoisseur's delight for topping off a meal.

PHEASANT UNDER GLASS: Wild, totally unique, a rare dish for people who appreciate original fare.

CARAFE OF WINE: Sparkling, effervescent, exuberant and joyful; outrageously free and liberating to the rest of us.

ESCARGOT AND OYSTERS: Priceless treasures of the sea once out of their shells; succulent, delicate and irreplaceable.

FRESH FRUIT: Vine-ripened, energy-filled, invigorating; the perfect treat after a heavy meal.

ITALIAN ICE CREAMS: Colorful, flavorful, delightfully childlike; the unexpected surprise in our group.

Thank You

How would you describe your experience with this group? Choose one of the animals below that best describes how your experience in this group affected your life. Then share your responses with the group.

WILD EAGLE: You have helped to heal my wings, and taught me how to soar again.

TOWERING GIRAFFE: You have helped me to hold my head up and stick my neck out, and reach over the fences I have built.

PLAYFUL PORPOISE: You have helped me to find a new freedom and a whole new world to play in.

COLORFUL PEACOCK: You have told me that I'm beautiful; I've started to believe it, and it's changing my life.

SAFARI ELEPHANT: I have enjoyed this new adventure, and I'm not going to forget it, or this group; I can hardly wait for the next safari.

LOVABLE HIPPOPOTAMUS: You have let me surface and bask in the warm sunshine of God's love.

LANKY LEOPARD: You have helped me to look closely at myself and see some spots, and you still accept me the way I am.

DANCING BEAR: You have taught me to dance in the midst of pain, and you have helped me to reach out and hug again.

ALL-WEATHER DUCK: You have helped me to celebrate life—even in stormy weather—and to sing in the rain.

Academy Awards

You have had a chance to observe the gifts and talents of the members of your group. Now you will have a chance to pass out some much deserved praise for the contribution that each member of the group has made to your life. Read out loud the first award. Then let everyone nominate the person they feel is the most deserving for that award. Then read the next award, etc., through the list. Have fun!

SPARK PLUG AWARD: for the person who ignited the group

DEAR ABBY AWARD: for the person who cared enough to listen

ROYAL GIRDLE AWARD: for the person who supported us

WINNIE THE POOH AWARD: for the warm, caring person when someone needed a hug

ROCK OF GIBRALTER AWARD: for the person who was strong in the tough times of our group

OPRAH AWARD: for the person who asked the fun questions that got us to talk

TED KOPPEL AWARD: for the person who asked the heavy questions that made us think

KING ARTHUR'S AWARD: for the knight in shining armor

PINK PANTHER AWARD: for the detective who made us deal with Scripture

NOBEL PEACE PRIZE: for the person who harmonized our differences of opinion without diminishing anyone

BIG MAC AWARD: for the person who showed the biggest hunger for spiritual things

SERENDIPITY CROWN: for the person who grew the most spiritually during the course—in your estimation

You Remind Me of Jesus

Every Christian reflects the character of Jesus in some way. As your group has gotten to know each other, you can begin to see how each person demonstrates Christ in their very own personality. Go around the circle and have each person listen while others take turns telling that person what they notice in him or her that reminds them of Jesus. You may also want to tell them why you selected what you did.

YOU REMIND ME OF ...

JESUS THE HEALER: You seem to be able to touch someone's life with your compassion and help make them whole.

JESUS THE SERVANT: There's nothing that you wouldn't do for someone.

JESUS THE PREACHER: You share your faith in a way that challenges and inspires people.

JESUS THE LEADER: As Jesus had a plan for the disciples, you are able to lead others in a way that honors God.

JESUS THE REBEL: By doing the unexpected, you remind me of Jesus' way of revealing God in unique, surprising ways.

JESUS THE RECONCILER: Like Jesus, you have the ability to be a peacemaker between others.

JESUS THE TEACHER: You have a gift for bringing light and understanding to God's Word.

JESUS THE CRITIC: You have the courage to say what needs to be said, even if it isn't always popular.

JESUS THE SACRIFICE: Like Jesus, you seem willing to sacrifice anything to glorify God.

Reflections

Take some time to evaluate the life of your group by using the statements below. Read the first sentence out loud and ask everyone to explain where they would put a dot between the two extremes. When you are finished, go back and give your group an overall grade in the category of Group Building, Bible Study and Mission.

◇ GROUP BUILDING

On celebrating life and having fun together, we were more like a ...
wet blanket _____ hot tub

On becoming a caring community, we were more like a ...
prickly porcupine_____cuddly teddy bear

📖 SPIRITUAL FORMATION (Bible Study)

On sharing our spiritual stories, we were more like a ...
shallow pond _____spring-fed lake

On digging into Scripture, we were more like a ...
slow-moving snail _____voracious anteater

◯ MISSION

On inviting new people into our group, we were more like a ...
barbed-wire fence _____wide-open door

On stretching our vision for mission, we were more like an ...
ostrich _____eagle

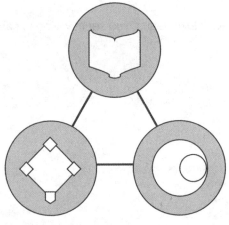

Human Bingo / Party Mixer

After the leader says "Go!" circulate the room, asking people the things described in the boxes. If someone answers "Yes" to a question, have them sign their initials in that box. Continue until someone completes the entire card—or one row if you don't have that much time. You can only use someone's name twice, and you cannot use your own name on your card.

can juggle	TP'd a house	never used an outhouse	sings in the shower	rec'd 6+ traffic tickets	paddled in school	watches Sesame Street
sleeps in church regularly	never changed a diaper	split pants in public	milked a cow	born out of the country	has been to Hawaii	can do the splits
watches soap operas	can touch tongue to nose	rode a motor-cycle	never ridden a horse	moved twice last year	sleeps on a waterbed	has hole in sock
walked in wrong restroom	loves classical music	skipped school	**FREE**	broke a leg	has a hot tub	loves eating sushi
is an only child	loves raw oysters	has a 3-inch + scar	doesn't wear PJ's	smoked a cigar	can dance the Charleston	weighs under 110 lbs.
likes writing poetry	still has tonsils	loves crossword puzzles	likes bubble baths	wearing Fruit of the Loom	doesn't use mouth-wash	often watches cartoons
kissed on first date	can wiggle ears	can play the guitar	plays chess regularly	reads the comics first	can touch palms to floor	sleeps with stuffed animal

Group Covenant

Any group can benefit from creating a group covenant. Reserve some time during one of the first meetings to discuss answers to the following questions. When everyone in the group has the same expectations for the group, everything runs more smoothly.

1. The purpose of our group is:

2. The goals of our group are:

3. We will meet for _____ weeks, after which we will decide if we wish to continue as a group. If we do decide to continue, we will reconsider this covenant.

4. We will meet _____ (weekly, every other week, monthly).

5. Our meetings will be from _____ o'clock to _____ o'clock, and we will strive to start and end on time.

6. We will meet at _____ or rotate from house to house.

7. We will take care of the following details: ☐ child care ☐ refreshments

8. We agree to the following rules for our group:

   ☐ PRIORITY: While we are in this group, group meetings have priority.

   ☐ PARTICIPATION: Everyone is given the right to their own opinion and all questions are respected.

   ☐ CONFIDENTIALITY: Anything said in the meeting is not to be repeated outside the meeting.

   ☐ EMPTY CHAIR: The group stays open to new people and invites prospective members to visit the group.

   ☐ SUPPORT: Permission is given to call each other in times of need.

   ☐ ADVICE GIVING: Unsolicited advice is not allowed.

   ☐ MISSION: We will do all that is in our power to start a new group.

bread. Once again food and eating appear in this section (vv. 2,5,19; see also 6:31,35–44,52).

dogs. The reference is to small, household dogs. This is a play on words. On one level, it means simply that the children have the first claim on the food (Jesus' prime ministry is to Israel). On another level, the Jews considered Gentiles "dogs" (using a harsher term which referred to wild street dogs). This woman probably knew this. Jesus echoes this traditional view (which he rejected when he said that nothing is unclean) in an ironic way, using the softened form of the word (lap dogs) and saying it, probably, with a smile on his face.

7:28 She catches on to his wordplay and replies, in essence, "Carry on with the meal you are serving Israel, but allow us a few scraps."

7:29 *For such a reply.* Jesus is impressed with the depth of her understanding as well as her clever and witty reply. In fact, this Gentile woman seems to understand more about Jesus than either the Twelve (6:45–56) or the Pharisees (vv. 1–13)!

7:31–37 Cycle one of this section concludes with the healing of a deaf and mute man, which seems to have symbolic significance for Mark. It is this sort of miracle of healing that the disciples need if they are to understand properly who Jesus is.

7:32 *deaf.* Apparently the result of an accident or disease and not a birth defect, since the man could speak some.

could hardly talk. This is a rare Greek word used only here and in the Greek version of Isaiah 35:5–6. Mark probably intends his readers to understand this healing in the light of the Isaiah passage which proclaims: "Then will the eyes of the blind be opened and the ears of the deaf unstopped. Then will the lame leap like a deer, and the mute tongue shout for joy."

7:33–35 A more complex healing than normal. Perhaps Jesus was using touch to communicate with this deaf man.

7:33 *he spit.* Saliva was regarded by Jews and Greeks as a healing agent.

7:34 *Ephphatha!* Mark continues to translate for his Roman readers.

7:36 *not to tell anyone.* This command stands in sharp contrast to what Jesus said on his previous visit to the region of the Decapolis. On that occasion, he told the ex-demoniac *to go and tell* the story of what the Lord had done for him (5:18–20). On this trip, Jesus sees the results of that man's witness. Instead of urgently requesting Jesus to leave as they had done on his previous visit (5:17), now not only do the townspeople bring a man to be healed, but they have developed expectations about who Jesus is and what he can do. Thus Jesus must now command silence, much as he has done regularly in Jewish regions.

they kept talking about it. Jesus has no better luck getting these Gentiles to be silent than he has had in keeping his healings a secret in Israel (e.g., 1:43–45)!

7:37 *He has done everything well.* By this statement Mark sums up the testimony of these Gentiles to Jesus. While they do not know who he is, they are struck by his power and affirm him as one who does good, unlike the religious leaders of Israel who declared his power was inspired by Satan (3:22).

13 Jesus Provides—Mark 8:1–26

THREE-PART AGENDA

ICE-BREAKER	BIBLE STUDY	CARING TIME
15 Minutes	30 Minutes	15–45 Minutes

> **LEADER:** *To help you identify an Apprentice / Leader for a new small group (or if you have a new person at this meeting), see the listing of appropriate ice-breakers on page M7 of the center section.*

TO BEGIN THE BIBLE STUDY TIME
(Choose 1 or 2)

1. Who sat where at your dinner table when you were age 7? What was your favorite meal then?

2. What kind of food are you most likely to "pig out" on: Ice cream? Chocolate? Chips? Pizza? Other?

3. What do you use to help you remember and keep track of things?

READ SCRIPTURE & DISCUSS
(If you don't have time for all the questions in this section, conclude the Bible Study [30 min.] by answering question #7.)

1. If everyone in this group came to your house right after this meeting, what would you feed them?

2. Whom do you relate with most in this story—someone in the crowd, the disciples, the Pharisees? Why?

3. Jesus had previously fed 5,000 people in a similar situation (6:30–56). Why was it important for Mark to include both of these accounts (see note on 8:1–10)?

Jesus Feeds the Four Thousand

8 *During those days another large crowd gathered. Since they had nothing to eat, Jesus called his disciples to him and said,* ²*"I have compassion for these people; they have already been with me three days and have nothing to eat.* ³*If I send them home hungry, they will collapse on the way, because some of them have come a long distance."*

⁴*His disciples answered, "But where in this remote place can anyone get enough bread to feed them?"*

⁵*"How many loaves do you have?" Jesus asked.*

"Seven," they replied.

⁶*He told the crowd to sit down on the ground. When he had taken the seven loaves and given thanks, he broke them and gave them to his disciples to set before the people, and they did so.* ⁷*They had a few small fish as well; he gave thanks for them also and told the disciples to distribute them.* ⁸*The people ate and were satisfied. Afterward the disciples picked up seven basketfuls of broken pieces that were left over.* ⁹*About four thousand men were present. And having sent them away,* ¹⁰*he got into the boat with his disciples and went to the region of Dalmanutha.*

¹¹*The Pharisees came and began to question Jesus. To test him, they asked him for a sign from heaven.* ¹²*He sighed deeply and said, "Why does this generation ask for a miraculous sign? I tell you the truth, no sign will be given to it."* ¹³*Then he left them, got back into the boat and crossed to the other side.*

The Yeast of the Pharisees and Herod

¹⁴*The disciples had forgotten to bring bread, except for one loaf they had with them in the boat.* ¹⁵*"Be careful," Jesus warned them. "Watch out for the yeast of the Pharisees and that of Herod."*

¹⁶*They discussed this with one another and said, "It is because we have no bread."*

¹⁷*Aware of their discussion, Jesus asked them: "Why are you talking about having no bread? Do you still not see or understand? Are your hearts hardened?* ¹⁸*Do you have eyes but fail to see, and ears but fail to hear? And don't you remember?* ¹⁹*When I broke the five loaves for the five thousand, how many basketfuls of pieces did you pick up?"*

"Twelve," they replied.

4. What "sign from heaven" did the Pharisees want? Why wouldn't Jesus give them a sign? What "sign" would help your faith?

5. The yeast of Herod and the Pharisees relates to their idea of who the Messiah should be. Jesus is the Messiah for the Jews *and* non-Jews, but the disciples had difficulty understanding this. What "yeast" (teaching that is contrary to God's purposes) do you need to avoid in your life?

6. Why did Jesus take the blind man out of the village before he healed him? Why did Jesus heal him in stages?

7. Who helped you receive your spiritual sight? What stage are you at in your spiritual growth?

CARING TIME

(Choose 1 or 2 of these questions before closing in prayer. Be sure to pray for the empty chair.)

1. Congratulations! You are halfway through Mark. What is the best thing you've learned so far?

2. In what way has God been at work in your life this past week?

3. How can this group help you in prayer?

> *²⁰"And when I broke the seven loaves for the four thousand, how many basketfuls of pieces did you pick up?"*
>
> *They answered, "Seven."*
>
> *²¹He said to them, "Do you still not understand?"*
>
> The Healing of a Blind Man at Bethsaida
>
> *²²They came to Bethsaida, and some people brought a blind man and begged Jesus to touch him. ²³He took the blind man by the hand and led him outside the village. When he had spit on the man's eyes and put his hands on him, Jesus asked, "Do you see anything?"*
>
> *²⁴He looked up and said, "I see people; they look like trees walking around."*
>
> *²⁵Once more Jesus put his hands on the man's eyes. Then his eyes were opened, his sight was restored, and he saw everything clearly. ²⁶Jesus sent him home, saying, "Don't go into the village."*

Notes—Mark 8:1–26

Summary. Mark begins a second, parallel cycle of stories. (Regarding how the disciples come to recognize Jesus as the Messiah in this passage, see Summary note in Session 11.) If Mark's intention had been simply to recount incidents that reveal Jesus' power, one cycle of stories would have sufficed. But this second cycle alerts the reader to the fact that more is going on here than meets the eye. They must pay attention to what these stories reveal about who Jesus is. These accounts are like parables. On the surface, they say something that is obvious (they are yet more stories about Jesus' power in ministry). But taken together, they add up to something more (they reveal that Jesus is the Messiah). And, like parables, the reader needs to "consider carefully what you hear" (Mark 4:24) in order to grasp their meaning.

8:1–10 The major difference between the feeding of the four thousand and the feeding of the five thousand is the difference in audience. This feeding included Gentiles (as well as Jews), whereas the earlier feeding involved Jews only. The feeding of the five thousand is about the coming salvation for Israel brought by Jesus, the one who fulfills the mission of Moses and David. The feeding of the four thousand promises this same salvation to Gentiles.

8:2 *three days.* The crowd had been with him for a few days in contrast to the five thousand, who gathered on the day they were fed (Mark 6:33–35).

8:3 *some of them have come a long distance.* This was a phrase used in the Greek Old Testament to describe those who came from Gentile lands (e.g., Isa. 60:4,9; Jer. 46:27). By this allusion, Mark hints at the eventual Gentile mission that will gather non-Jews into the church.

8:5 *loaves.* Though fish is once again mentioned (v. 7), the emphasis is on bread, both in terms of the feeding stories and in terms of the lessons of these events (vv. 14–21; 6:52).

Seven. This is a number often associated with Gentiles.

8:7 *he gave thanks.* This term is used to describe the typical grace that would be said before a meal by Mark's Gentile readers. In contrast, the term used for Jesus' prayer prior to the feeding of the five thousand, though translated "he gave thanks," is literally "he blessed [God]," which is a typical Jewish blessing.

8:10 *Dalmanutha*. It is not certain where this town is located. Possibly it is Magdala, a town near Tiberias on the west side of the lake. The point, however, is clear. At this time Jesus left the Gentile region where he was ministering and returned to Jewish soil.

8:11 *test*. Having just shown who he is by the great miracle of feeding, the Pharisees now want Jesus to prove that he is from God! This is what Jesus has been doing all along, but they are too blind to see it. Jesus refuses their request. Even if he granted it, his sign would probably have been rejected, given the Pharisees' conviction that he was empowered by an evil spirit (see Mark 3:22,30). They would have condemned him on the basis of Deuteronomy 13:1–5, which warns against following those who do signs and wonders and seek to get people to follow another god.

***a sign from heaven*.** What they probably had in mind was something like a vivid display in the sky, or knocking over a house by a word of power. Jesus will not give a sign for its own sake, especially when the request springs from unbelief. His miracles are always in aid of others. Jesus is not just a wonder-worker (see Mark 4:35–6:29).

8:12 *He sighed deeply*. Perhaps in weariness over the seemingly futile disputing with the Pharisees. They just don't get it. This is yet another example of Mark informing the reader about Jesus' emotions (1:41; 3:5; 6:6; 10:14; 14:34).

8:15 *yeast*. To the Jew, yeast was connected with fermentation, which they saw as a form of rotting. So yeast became a metaphor for evil and its expansion. Here it stands for the misunderstanding of the Pharisees, which seems to have spread now even to the disciples (see vv. 17–21). It takes only a small amount of yeast to infiltrate a whole batch of bread dough, producing spectacular results. Jesus is not talking about literal yeast (as the disciples took his words to mean—v. 16). He is using yeast as a symbol of something else—which is yet another indication of the symbolic nature of this whole passage.

8:16 *They discussed this with one another*. This was probably a quarrel over who forgot the bread.

That they should worry about not having enough bread after what had just happened with the four thousand is incredible.

8:17 *Do you still not see or understand?* Jesus asks this question twice in these verses (vv. 14–21). This is the issue. Although exposed to ample evidence of who Jesus is, they still fail to put it together.

***hearts hardened*.** This is the problem (see Mark 3:5; 6:52). Their hearts are stone-like. The seed of the word can't penetrate (see Mark 4:15).

8:18 This is actually a quote from Jeremiah 5:21.

eyes but fail to see, and ears but fail to hear? Now the point of the two healings becomes clear. The disciples are like the deaf man (Mark 7:31–35) and the blind man (vv. 22–25). They too need a miracle from Jesus in order to see and hear properly. That such a miracle takes place becomes evident in the final story in this passage: the confession at Caesarea Philippi that Jesus is the Messiah (Mark 8:27–29).

8:19–21 A notoriously difficult passage to interpret.

8:19 *how many*. Jesus' repetition of this question points to the fact that the numbers are important in understanding the meaning of the feedings. They reveal him to be the long-expected Messiah who brings salvation to Israel and to the whole world.

***Twelve*.** A symbol standing for Israel.

8:20 *Seven*. A symbol standing for the Gentile nations.

8:22–26 There are clear parallels between this healing and the healing of the deaf and mute man in 7:31–37. The healing of this blind man is unusual in that it requires two touches on the part of Jesus. As with so much else in this unit, this healing symbolizes something else. Specifically, the "blind" disciples (vv. 17–18) are about to receive their "first touch" of healing. In the next story, Peter will declare that they know that Jesus is the Messiah (Mark 8:27–30). This is a great step forward in their understanding. However, they have not fully understood who Jesus is, as Peter's vigorous rejection of Jesus' teaching about the Messiah demonstrates (Mark 8:31–33). They need a second touch to open their eyes completely. This will not come until Jesus dies and rises again.

8:24 *they look like trees*. He probably once had his sight, since he knows what a tree looks like.

14 Peter's Confession—Mark 8:27–9:1

THREE-PART AGENDA

ICE-BREAKER
15 Minutes

BIBLE STUDY
30 Minutes

CARING TIME
15–45 Minutes

> **LEADER:** Check page M7 in the center section for a good ice-breaker, particularly if you have a new person at this meeting. In the Caring Time, is everyone sharing and are prayer requests being followed up?

TO BEGIN THE BIBLE STUDY TIME
(Choose 1 or 2)

1. What's your favorite TV game show or question-and-answer game?

2. What is one person, place or thing you have always wanted to see but have not had the opportunity?

3. When you misbehaved as a child, what did your parents say that made you feel most ashamed of what you had done?

READ SCRIPTURE & DISCUSS
(If you don't have time for all the questions in this section, conclude the Bible Study [30 min.] by answering question #7.)

1. If your closest friends were asked what one word best describes you, what might they say?

2. Why is the question "Who do you say I am?" (v. 29) so important?

3. Who did the people of Jesus' day think he was (v. 28)? Who do people today say Jesus is? What about you, and how has your answer changed over time?

Peter's Confession of Christ

27Jesus and his disciples went on to the villages around Caesarea Philippi. On the way he asked them, "Who do people say I am?"

28They replied, "Some say John the Baptist; others say Elijah; and still others, one of the prophets."

29"But what about you?" he asked. "Who do you say I am?"

Peter answered, "You are the Christ.ª"

30Jesus warned them not to tell anyone about him.

Jesus Predicts His Death

31He then began to teach them that the Son of Man must suffer many things and be rejected by the elders, chief priests and teachers of the law, and that he must be killed and after three days rise again. 32He spoke plainly about this, and Peter took him aside and began to rebuke him.

33But when Jesus turned and looked at his disciples, he rebuked Peter. "Get behind me, Satan!" he said. "You do not have in mind the things of God, but the things of men."

34Then he called the crowd to him along with his disciples and said: "If anyone would come after me, he must deny himself and take up his cross and follow me. 35For whoever wants to save his lifeᵇ will lose it, but whoever loses his life for me and for the gospel will save it. 36What good is it for a man to gain the whole world, yet forfeit his soul? 37Or what can a man give in exchange for his soul? 38If anyone is ashamed of me and my words in this adulterous and sinful generation, the Son of Man will be ashamed of him when he comes in his Father's glory with the holy angels."

9 *And he said to them, "I tell you the truth, some who are standing here will not taste death before they see the kingdom of God come with power."*

ª29 or *Messiah.* "The Christ" (Greek) and "the Messiah" (Hebrew) both mean "the Anointed One."
ᵇ35 The Greek word means either *life* or *soul*, also in verse 36.

4. What four things does Jesus prophesy about himself in verses 31 and 32?

5. How did Peter go from "star pupil" (v. 29) to being in the doghouse (v. 33)?

6. According to verses 34–38, what is involved in being a follower of Christ?

7. How does your relationship with Christ affect how you live? In what area of ministry do you feel most called to follow Jesus?

CARING TIME

(Choose 1 or 2 of these questions before closing in prayer. Be sure to pray for the empty chair.)

1. Rate this past week on a scale of 1 (terrible) to 10 (great). What's the outlook for this week?

2. How is this group helping you to keep in mind "the things of God" rather than "the things of men"?

3. How would you like this group to pray for you?

8:27–30 This is a pivotal passage in the Gospel of Mark. The disciples declare (through Peter, who seems to have become their spokesman) that in contrast to the crowds, they recognize who Jesus is. He is the long-expected Messiah. To be sure, they have the wrong idea about the nature and role of the Messiah. But at least they have grasped accurately that Jesus is not just an exceptional rabbi, nor just a wonder-worker.

8:27 *Caesarea Philippi.* A beautiful city on the slopes of Mt. Hermon, 25 miles north of Bethsaida. This region reeked with religion. It had been a center of Baal worship, and was said to be the birthplace of the god Pan. It was also the place where the River Jordan began. At the time when Jesus and his disciples visited there, up on the hill was a gleaming, white marble temple dedicated to the godhead of Caesar. It is fitting that in this place with rich associations to the religions of the world, Jesus, the Galilean, asks his disciples if they understand that he is the Anointed One sent by God.

8:29 *Who do you say I am?* This is *the* crucial question in Mark's Gospel. By it the author forces his readers to consider how they will answer the question as well.

You are the Christ. Peter correctly identifies him as the Messiah. "Christ" is the Greek term for "Messiah" (which is a Hebrew word). In the context of Jewish thought, this meant the prophesied future king of Israel who would deliver Israel from bondage into an era of freedom, power, influence and prosperity.

8:30 *not to tell anyone.* Jesus urges them to be silent about what they know. The problem is that although they know that he is the Messiah, they do not yet know what kind of Messiah he is. This recognition of Jesus follows immediately after the strange two-stage healing of the blind man (8:22–26) meant to be an enacted parable of the disciples' insight. Like the blind man, the disciples have received the "first touch" of healing. Their spiritual blindness, which thus far prevented them from understanding Jesus, is beginning to be healed but they are not yet totally restored to full sight as the next incident shows (8:31–33).

8:31–9:1 This begins a new major section which runs through 10:32. In this section the focus is on Jesus in his role as teacher. Specifically, he seeks to teach the Twelve what kind of Messiah he is, over against their erroneous cultural assumptions which viewed the Messiah as a military hero who would be crowned king after leading a literal army in a triumphant battle against the Roman oppressors. This section is organized around Jesus' three predictions that he will die and rise again (8:31; 9:31 and 10:32–34). In each case the disciples fail to grasp what he is saying. It is not until they receive a "second touch" that they are able to see clearly. Fittingly, the unit ends with the healing of blind Bartimaeus which introduces the events that lead to his death and resurrection after which the disciples do, finally, grasp his divinity and the spiritual, universal nature of his role as Messiah. In addition, this section contains Jesus' teaching regarding what it means to be his disciple (8:34–38; 9:33–36; 10:35–45); relationships between disciples (9:33–50); who his disciples are (9:38–41; 10:13–31) and how to treat those who are his disciples (9:36–49).

> *Discipleship is a matter of following in the ways of one's teacher.*

8:31 This is the first of the three predictions. To predict one's death is rare, but not unknown. However, to predict that one will rise from the dead is startling. No wonder the disciples had trouble taking in what he was saying. The repetition three times of this prediction of death and resurrection draws attention to its central importance in understanding who Jesus is.

He then began to teach them. For the remainder of this unit (8:31–10:52), Jesus seeks to teach the Twelve what kind of Messiah he is. They think of him in popular terms: as a military hero who will lead a literal army in battle against the Romans from which he will emerge triumphant and be crowned king.

Son of Man. This is the title that Jesus prefers for himself. In the first century it was a rather colorless, indeterminate title (with some messianic overtones) which could be translated as "man" or even "I." This allows Jesus to fill it with new meaning and to convey what kind of Messiah he actually is.

rejected by the elders, chief priests and teachers of the law. These three groups made up the

Sanhedrin, the ruling Jewish body. Jesus is predicting that he will be officially rejected by Israel (see Mark 14:55).

must be killed. The death of the Messiah at the hands of Israel's official governing body played no part in popular ideas about the Messiah. This was a startling, incomprehensible announcement. For Jesus, his death was mandated by a divine necessity. Passages such as Isaiah 53 and Psalm 22 appear to have shaped his realization of what his future would involve.

8:32 rebuke. Peter, who moments before identifies Jesus as the Messiah, is startled by his teaching that the Messiah will suffer, be rejected, killed, and then rise from the dead. He felt compelled to take Jesus aside and urge him to stop this line of teaching. The word "rebuke" is the same one used to describe the silencing of demons.

8:33 Get behind me, Satan! By urging Jesus to back away from his teaching about suffering and death, Peter is doing what Satan did: tempting Jesus with the promise that he can have the whole world without pain (Matt. 4:8–10).

8:34–38 Jesus defines what following him means. It involves denial, cross-bearing, and losing one's life. The original recipients of the letter (the Christians in Rome) were doing this very thing: suffering for the sake of Jesus.

8:34 the crowd. This message is intended to be heard by everyone who wishes to follow Jesus. While the miracles might have made it appear that the kingdom of God simply meant fulfillment and joy, Jesus makes it clear that the way to the kingdom involves self-denial and sacrifice. Mark appears to have especially directed these words to the situation faced by the original recipients of the Gospel, the Christians in Rome who were in fact suffering for the sake of Jesus during the persecution under Nero.

come after me. Discipleship is a matter of following in the ways of one's teacher.

deny himself / take up his cross / follow me. To "take up a cross" was something done only by a person sentenced to death by crucifixion, a reality that had faced some of the comrades of Mark's readers who had been executed by Nero. This stark image

points out that to be a follower of Jesus means loyalty to him must precede all desires and ambitions, including the natural desire for self-preservation. Like Jesus, his followers are to single-mindedly pursue God's way even when it means suffering and death.

> *Like Jesus, his followers are to single-mindedly pursue God's way even when it means suffering and death.*

8:35 save his life. The image is of a trial in which one is called upon to renounce Jesus in order to live. This would have immediate application to the Christians in Rome who were pressed with the decision of considering whether to affirm their loyalty to Jesus and face the persecution of the state or deny their association with Jesus and be allowed to live.

will lose it. That is, the person will ultimately face the judgment of God for his or her denial of Christ.

whoever loses his life ... will save it. In this Gospel, John the Baptist represents such a faithful person (6:14–29).

8:36–37 These two rhetorical questions press home the critical nature of the decision to remain loyal to Jesus.

8:38 ashamed of me. This would be indicated by failing to persist in one's Christian testimony in times of persecution.

adulterous and sinful generation. This is reminiscent of the language of the Old Testament prophets who used adultery as a metaphor for Israel's disloyalty to God.

Son of Man / Father's glory / holy angels. This is apocalyptic imagery borrowed from Daniel 7:13ff. The Jewish expectation was that God's kingdom would one day be decisively and dramatically ushered in.

9:1 Jesus announces that a momentous event (which will demonstrate that the kingdom of God has indeed come) will soon take place. Six days later the Transfiguration occurs (9:2–8).

15 The Transfiguration—Mark 9:2–32

THREE-PART AGENDA

ICE-BREAKER
15 Minutes

BIBLE STUDY
30 Minutes

CARING TIME
15–45 Minutes

> *LEADER: If there's a new person in this session, start with an ice-breaker from the center section (see page M7). Remember to stick closely to the three-part agenda and the time allowed for each segment. Is your group praying for the empty chair?*

TO BEGIN THE BIBLE STUDY TIME
(Choose 1 or 2)

1. What's the tallest mountain you've ever been on?

2. When is a time you really put your foot in your mouth?

3. If you were to plan a getaway with three friends, who would you take and where would you go?

READ SCRIPTURE & DISCUSS
(If you don't have time for all the questions in this section, conclude the Bible Study [30 min.] by answering question #7.)

1. How would you describe your relationship with God right now: In the valley? On the mountaintop? Climbing? Other?

2. Why was Peter's response to what he had just seen inappropriate? What caused him to react this way?

3. What questions did Peter, James and John have as they came down the mountain? What questions would you be asking?

4. How would this experience be a help and encouragement to Jesus as he drew nearer to his time of suffering and death?

The Transfiguration

²After six days Jesus took Peter, James and John with him and led them up a high mountain, where they were all alone. There he was transfigured before them. ³His clothes became dazzling white, whiter than anyone in the world could bleach them. ⁴And there appeared before them Elijah and Moses, who were talking with Jesus.

⁵Peter said to Jesus, "Rabbi, it is good for us to be here. Let us put up three shelters—one for you, one for Moses and one for Elijah." ⁶(He did not know what to say, they were so frightened.)

⁷Then a cloud appeared and enveloped them, and a voice came from the cloud: "This is my Son, whom I love. Listen to him!"

⁸Suddenly, when they looked around, they no longer saw anyone with them except Jesus.

⁹As they were coming down the mountain, Jesus gave them orders not to tell anyone what they had seen until the Son of Man had risen from the dead. ¹⁰They kept the matter to themselves, discussing what "rising from the dead" meant.

¹¹And they asked him, "Why do the teachers of the law say that Elijah must come first?"

¹²Jesus replied, "To be sure, Elijah does come first, and restores all things. Why then is it written that the Son of Man must suffer much and be rejected? ¹³But I tell you, Elijah has come, and they have done to him everything they wished, just as it is written about him."

The Healing of a Boy With an Evil Spirit

¹⁴When they came to the other disciples, they saw a large crowd around them and the teachers of the law arguing with them. ¹⁵As soon as all the people saw Jesus, they were overwhelmed with wonder and ran to greet him.

¹⁶"What are you arguing with them about?" he asked.

¹⁷A man in the crowd answered, "Teacher, I brought you my son, who is possessed by a spirit that has robbed him of speech. ¹⁸Whenever it seizes him, it throws him to the ground. He foams at the mouth, gnashes his teeth and becomes rigid. I asked your disciples to drive out the spirit, but they could not."

5. When have you felt like the father of the boy with an evil spirit, one moment saying, "I do believe," and the next, "Help me overcome my unbelief" (v. 24)?

6. What kind of doubts hit you the hardest: Future concerns? Faith issues? Self-image issues?

7. What would help silence the doubts you feel: Admitting them? Praying more? Experiencing a miracle? Asking others to pray for you?

CARING TIME

(Choose 1 or 2 of these questions before closing in prayer. Be sure to pray for the empty chair.)

1. On a scale of 1 to 10, how closely have you been walking with Jesus this week? What has taken your attention away from him?

2. What would you like to do this week in order to walk more closely with him?

3. How can this group support you in prayer this week?

¹⁹*"O unbelieving generation," Jesus replied, "how long shall I stay with you? How long shall I put up with you? Bring the boy to me."*

²⁰*So they brought him. When the spirit saw Jesus, it immediately threw the boy into a convulsion. He fell to the ground and rolled around, foaming at the mouth.*

²¹*Jesus asked the boy's father, "How long has he been like this?"*

"From childhood," he answered. ²²*"It has often thrown him into fire or water to kill him. But if you can do anything, take pity on us and help us."*

²³*" 'If you can'?" said Jesus. "Everything is possible for him who believes."*

²⁴*Immediately the boy's father exclaimed, "I do believe; help me overcome my unbelief!"*

²⁵*When Jesus saw that a crowd was running to the scene, he rebuked the evil^a spirit. "You deaf and mute spirit," he said, "I command you, come out of him and never enter him again."*

²⁶*The spirit shrieked, convulsed him violently and came out. The boy looked so much like a corpse that many said, "He's dead."* ²⁷*But Jesus took him by the hand and lifted him to his feet, and he stood up.*

²⁸*After Jesus had gone indoors, his disciples asked him privately, "Why couldn't we drive it out?"*

²⁹*He replied, "This kind can come out only by prayer.^b"*

³⁰*They left that place and passed through Galilee. Jesus did not want anyone to know where they were,* ³¹*because he was teaching his disciples. He said to them, "The Son of Man is going to be betrayed into the hands of men. They will kill him, and after three days he will rise."* ³²*But they did not understand what he meant and were afraid to ask him about it.*

^a25 Greek *unclean*   ^b29 Some manuscripts *prayer and fasting*

Notes—Mark 9:2–32

Summary. Events begin to gather speed. The disciples have discovered that Jesus is no mere teacher (no matter how gifted and special he is), nor is he simply a prophet (no matter how powerful he might be). He is the Messiah—God's Anointed Servant who has come to bring a new order in the world. Here in the Transfiguration, God affirms once again that Jesus is his beloved Son, and he declares to the people (via the three apostles who witness these events) that Jesus is, indeed, the Promised One whose coming was foretold in the Old Testament. The account of the Transfiguration parallels in some interesting ways the baptism of Jesus (1:9–11). In the same way that the baptism of Jesus opened the first half of the Gospel (after some preliminary words from the Old Testament and from John the Baptist), the Transfiguration opens the second half (following some defining words by Jesus). In both incidents, the voice of God affirms that Jesus is his special Son. Both draw heavily on the Old Testament for their meaning. The baptism of Jesus prefigures his death; the Transfiguration, his resurrection.

9:2 *After six days.* By this phrase Mark connects the Transfiguration with Jesus' prediction that "some who are standing here will not taste death before they see the kingdom of God come with power" (9:1). The mention of "six days" is probably also an allusion to Exodus 24:15–18, where the story is told of Moses going up the mountain and remaining there six days until he is summoned into the presence of God. Thus the readers are alerted to the fact that another revelation of God is about to take place.

Peter, James and John. These three emerge as an inner circle around Jesus. Mark has pointed out that Jesus took only these three disciples with him when he raised Jairus' daughter (5:37–41). Here he selects them to accompany him up the mountain. These are three of the first four disciples Jesus chose (1:14–20).

a high mountain. This may well be Mt. Hermon, a 9,000 foot mountain located some 12 miles from Caesarea Philippi (though early tradition says it is Mt. Tabor, located southwest of the Sea of Galilee). The physical location of the mountain is not as significant as its theological meaning since mountains were the places in times past that God revealed himself to the leaders of Israel in special ways. For example, to Moses on Mt. Sinai (Ex. 24) and to Elijah on Mt. Horeb (1 Kings 19). This sets the stage for another dramatic revelation of God to a leader of God's people.

transfigured. The word used here is *metamorphothe* (from which the English word "metamorphosis" comes). It means, literally, "to change one's form."

9:3 *dazzling white.* The word "dazzling" (or "radiant") was used to describe the glistening of highly polished metal or the sparkling of sunlight. The phrase "white as snow" is found in Daniel 7:9, where it is used to describe the clothing of God when he appeared in a vision. Here the disciples witness Jesus being changed into a form just like God. In Revelation 1:9–18, the resurrected, glorified Jesus is described in similar terms. Brilliant, radiant light is often associated with appearances of God in the Old Testament.

9:4 *Elijah.* Elijah was a great prophet. The Jews expected that he would return just prior to the coming of the salvation they had been promised. And indeed, he is there on the mountain as the forerunner of the Messiah.

Moses. Moses was the greatest figure in the Old Testament. It was to him God gave the Law which became the very heart of the nation. It was he who brought the religion of Israel into being. And it was Moses who prophesied that God would one day send another prophet to lead his people (Deut. 18:15). The early Christians took this to be a prophecy about Jesus (Acts 3:22–26; 7:35–37). The presence of both Moses and Elijah on the mountain is meant to indicate that the Old Testament Law and the Prophets, which form the core of Israel's identity, endorse Jesus as God's appointed Messiah. They witness to his greatness and superiority over them.

> *Throughout the Bible, whenever God is manifested before people the human response is one of fear and of being undone.*

9:5 *shelters.* Peter might have had in mind the huts of intertwined branches which were put up at the Festival of Tabernacles to commemorate Israel's time in the wilderness. Or he might be thinking of the "tent of meeting" where God met with Moses. In making this suggestion, Peter shows his (quite understandable) confusion about this event. Did it mark the full arrival of the kingdom? Did this mean that Jesus had come into his glory without the suffering he told them about? How should he respond to such an amazing experience?

9:6 *frightened.* Throughout the Bible, whenever God is manifested before people the human response is one of fear and of being undone (Ex. 3:5–6; 20:18–19; Judges 6:20–23; Isaiah 6:5; Dan. 10:7–8; Rev. 1:17).

9:7 This verse is full of Old Testament allusions that are meant to confirm Jesus' divine authority.

a cloud. The Old Testament often speaks of clouds as one of the phenomena which accompanies an appearance of God (Ex. 16:10; 19:9; 24:15–18; 40:34–38). Clouds are signs of his majesty and serve to veil his full glory from the eyes of mortals (who would otherwise be totally overwhelmed). This cloud is a symbol of the presence of God.

a voice. Once again, as he did at the baptism of Jesus (1:11), God proclaims that Jesus is his Son.

This is my Son, whom I love. By means of this event, it is revealed that not only is Jesus the Messiah (as the disciples have just confessed), he is also the Son of God. Both titles are necessary for a full understanding of his nature and role. In the Old Testament, the phrase "son of God" was used as a title for God's appointed king over Israel (Ps. 2:7). In and of itself, it neither carries a connotation of deity nor implies anything unique about the means of Jesus' conception. It simply asserts his authority as the one God has chosen to be king. Yet the miracles Jesus has performed earlier in the Gospel (in which he performs the acts of God, such as in calming the sea) indicate that in his case this title has a special meaning unparalleled by its former uses.

Listen to him! This is a quotation from Moses' prophecy about the coming prophet (see note for 9:4). The new prophet, whose authority and glory

superseded that of Moses, was on the scene. This is a divine attestation to his authority.

> *The Old Testament often speaks of clouds as one of the phenomena which accompanies an appearance of God. Clouds are signs of his majesty and serve to veil his full glory from the eyes of mortals (who would otherwise be totally overwhelmed). This cloud is a symbol of the presence of God.*

9:8 In an instant, the overwhelming experience of God's glory was gone. Moses, Elijah and God himself had all borne witness to these three disciples regarding the person of Jesus. Mark has answered once for all the question about Jesus' identity that had been building all throughout the first eight chapters of his Gospel. Now the disciples are to learn more fully what discipleship to the Messiah, the Son of God, really involves.

9:9–11 The disciples discuss the Jewish expectation that Elijah will come to inaugurate the kingdom. They do not really grasp the significance of the Transfiguration (nor the need for suffering and death on the part of the Messiah), nor can they until after Jesus' resurrection. Their two questions spring from confusion over Jesus' radically new teaching (about suffering, death and resurrection) in light of popular expectations about the Messiah.

9:9 *not to tell.* Once again, Jesus commands silence. The meaning of this event cannot be understood until Jesus dies and rises again. Then it will be clear what kind of Messiah he is and what it means to be the Son of God.

9:11 *Elijah must come first.* Since Elijah, a prophet who had called Israel to be faithful to God during a time of widespread apostasy, never died but was taken up into heaven by God (2 Kings 2:1–2), the Jews believed that God would send Elijah back before the Messiah appeared to again call Israel to faithfulness (Mal. 4:5).

9:12 Why then is it written. Jesus does not specify which Old Testament passage he has in mind, though a passage like Isaiah 53:3 would explain his statement here and in 8:31 that the Son of Man "must suffer" and die. While it seems incongruous to the disciples that the Messiah must suffer, Jesus reminds them that Elijah himself suffered at the hands of King Ahab and Queen Jezebel (1 Kings 19:1–10).

9:13 Elijah has come. Here, in the Transfiguration, the long-expected Elijah comes. However, Elijah has come in a second sense. John the Baptist has played the role of Elijah by being the forerunner of the Messiah.

9:14–32 Jesus and his three disciples descend from the "high" of this mountaintop experience to the valley, where the other disciples are arguing with the religious leaders about their failure to cast out a demon. They go from the experience of God's power and presence to the experience of Satan's power and presence. The movement from transfiguration to confrontation with evil parallels the earlier movement of Jesus from baptism to the wilderness of temptation. This also parallels Moses' experience when he came down from the mountain to find the people of Israel worshiping a golden calf (Ex. 32). This is the final exorcism in the Gospel of Mark.

9:18 The symptoms closely resemble those of a certain form of epilepsy.

they could not. The faith of the disciples is shown once again to be incomplete.

9:19 O unbelieving generation. This is the cry of anguish and loneliness of one who knows so clearly the way things really are, and yet is constantly confronted with disbelief in various forms.

how long shall I stay with you? The time will come when the disciples are on their own to carry on the work of the kingdom.

9:23 'If you can'? By this phrase, the man indicates that he is not sure if Jesus can perform such a miracle (after all, his disciples have failed). By highlighting his doubts Jesus pinpoints the real issue: the question is not whether Jesus has the ability to heal (which has been amply demonstrated); the issue is the man's ability to believe.

9:24 believe. Belief or "faith is the assertion of a possibility against all probabilities, in spite of any contrary indications provided by our experience of life or of the realities of the world. … What is it that differentiates this faith from mere illusion …? It is not a faith which reaches vaguely into the void, but one that firmly trusts Jesus Christ" (Lane).

unbelief. The problem here is one of *doubt* (being in two minds about an issue) not one of *disbelief* (certainty that something is not true). The father did not disbelieve. After all, he had brought his son to Jesus to be healed (v. 17). His faith has been shaken, however, by the failure of the disciples to heal his son (v. 18) so that now, even though he desperately wants his child to be free of this demon, he wonders if it is possible (v. 22).

9:29 prayer. The disciples have been given the authority to cast out demons (6:7) and have, in fact, done so (6:13). However, as this incident makes clear, this power was not their own. It required continuing dependence upon God.

9:31 For the second time, Jesus warns them of what lies ahead.

betrayed. This is a new note in his teaching. It is not just that he will be rejected by the leaders of Israel. There will be an element of treachery involved. This same word is used again by Mark in 14:41–42 to describe Judas' betrayal of Jesus.

9:32 Once again they fail to grasp what Jesus is saying. His talk of betrayal, death, and resurrection is so far from their understanding of what the Messiah would be like that they simply cannot take in his words.

16 True Greatness—Mark 9:33–10:12

THREE-PART AGENDA

ICE-BREAKER
15 Minutes

BIBLE STUDY
30 Minutes

CARING TIME
15–45 Minutes

> **LEADER: How is the group progressing on reaching its mission goal? Does the group need to review pages M3 and M6 in the center section? If you have a new person at the meeting, remember to do an ice-breaker from the center section.**

TO BEGIN THE BIBLE STUDY TIME
(Choose 1 or 2)

1. If you could be "king or queen for a day," what would be your first order?

2. What do you like most about going to weddings?

3. If you could recapture one quality you had as a child, what would it be? Why?

READ SCRIPTURE & DISCUSS
(If you don't have time for all the questions in this section, conclude the Bible Study [30 min.] by answering question #7.)

1. When have you felt you were not given the recognition you deserved?

2. Why were the disciples concerned about which of them was the greatest (see note on v. 34)?

3. How does Jesus define true greatness (v. 35)? How does this differ from the success portrayed by television or pursued by most people?

Who Is the Greatest?

³³They came to Capernaum. When he was in the house, he asked them, "What were you arguing about on the road?" ³⁴But they kept quiet because on the way they had argued about who was the greatest.

³⁵Sitting down, Jesus called the Twelve and said, "If anyone wants to be first, he must be the very last, and the servant of all."

³⁶He took a little child and had him stand among them. Taking him in his arms, he said to them, ³⁷"Whoever welcomes one of these little children in my name welcomes me; and whoever welcomes me does not welcome me but the one who sent me."

Whoever Is Not Against Us Is for Us

³⁸"Teacher," said John, "we saw a man driving out demons in your name and we told him to stop, because he was not one of us."

³⁹"Do not stop him," Jesus said. "No one who does a miracle in my name can in the next moment say anything bad about me, ⁴⁰for whoever is not against us is for us. ⁴¹I tell you the truth, anyone who gives you a cup of water in my name because you belong to Christ will certainly not lose his reward.

Causing to Sin

⁴²"And if anyone causes one of these little ones who believe in me to sin, it would be better for him to be thrown into the sea with a large millstone tied around his neck. ⁴³If your hand causes you to sin, cut it off. It is better for you to enter life maimed than with two hands to go into hell, where the fire never goes out.ᵃ ⁴⁵And if your foot causes you to sin, cut it off. It is better for you to enter life crippled than to have two feet and be thrown into hell.ᵇ ⁴⁷And if your eye causes you to sin, pluck it out. It is better for you to enter the kingdom of God with one eye than to have two eyes and be thrown into hell, ⁴⁸where

> *" 'their worm does not die,*
> *and the fire is not quenched.'ᶜ*

⁴⁹Everyone will be salted with fire.

4. Jesus said that someone who gave one of his people a cup of water in his name would not lose his reward (v. 41). What simple, everyday skills do you have that you can do for someone in Jesus' name?

5. Short of amputating body parts, what do you need to cut out of your life in order to avoid sin?

6. What was God's intention for marriage? What causes so much divorce today?

7. What can you do in the coming week to keep your heart soft toward the ways of God?

CARING TIME
(Choose 1 or 2 of these questions before closing in prayer. Be sure to pray for the empty chair.)

1. How has being in this group helped you believe in Christ more fully?

2. What is your biggest concern about the future? About the coming week?

3. How can this group pray for you this week?

⁵⁰"Salt is good, but if it loses its saltiness, how can you make it salty again? Have salt in yourselves, and be at peace with each other."

Divorce

10 Jesus then left that place and went into the region of Judea and across the Jordan. Again crowds of people came to him, and as was his custom, he taught them.

²Some Pharisees came and tested him by asking, "Is it lawful for a man to divorce his wife?"

³"What did Moses command you?" he replied.

⁴They said, "Moses permitted a man to write a certificate of divorce and send her away."

⁵"It was because your hearts were hard that Moses wrote you this law," Jesus replied. ⁶"But at the beginning of creation God 'made them male and female.'ᵈ ⁷'For this reason a man will leave his father and mother and be united to his wife,ᵉ ⁸and the two will become one flesh.'ᶠ So they are no longer two, but one. ⁹Therefore what God has joined together, let man not separate."

¹⁰When they were in the house again, the disciples asked Jesus about this. ¹¹He answered, "Anyone who divorces his wife and marries another woman commits adultery against her. ¹²And if she divorces her husband and marries another man, she commits adultery."

ᵃ43 Some manuscripts out, 44where / " 'their worm does not die, / and the fire is not quenched.'
ᵇ45 Some manuscripts hell, 46where / " 'their worm does not die, / and the fire is not quenched.'
ᶜ48 Isaiah 66:24
ᵈ6 Gen. 1:27
ᵉ7 Some early manuscripts do not have and be united to his wife.
ᶠ8 Gen. 2:24

Summary. In this section Jesus teaches about discipleship. Specifically, the focus of this teaching is relationships between people, i.e., how to move from argument (v. 33) to peace (v. 50). By comparison with where this material appears in Matthew and Luke, it would appear that once again (as he did in 4:1–34), Mark has collected into one unit teachings given by Jesus on various occasions. These sayings are linked together by various "catch words." Furthermore, the topic which began this section (the disciples arguing with each other) is resolved at the end (with the injunction in v. 50 to "be at peace with each other"). This was a common device used in the first century to aid memorization in an era when books were not widely available.

9:33–37 For the second time following the Lord's words about what will happen to him, there is an incident which demonstrates that the disciples have not grasped what he is saying (see also 8:31, followed by 8:32–33). In this case, despite Jesus' teaching about betrayal and death, the disciples continue to have visions of a literal kingdom to be established on earth with Jesus as its head. They are arguing about who will have what position in that kingdom.

9:34 greatest. Once again the disciples have missed the point. In the face of Jesus' teaching about suffering and death, they are concerned about their position and personal power. That such a topic should be debated was not unexpected, since concern for rank was common in those days. Rabbis disputed about who would be the greatest in the new age. Each year the religious sect at Qumran ranked each member of the community in accord with his worthiness.

9:35 Once again (as he did in 8:35, when he spoke about losing one's life to save it), Jesus turns their understanding upside down. The real issue is not who is greatest, he says, but who serves best. Service, not power, is the prime value in his kingdom.

9:36–37 This is the first of several dramatized parables in Mark whereby Jesus uses an object in a symbolic way to make his point (e.g., 11:12–14,20–21). The child is a symbol standing for Jesus' followers (in Aramaic and in Greek, the same word can be translated child or servant, thus referring back to his previous point in v. 35). His point is that they must welcome his followers. All of his followers need to be treated with respect. Verse 37 accents the strong identity between Jesus and his followers: how one treats even the most (seemingly) insignificant disciple is seen as evidence of how one actually treats Jesus.

9:38–41 From the issue of how to treat Jesus' disciples, Mark deals with the way to recognize these disciples. The point is that those who claim to be his followers must be accepted as such.

9:38 John. Following each of the three predictions of his death and resurrection, it is one of the three disciples closest to Jesus who is shown to be missing the point: Peter in 8:32, John here, and James (along with John) in 10:35–37.

> *The real issue is not who is greatest, Jesus says, but who serves best. Service, not power, is the prime value in his kingdom.*

a man driving out demons in your name. Acts 19:13–16 describes the successful use by Jewish exorcists of Jesus' name to drive out demons. In exorcism, it was the power of the name that dominated (see notes on 1:24 in Session 2 and 5:6–9 in Session 8). This unnamed exorcist is an example of one of his followers who is to be welcomed (thus illustrating the point Jesus just made in v. 37).

9:39 Do not stop him. The attempt by the disciples to stop this unauthorized exorcism is an abuse of their authority (demonstrating once again that this is what they are thinking about), made all the more ironic by their own failure to cast out the demon from the epileptic boy (9:17–18).

9:40 This sums up Jesus' point. Anyone who, in the name of Jesus, engages in his work is to be seen as an ally, even if he or she is not part of "our" community.

9:41 a cup of water. Echoing the principle in verse 37, this saying illustrates the point of verse 40.

Service done to a disciple is seen as service to Jesus. "The reference to 'his reward' ... stresses God's awareness of all who share in the extension of Jesus' work, and to emphasize that there are no distinctions between 'trivial' and 'important' tasks" (Lane).

9:42–50 Mark adds to the two previous incidents a collection of other related sayings (much as he added the sayings in 4:21–34 to the Parable of the Sower in 4:1–20).

9:42 This saying, which thematically probably belongs to verses 38–41, accents the severity of judgment that will come upon any who cause a "little one" (i.e., a follower of Christ) to sin. This saying is an example of Jesus' frequent use of using dramatic, exaggerated language in order to make his point.

9:42 *these little ones who believe in me.* The reference is to Jesus' followers (see v. 37).

causes ... to sin. Literally, something which snares a person or animal; which causes them to trip up or entices them to stray.

the sea. Jews were terrified of the sea.

a large millstone. There are two words for millstone. One refers to a small hand mill used in a home; the other (which Jesus uses here) refers to the huge upper stone of a community mill, so big that it had to be drawn around by a donkey. Jesus uses hyperbole to make his point.

9:43 *cut it off.* Another hyperbole. That Jesus is not calling for his followers to indulge in physical mutilation (which was forbidden by the Old Testament) is demonstrated by the fact that the early Christians were not noted for being eyeless or legless.

life. Spiritual life; life in the kingdom of God (see v. 47).

hell. Literally, Gehenna—a ravine outside Jerusalem where children were once sacrificed and where garbage was burned during the time of Jesus. Gehenna became a symbol for extreme horror, the place of punishment and spiritual death.

9:48 Gehenna is a place where horrid worms live in the refuse and where the fire smolders constantly. Mark's point in this section is that any sacrifice is worth avoiding Gehenna.

9:49 The allusion is to the practice of sprinkling salt on the sacrifices that were to be burned on the altar (see Lev. 2:13). While verses 43–48 warned the disciples not to compromise with sin, here they are warned that, like sacrifices offered to God, they will be "salted" with fire, a metaphor for the suffering and trials they will experience because of their loyalty to Jesus (see 1 Peter 1:7; 4:12).

9:50 *Salt.* Salt does not normally lose its taste, but salt from the Dead Sea was mixed with impurities and over time could acquire a stale taste. If his followers lose their salt (probably meaning their sense of servanthood—see v. 35), this is not easily restored.

be at peace with each other. However, when his followers have such a sense of service, peace is the outcome. Had the disciples grasped this concept of servanthood instead of opting for power and greatness, they would not have been arguing on the road (9:33). Thus, Mark returns back to the issue which began this teaching section.

10:1–12 Chapter 10 records the incidents en route from Capernaum to Jerusalem on Jesus' final journey, a trip that will culminate in his death. Its stories all relate to various aspects of a disciple's relationships with others.

10:1 Jesus goes south, over the hills into Samaria, following the traditional route of pilgrims on their way to Jerusalem.

that place. He begins his journey to Jerusalem in Capernaum (see 9:33), the place where his ministry began in the Gospel of Mark (1:16–45).

Judea. A Roman province in the south of Palestine, similar in size and location to the land of Judah in the Old Testament.

across the Jordan. This is a reference to a specific region called Perea, which was a narrow corridor on the east side of the Jordan. Pious Jews would cross over the Jordan into Perea to avoid traveling through Samaria (where they would become ritually unclean). This is the territory of Herod Antipas, the ruler who beheaded John the Baptist.

10:2 *tested him.* It is not by chance that the Pharisees question Jesus about divorce. It was this issue that led to John the Baptist's death (see 6:17–28). If Jesus responded that divorce was lawful, then the leaders could criticize him as being in opposition to John the Baptist whom the people greatly respected for his courage in opposing Herod's sin. However, if Jesus said it was not lawful, then the leaders might be able to get Herod to arrest him as well. It is important to remember this context as one interprets the meaning of Jesus' words about divorce. He was responding here to a trap, not to a sincere question asked by someone in a difficult marital relationship.

> *The casual attitude of the Pharisees toward divorce and remarriage amounted to no more than legalized adultery, and Jesus makes sure that his disciples realize they are not to share that attitude.*

divorce. All the Jewish parties agreed (on the basis of Deut. 24:1–4) that divorce was allowed. The issue in this debate concerned the grounds on which such divorce was permissible. The strict rabbis allowed divorce only on the basis of adultery. Liberal teachers allowed divorce for a host of reasons: e.g., if a woman spoiled her husband's dinner, or if her husband found her less attractive than someone else. In any case, it was only the husband who had the right of divorce. The most that a wife could do was to ask her husband to divorce her.

10:4 *a certificate of divorce.* This was issued to the woman as a form of protection, verifying her release from marriage and giving her the right to remarry.

10:5–9 Jesus attacks the way Deuteronomy 24:1–4 had come to be used by the religious leaders of his day. Originally its aim was to prohibit a divorced and remarried woman from remarrying her former husband. However, it came to be taken as a sanction for divorce, which in that era had become very easy for husbands to obtain. Jesus quotes from the account of creation (in Gen. 1–2) to make his point that the original intention of God was an indissoluble union whereby two people become one. God joins the couple together (v. 9) and they are responsible to each other for maintaining this union (vv. 7–8). The point is that while the leaders wanted to argue about the legalities of divorce, Jesus asserts that his disciples are to build their marriages on the foundation that marriage is intended to be a nurturing, unifying, secure relationship of love and trust. The fact that how such permanency might be nurtured and protected was not a concern of Israel's religious leaders revealed their hardness of heart toward God's law. Thus, Jesus turned the test around to expose their resistance to God.

10:11 *commits adultery against her.* In the Jewish law of that era, adultery was always considered to be an offense against the man. Here, Jesus asserts the responsibility of the husband to be faithful to his wife, who is his equal in relation to God's command. The casual attitude of the Pharisees toward divorce and remarriage amounted to no more than legalized adultery, and Jesus makes sure that his disciples realize they are not to share that attitude.

10:12 This verse, not found in the parallel passage in Matthew 19, may be an editorial comment by Mark relating to the Roman situation in which a woman could initiate divorce. However, it might also have been a comment by Jesus indicating his support for Herodias' marriage to Herod as unlawful (6:17–18) since she had essentially deserted her former husband to marry Herod.

17 True Wealth—Mark 10:13–31

THREE-PART AGENDA

ICE-BREAKER
15 Minutes

BIBLE STUDY
30 Minutes

CARING TIME
15–45 Minutes

> **LEADER:** To help you identify an Apprentice / Leader for a new small group (or if you have a new person at this meeting), see the listing of appropriate ice-breakers on page M7 of the center section.

TO BEGIN THE BIBLE STUDY TIME
(Choose 1 or 2)

1. What is a happy memory you have from your childhood?

2. You've just inherited $5 million dollars from a distant uncle. What are you going to do with the money?

3. What three things would you be most upset about losing in a fire (assuming all people and pets are safe)?

READ SCRIPTURE & DISCUSS
(If you don't have time for all the questions in this section, conclude the Bible Study [30 min.] by answering question #7.)

1. What was the last field trip or activity you attended with lots of small children? How did you feel by the end of the day?

2. Why would the disciples want to keep the children away from Jesus? What childlike qualities was Jesus encouraging?

3. Why did the rich young man ask the question in verse 17? What might have been missing in his life?

4. By choosing his wealth over a loving relationship with Christ, what was the rich young man gaining? What was he forfeiting?

The Little Children and Jesus

¹³People were bringing little children to Jesus to have him touch them, but the disciples rebuked them. ¹⁴When Jesus saw this, he was indignant. He said to them, "Let the little children come to me, and do not hinder them, for the kingdom of God belongs to such as these. ¹⁵I tell you the truth, anyone who will not receive the kingdom of God like a little child will never enter it." ¹⁶And he took the children in his arms, put his hands on them and blessed them.

The Rich Young Man

¹⁷As Jesus started on his way, a man ran up to him and fell on his knees before him. "Good teacher," he asked, "what must I do to inherit eternal life?"

¹⁸"Why do you call me good?" Jesus answered. "No one is good—except God alone. ¹⁹You know the command-ments: 'Do not murder, do not commit adultery, do not steal, do not give false testimony, do not defraud, honor your father and mother.' "

²⁰"Teacher," he declared, "all these I have kept since I was a boy."

²¹Jesus looked at him and loved him. "One thing you lack," he said. "Go, sell everything you have and give to the poor, and you will have treasure in heaven. Then come, fol-low me."

²²At this the man's face fell. He went away sad, because he had great wealth.

²³Jesus looked around and said to his disciples, "How hard it is for the rich to enter the kingdom of God!"

²⁴The disciples were amazed at his words. But Jesus said again, "Children, how hard it is to enter the kingdom of God! ²⁵It is easier for a camel to go through the eye of a needle than for a rich man to enter the kingdom of God."

²⁶The disciples were even more amazed, and said to each other, "Who then can be saved?"

²⁷Jesus looked at them and said, "With man this is impossible, but not with God; all things are possible with God."

²⁸Peter said to him, "We have left everything to follow you!"

5. Why is it so hard for a rich man to enter the kingdom of heaven (vv. 23–25)?

6. According to verses 29–31, what might you lose by following Christ? What will you gain? Which carries the greater sacrifice?

7. Name one thing you can do this week to let go of material things and embrace God's kingdom more fully.

CARING TIME
(Choose 1 or 2 of these questions before closing in prayer. Be sure to pray for the empty chair.)

1. How is the book of Mark making you feel? Why? What has surprised you about God or about this book?

2. What season are you experiencing in your spiritual life: Warmth of summer? Spring is just beginning to bud? Dead of winter? Fall is in the air?

3. What prayer requests would you like to share with this group?

> ²⁹"I tell you the truth," Jesus replied, "no one who has left home or brothers or sisters or mother or father or children or fields for me and the gospel ³⁰will fail to receive a hundred times as much in this present age (homes, brothers, sisters, mothers, children and fields—and with them, persecutions) and in the age to come, eternal life. ³¹But many who are first will be last, and the last first."

Notes—Mark 10:13–31

Summary. These two scenes are set together to provide insight into the nature of true discipleship. Whereas the children represent people who are considered insignificant in society, the rich young man stands for all that the society of the time valued. However, for the second time in this passage on discipleship (8:31–10:52), children become a model of what Jesus is looking for in his followers (see 9:36–37).

10:13–16 From women and marriage, the subject moves to children. Jesus affirms women and children. This was uncharacteristic of his age, in which both groups were considered to be inferior.

10:13 *little children.* The age is uncertain. The term was used to describe infants and children up to 12 years old. Children are dependent upon others and receptive to what they are given. It is this spirit of openness and dependence that Jesus commends.

the disciples rebuked them. The demands on Jesus were ceaseless (e.g., 6:30–31). The disciples wanted to protect him, and so in an era when children were expected to be kept in the background, it was not unreasonable that they would attempt to curb this particular demand.

10:14 Once again Jesus does the unexpected. He invites the weak and the helpless into his kingdom. It is only as adults realize that they, like children, have no position or status by which to earn access to God's kingdom that they will be able to receive it as a gift of God's grace.

do not hinder them. This is the same phrase as Jesus used in 9:39 in relation to the exorcist who was performing the works of the kingdom of God even though he was not part of the disciples' band. Once again, the disciples are using their position to try to stop what is in reality a manifestation of God's kingdom!

> *Jesus points out that accumulation of wealth can hinder participation in God's kingdom.*

the kingdom of God belongs to such as these. The point is not that children are innocent. Rather, the emphasis is on the fact that children were considered insignificant. In that time, they would not assume they could lay claim to any rights or privilege or status; they are dependent upon others and receptive to what they are given. It is this spirit of humility, openness and dependence that Jesus is commending.

10:17–31 In contrast to children, Jesus next meets one who is wealthy and powerful. He turns away the rich young man by the severity of his demand.

10:17 *a man.* Luke describes him as a ruler (Luke 18:18); Matthew calls him young (Matt. 19:20).

Good teacher. His assumption is that some people are good (and merit eternal life), while others are not. This is a distinction which Jesus does not accept. Instead, he casts the whole question into terms of dependence and openness (vv. 14–15).

what must I do. This emphasis on doing is in sharp contrast to Jesus' teaching about receiving the kingdom as a gift that is grasped by faith (see v. 15).

inherit. Gain entrance to; possess.

eternal life. What he is asking for is entrance to the kingdom of God (see vv. 23,25). The view in that era was that the present age would end, at which time the righteous would enter the new age where they will experience eternal life. He wants to be part of this company.

10:18 In the Old Testament only God is called "good" (see v. 17). Does this young man really grasp what is implied in this title that he so easily gives to Jesus?

10:19 *the commandments.* Those which Jesus lists all come from the Ten Commandments, with the exception of "do not defraud" (though by this he may refer to the tenth commandment not to covet).

10:20 He kept the commandments, yet he is unsure whether he has gained eternal life. This was the insecurity of a system based on works-righteousness.

since I was a boy. A Jewish boy was responsible from age 13 onward to keep the commandments.

10:21 *loved him.* Mark is the only Gospel to note Jesus' affection for this earnest and sincere young man.

Go, sell everything. It was felt in the Old Testament that riches by themselves were no hindrance to spiritual pursuit. But Jesus points out that accumulation of wealth can hinder participation in God's kingdom. This is not a general call to poverty in order to follow Jesus, as is evident from his other teachings. By telling the young man to sell all his goods, it became evident to the youth that his faith was in his possessions, not Jesus. Since he will not change his mind (repent), he walks away.

follow me. The emphasis is not on selling all, but on following Jesus.

10:24 *amazed.* The disciples are astonished because traditional Jewish wisdom saw wealth as a sign of God's favor (e.g., Job 1:10; 42:10; Ps. 128:1–2).

how hard it is. Jesus repeats his statement, but now drops the reference to the rich.

10:25 Once again Jesus makes his point by using humorous hyperbole. The camel was the largest animal in Palestine, and certainly couldn't get through the smallest opening known to most people ("the eye of a needle"). Contrary to popular belief, there was no gate into Jerusalem called "The Needle's Eye."

10:26 *even more amazed.* The disciples are even more bewildered than before. What Jesus says directly confronts their assumptions about salvation.

Who then can be saved? They realize the radical nature of Jesus' statement and wonder about their own fate. If it is difficult for anyone to enter the kingdom, then what chance have they got?

10:27 This is Jesus' point. It is, indeed, impossible for a man to make his own way into the kingdom. It is God who grants this gift.

10:29 *for me and the gospel.* That for which the sacrifice of leaving home and family is made is Jesus and the work of his kingdom.

10:30 There is a certain irony in Jesus' words. Those who leave a settled life to follow Jesus will be given a new place, a new family, and the support from new fields. That this is not to be taken as a promise of worldly blessing is made clear by Mark's addition of "persecutions" as part of what they will gain.

10:31 Once again Jesus reverses expectations. Many (but not all) of those who think they are worthy of God's favor will find that they do not have it; while many of those who are at the bottom (e.g., tax collectors, sinners) will gain that favor. This pithy statement by Jesus is used here as a summary of his teaching on discipleship in 9:33–10:31.

18 Jesus Predicts—Mark 10:32–52

THREE-PART AGENDA

ICE-BREAKER
15 Minutes

BIBLE STUDY
30 Minutes

CARING TIME
15–45 Minutes

> **LEADER: How is the process going of identifying an Apprentice / Leader to start a new small group (see page M6 in the center section)? Check the list of ice-breakers on page M7, especially if you have a new person in this session.**

TO BEGIN THE BIBLE STUDY TIME
(Choose 1 or 2)

1. Who is the most competitive person in your family? Do you see competitiveness as a positive or negative quality?

2. For what famous person would you like to be the "right-hand man" or "right-hand woman"?

3. If you had one week to live, how would you spend your time?

READ SCRIPTURE & DISCUSS
(If you don't have time for all the questions in this section, conclude the Bible Study [30 min.] by answering question #7.)

1. What is the most frightening situation you have ever been in? What happened?

2. How do you think the disciples felt when Jesus described what was going to happen to him in Jerusalem?

3. Why do you think James and John asked Jesus for this special honor (v. 37)?

Jesus Again Predicts His Death

32They were on their way up to Jerusalem, with Jesus leading the way, and the disciples were astonished, while those who followed were afraid. Again he took the Twelve aside and told them what was going to happen to him. 33"We are going up to Jerusalem," he said, "and the Son of Man will be betrayed to the chief priests and teachers of the law. They will condemn him to death and will hand him over to the Gentiles, 34who will mock him and spit on him, flog him and kill him. Three days later he will rise."

The Request of James and John

35Then James and John, the sons of Zebedee, came to him. "Teacher," they said, "we want you to do for us whatever we ask."

36"What do you want me to do for you?" he asked.

37They replied, "Let one of us sit at your right and the other at your left in your glory."

38"You don't know what you are asking," Jesus said. "Can you drink the cup I drink or be baptized with the baptism I am baptized with?"

39"We can," they answered.

Jesus said to them, "You will drink the cup I drink and be baptized with the baptism I am baptized with, 40but to sit at my right or left is not for me to grant. These places belong to those for whom they have been prepared."

41When the ten heard about this, they became indignant with James and John. 42Jesus called them together and said, "You know that those who are regarded as rulers of the Gentiles lord it over them, and their high officials exercise authority over them. 43Not so with you. Instead, whoever wants to become great among you must be your servant, 44and whoever wants to be first must be slave of all. 45For even the Son of Man did not come to be served, but to serve, and to give his life as a ransom for many."

Blind Bartimaeus Receives His Sight

46Then they came to Jericho. As Jesus and his disciples, together with a large crowd, were leaving the city, a blind man, Bartimaeus (that is, the Son of Timaeus), was sitting by the roadside begging. 47When he heard that it was Jesus

4. What cup and baptism is Jesus talking about in verse 39? Did James and John know what they were asking for?

5. How do you feel about following the servant's path to greatness (vv. 43–44)?

6. How does the blind man get Jesus' attention? In what area of your life would you like Jesus to open your eyes so you could "see" more clearly?

7. Jesus asked James, John and Bartimaeus the question, "What do you want me to do for you?" If Jesus asked you that question, how would you answer him?

CARING TIME

(Choose 1 or 2 of these questions before closing in prayer. Be sure to pray for the empty chair.)

1. What was the high point of last week for you? What was the low point?

2. What challenge are you facing this week or in the near future?

3. How do you need the group to pray for you during the coming week?

> of Nazareth, he began to shout, "Jesus, Son of David, have mercy on me!"
>
> ⁴⁸Many rebuked him and told him to be quiet, but he shouted all the more, "Son of David, have mercy on me!"
>
> ⁴⁹Jesus stopped and said, "Call him."
>
> So they called to the blind man, "Cheer up! On your feet! He's calling you." ⁵⁰Throwing his cloak aside, he jumped to his feet and came to Jesus.
>
> ⁵¹"What do you want me to do for you?" Jesus asked him.
>
> The blind man said, "Rabbi, I want to see."
>
> ⁵²"Go," said Jesus, "your faith has healed you." Immediately he received his sight and followed Jesus along the road.

Notes—Mark 10:32–52

10:32–34 For the the third and final time, Jesus predicts his death and resurrection. This is the fullest of his three predictions. In addition to what he has already said, he points out *where* these events will take place (Jerusalem) and what the *role of the Gentiles* will be (they will torment him and then do the actual killing). The progression from condemnation to mocking, being spit on, flogging, and finally death makes clear that the focus of coming events is his death.

10:32 *Jerusalem.* Jesus' destination is now revealed as is the site of his betrayal, death, and resurrection (see v. 33).

astonished / afraid. Given the increasingly hostile response toward Jesus by the leaders, it was frightening that Jesus was heading directly into a confrontation with them.

10:35–45 The three predictions of his passion (8:31; 9:31; 10:33–34) are followed by three failures of the disciples to understand what he is saying (8:32–33; 9:32–34; 10:35–40), followed in turn by three teaching sessions in which Jesus explains what discipleship means (8:34–38; 9:35–37; 10:42–45).

10:35 *James and John.* Perhaps it is because they are closest to Jesus that they presume to make such a request.

10:37 James and John expect that Jesus will come into a position of authority as the new king of Israel. (This was the general assumption in those days about the Messiah.) Those who sit on his right and his left will be his chief lieutenants.

10:38 *drink the cup.* This is a phrase which means "share the same fate." In the Old Testament, the cup is a metaphor for wrath (e.g., Ps. 75:8 and Isa. 51:17–22).

baptism. In the Old Testament, the image of a deluge or flood overwhelming one is used as a metaphor for disaster (e.g., Ps. 42:7 and Isa. 43:2). Both the cup and the baptism refer to Jesus' coming suffering and death for the sins of the world. Both would remind Mark's readers of the sacraments of Communion and baptism and help them understand that to participate in these is to open themselves up to suffering and death—an apt word for those facing death in the coliseum.

10:39–40 Their leadership will not be expressed

through positions of authority, but through suffering and death.

10:39 *We can.* The disciples answer too readily Jesus' question as to whether they can share his cup and his baptism. They do not grasp what he means by this question, thinking perhaps that it is referring to being in fellowship with him. Their leadership will not be expressed through positions of authority but through suffering and death.

10:41 *they became indignant.* As self-serving as the request of James and John had been, the response of the other 10 disciples is not much better. They get angry when they hear what happened. James and John want to have positions ahead of them! All 12 share the same view of the kingdom, it seems, namely that it will be earthly and political, with Jesus as the reigning king and them as his chief lieutenants (as is seen in what Jesus has to say to them in vv. 42–45).

10:42–45 With this final statement, Mark ends this long section (which began in 8:31) in which Jesus is shown primarily in his role as teacher. Jesus' teaching has been structured around three attempts to get the disciples to understand what kind of Messiah he is. In the course of doing this, he teaches them what it means to be his disciple. His words here sum up what he has said: in the same way that the Messiah came to serve, so too must his disciples. They are not to seek power and authority over others, but rather they are to serve them. Jesus' teaching throughout this section has been characterized by reversals of expectation (see 9:35; 10:15,23,31). Here is the ultimate reversal. The Messiah has come to give his life away for the sake of others, not to conquer Rome by force and set up an earthly kingdom.

10:43 *servant.* Rather than become masters (and exercise authority), they are to become servants (and meet the needs of others). The Greek word for servant (*diakonos,* from which the English word "deacon" is derived) became the most common description of church leaders in the early church.

10:45 Jesus now reveals why he must suffer and die. It is in order to redeem the many. This statement of Jesus also defines the theme of the final section of Mark's Gospel (which begins in a few verses): the suffering and death of Jesus on behalf of humanity.

ransom. In the first century, a slave or a prisoner could gain freedom if a purchase price (ransom) was paid. Jesus would pay the ransom price "for many" by his death (see Titus 2:14; 1 Peter 1:18–19).

10:46–52 There is one final event that must take place before the start of Holy Week (the last week of Jesus' life). The disciples need a second touch so that they can see clearly the meaning of the coming events. They are like the man healed at Bethsaida (8:22–26): they have begun to see again but their vision is fuzzy. They see that Jesus is the Messiah, but they do not see what kind of Messiah he is (as Mark has just shown). So here, once again, Mark uses a healing in a symbolic way. The healing of blind Bartimaeus signals the second touch of healing that will cure the blindness of the Twelve.

10:46 *Jericho.* They have almost completed their journey from Galilee (see 9:33; 10:1). Jericho is a city some 18 miles east of Jerusalem and the place where travelers recrossed the Jordan back into Israel.

a large crowd. These were pilgrims on their way to Jerusalem for the Passover Feast. Every male over 12 years of age living within a 15-mile radius of Jerusalem was expected to attend.

10:47 *Jesus, Son of David.* A debate was going on as to who the Messiah would be. Would he come from the tribe of Levi, or was he a king in the line of David? Clearly this is a Messianic title by which Bartimaeus hails Jesus. Interestingly, Jesus does not silence him as he has done so often in the past when his identity is revealed. The time for secrecy is past. He accepts the title. This is the only use in Mark of this particular title, on the eve of Jesus' entry into Jerusalem as messianic king.

10:52 *your faith has healed you.* Bartimaeus demonstrated his faith in several ways: by his title for Jesus (showing that he grasped who Jesus was), by his persistence (he will not let this opportunity go by), and by his request for healing (showing that he believed Jesus could do so).

19 Triumphant Entry—Mark 11:1–25

THREE-PART AGENDA

ICE-BREAKER
15 Minutes

BIBLE STUDY
30 Minutes

CARING TIME
15–45 Minutes

> *LEADER: How is the process going of identifying an Apprentice / Leader to start a new small group (see page M6 in the center section)? Check the list of ice-breakers on page M7, especially if you have a new person in this session.*

TO BEGIN THE BIBLE STUDY TIME
(Choose 1 or 2)

1. What do you like best about parades?

2. What is your favorite fresh fruit or vegetable?

3. When you see something wrong, are you more likely to act without thinking or think without acting?

READ SCRIPTURE & DISCUSS
(If you don't have time for all the questions in this section, conclude the Bible Study [30 min.] by answering question #7.)

1. How are you greeted when you come home? What would you like to change about your homecoming? What would you keep?

2. What was unexpected about the way Jesus entered Jerusalem?

3. What kind of Messiah did the crowd think he was? How do you think Jesus felt in light of their incorrect perceptions of the kind of Messiah he was?

4. In what ways had the temple area been made into "a den of robbers" (v. 17)?

The Triumphal Entry

11 As they approached Jerusalem and came to Bethphage and Bethany at the Mount of Olives, Jesus sent two of his disciples, ²saying to them, "Go to the village ahead of you, and just as you enter it, you will find a colt tied there, which no one has ever ridden. Untie it and bring it here. ³If anyone asks you, 'Why are you doing this?' tell him, 'The Lord needs it and will send it back here shortly.' "

⁴They went and found a colt outside in the street, tied at a doorway. As they untied it, ⁵some people standing there asked, "What are you doing, untying that colt?" ⁶They answered as Jesus had told them to, and the people let them go. ⁷When they brought the colt to Jesus and threw their cloaks over it, he sat on it. ⁸Many people spread their cloaks on the road, while others spread branches they had cut in the fields. ⁹Those who went ahead and those who followed shouted,

"Hosanna!ᵃ"

"Blessed is he who comes in the name of the Lord!"ᵇ

¹⁰"Blessed is the coming kingdom of our father David!"

"Hosanna in the highest!"

¹¹Jesus entered Jerusalem and went to the temple. He looked around at everything, but since it was already late, he went out to Bethany with the Twelve.

Jesus Clears the Temple

¹²The next day as they were leaving Bethany, Jesus was hungry. ¹³Seeing in the distance a fig tree in leaf, he went to find out if it had any fruit. When he reached it, he found nothing but leaves, because it was not the season for figs. ¹⁴Then he said to the tree, "May no one ever eat fruit from you again." And his disciples heard him say it.

¹⁵On reaching Jerusalem, Jesus entered the temple area and began driving out those who were buying and selling there. He overturned the tables of the money changers and the benches of those selling doves, ¹⁶and would not allow anyone to carry merchandise through the temple courts. ¹⁷And as he taught them, he said, "Is it not written:

5. How do you feel about expressing anger? Have you ever expressed righteous anger? What happened?

6. If your spiritual life were like a tree, what would you need to produce more fruit: A good pruning? Transplanted to a different place? More water? Fertilizer? An orchard of similar trees surrounding you? Explain your answer.

7. How will you apply verses 22–25 to your prayer life this week?

CARING TIME
(Choose 1 or 2 of these questions before closing in prayer. Be sure to pray for the empty chair.)

1. What do you look forward to the most about these meetings?

2. What keeps you from making your life more of a "house of prayer"?

3. How can the group pray for you during the coming week?

> " 'My house will be called
> a house of prayer for all nations'[c]?
>
> But you have made it 'a den of robbers.'[d]"
>
> [18]The chief priests and the teachers of the law heard this and began looking for a way to kill him, for they feared him, because the whole crowd was amazed at his teaching. [19]When evening came, they[e] went out of the city.
>
> The Withered Fig Tree
>
> [20]In the morning, as they went along, they saw the fig tree withered from the roots. [21]Peter remembered and said to Jesus, "Rabbi, look! The fig tree you cursed has withered!" [22]"Have[f] faith in God," Jesus answered. [23]"I tell you the truth, if anyone says to this mountain, 'Go, throw yourself into the sea,' and does not doubt in his heart but believes that what he says will happen, it will be done for him. [24]Therefore I tell you, whatever you ask for in prayer, believe that you have received it, and it will be yours. [25]And when you stand praying, if you hold anything against anyone, forgive him, so that your Father in heaven may forgive you your sins.[g]"
>
> [a9] A Hebrew expression meaning "Save!" which became an exclamation of praise; also in verse 10
> [b9] Psalm 118:25,26   [c17] Isaiah 56:7   [d17] Jer. 7:11
> [e19] Some early manuscripts he   [f22] Some early manuscripts If you have
> [g25] Some manuscripts sins. [26]But if you do not forgive, neither will your Father who is in heaven forgive your sins.

Notes—Mark 11:1–25

Summary. Having been proclaimed by Bartimaeus as the Son of David, a new note of openness about Jesus' identity is sounded. Jesus so arranges his entry into Jerusalem that he arrives, openly, as the Messiah, the King like David. The time for secrecy so prominent earlier in the Gospel (i.e., 8:30; 9:9) is past. From the obvious intent to fulfill specific prophecies (Zech. 9:9; 14:4), to the royal greetings (e.g., 2 Kings 9:13), to the cries to God to "Save now," his whole arrival rings of messianic expectations. However, even still Jesus' messianic claims are ambiguous and veiled. The shouts and actions of the crowd in verses 8–10 are akin to those that

might happen when any group of pilgrims first caught sight of the temple and began praising God using the psalms commonly used upon arrival at Jerusalem. Their insight regarding the identity of Jesus is still very much partial.

The cursing and withering of the fig tree is the only incident of a miracle that is destructive in nature. Between the curse (v. 14) and its withering (v. 20) Mark sandwiches the story of the cleansing of the temple. Each story helps interpret the other. Both illustrate the judgment that is coming on Jerusalem. The disciples surprise upon discovering the fig tree leads into a discussion about prayer.

11:1 *Jerusalem.* Traditionally, it is understood that Jesus is arriving into Jerusalem, the spiritual heart of the nation, at the time of Passover, a feast that celebrated God's deliverance of Israel from Egypt centuries before and anticipated the ultimate, coming deliverance from Roman and all other oppressors as well. At this time, the population of Jerusalem would be swelled by Jews from all over the known world who would come to the city for the festival.

Bethphage. This was a village near Jerusalem, probably across a ravine from Bethany.

Bethany. A small village some two miles east of Jerusalem, site of the eastern slope of the Mount of Olives. This is where Jesus and his disciples were lodged during the Passover.

Mount of Olives. This place was associated in popular understanding with the coming of the Messiah. According to Zechariah 14:4–5, this is the place where God will commence the final judgment of Israel's enemies. It is not by accident that Jesus chose this place to prepare his entry into Jerusalem.

Jesus sent. Having come to the right spot, his next step is to send two disciples to secure the colt on which he will ride into Jerusalem. Clearly Jesus is consciously preparing his entry. His arrival will reveal who he is.

11:2 *a colt.* According to Zechariah 9:9, the King would come riding on a colt. Jesus will not simply enter Jerusalem. He will come as the Messianic King. However, he will not come as a Warrior-King (as the people expected) riding a war horse. Matthew 21:2 states this was a donkey, specifically fulfilling Zechariah's prophecy and emphasizing the peaceful, gentle nature of the Messiah.

tied there. In a prophetic word about the tribe of Judah, Genesis 49:8–12 speaks of a colt tethered to a choice vine. This was understood by many to be a prophecy that the Messiah would arise out of the tribe of Judah.

which no one has ridden. This colt had never been put to ordinary use and so was ideal for this very special purpose (see Num. 19:2; 1 Sam. 6:7–8).

11:3 *If anyone asks you ... tell him.* It is probable that Jesus has arranged all this with the colt's owner ahead of time. The words the disciples are to say will identify them to the owner as those Jesus has sent.

The Lord. Thus far in the Gospel, Jesus has not referred to himself by this title. While it can simply be a formal term for a master, the context of this occasion indicates he was implying divine authority as well.

11:8 *spread their cloaks.* This was a gesture of respect, given to kings (see 2 Kings 9:12–13). Media representations of this scene picture a huge throng of people convinced that Jesus is the Messiah. However, given that there was no opposition from Roman authorities (who at such feasts would be vigilant in their watch for anyone making claims that might threaten Rome), it is probable that this was simply a particular group of pilgrims who were traveling together, not a spontaneous gathering of multitudes. It is unlikely that the crowd as a whole realized the significance of what they were doing: they were merely rejoicing that they had finally arrived at their destination.

11:9–10 The shouts of joy were typical of pilgrims en route to Jerusalem for a feast. Here it adds to the prophetic sense of what was taking place. This time the real King is, indeed, arriving in the Holy City. How many recognized this fact is difficult to assess. Still, by enacting this ancient ritual, they were (unknowingly for many) welcoming the true King.

11:9 *Blessed is he.* While the psalm from which this cry is taken (Ps. 118:26), originally served as a tribute to the king of Israel, it was applied to any pilgrim who traveled to Jerusalem for the Feasts. It was later understood by the rabbis to be a messianic psalm, referring to the final redemption that would be ushered in by the Messiah.

11:10 *our father David.* King David was considered to be the model king of Israel, a man who was devoted to God and through whose line God had promised to build an everlasting kingdom. The people expected the Messiah to be a military hero like David who had delivered them from the hands of their enemies and been crowned king both by divine appointment and popular acclaim. This is the title used for Jesus from 10:46–12:44.

11:11 *temple.* This was the third temple to be built on Mount Zion. It was built by Herod the Great in 20 B.C. and was a magnificent structure covering some 30 acres. The temple consisted of four concentric courts ringed by enormous walls. The following scene tells of the judgment which Jesus, as the messianic King, brought upon the temple because of the abuses that were going on within it.

11:13 *fig tree.* On the Mount of Olives, fig trees are in leaf by early April, but they would not have ripe fruit until June, long after the Passover. Fig trees were a common prophetic symbol. They were associated with Israel and with judgment (e.g., Jer. 8:13; Hos. 9:10–11; Mic. 7:1). Thus it was no accident that Jesus chose a fig tree for this particular drama.

11:14 *his disciples heard him say it.* Jesus has done something so seemingly out of character (cursing a fig tree for not doing what it could not do) that the disciples cannot help but notice. Since there is no obvious reason for his action (Mark has taken care to point out that "it was not the season for figs"), they are forced to ponder why he did this. In the same way that he often used extravagant language to make his point (e.g., 9:42–43), here Jesus uses extravagant actions to get across this crucial point. Such acted-out parables were very much a part of how the Old Testament prophets communicated (see, for example, Isa. 20 and Ezek. 4–5).

11:15–19 Jesus' first act following his triumphal entry is to go into the temple and (by his actions) call to account the religious leadership of Israel. It is significant that he challenges these leaders in the temple, the very center of their power. Once again Jesus conveys his message by means of dramatic action. Jesus' action in the temple would have shocked everyone as he totally disrupted "normal" business and drastically interfered in religious observances. The prophet Malachi had said that "the Lord you are seeking will come to his temple. ... But who can endure the day of his coming? Who can stand when he appears?" (Mal. 3:1–2). Jesus' actions in the temple are a foreshadowing of the judgment to come upon Israel (and, at some point) the whole world for its sins.

11:15 *buying and selling.* Worship in the temple centered on sacrifice. Those wishing to participate were required to offer an unblemished animal, and apparently temple inspectors approved only those animals bought from certified vendors (who sold animals at a huge markup). During this era, these merchants worked for members of the high priest's family. There was profiteering on the part of priests and others, who were taking advantage of the religious obligations of the people.

money changers. At Passover, each Jew was required to pay a temple tax of one-half shekel (nearly two days' wages). No other currency was acceptable, necessitating money changes to exchange the money of pilgrims coming from outside. The money changers, however, charged exorbitant amounts for the simple act of exchanging currency: up to one-half day's wages of working people.

those selling doves. A dove was the lowliest of all sacrifices. While a lamb was normally required, the law had a provision that those too poor to afford a lamb could offer a dove instead (Lev. 5:7). While this provision was still observed, temple vendors charged 20 times what it cost to buy a dove outside the temple.

11:16 *carry merchandise.* Merchants used the temple court as a convenient walkway from one part of the city to another. Rather than respecting the sanctity of the temple by carrying their wares around it, they simply walked on through. The temple court had become only an extension of the marketplace. In attacking this abuse, Jesus was, in fact, simply enforcing a recognized rule from the Mishnah (a collection of Jewish traditions): "A man may not enter into the temple mount with his staff or his sandal or his wallet, or with the dust upon his feet, nor may he make of it a short by-path."

11:17 *a house of prayer for all nations.* The outermost area of the temple where all these activities were taking place was called the Court of the Gentiles. It was intended to be a place where pious Gentiles could pray. Instead it had been turned into a raucous oriental bazaar, making prayer impossible and thus doing away with the only place in the temple where non-Jews could come before the true God.

a den of robbers. This quote is from Jeremiah 7:11. In the days of Jeremiah, the religious authorities likewise masked their corruption with the veneer of religion. By using this phrase, Jesus implies that the judgment Jeremiah pronounced upon the leaders of his day applies to these leaders as well.

11:18 *chief priests.* These were Sadducees.

teachers of the law. These were typically Pharisees. The two sects normally did not cooperate together since they had so many differences between them, but they acted as one in their decision regarding Jesus. Rather than responding with repentance, the religious leaders plotted how to kill Jesus.

11:19 *they went out of the city.* Pilgrims coming to Jerusalem for Passover would often stay outside the city at night.

11:20 *the fig tree withered from the roots.* In light of the cleansing of the temple, the meaning of the withered fig tree becomes clear. This is what will happen to Israel. Judgment is coming on Jerusalem and on the temple in particular. "Just as the leaves of the tree concealed the fact that there was no fruit to enjoy, so too the magnificence of the Temple and its ceremony conceals the fact that Israel has not brought forth the fruit of righteousness demanded by God" (Lane). (See also Mark 7:6.) The fig tree's fate will be the temple's fate. The temple was, in fact, destroyed in A.D. 70. after a violent Jewish revolt against the empire. It has never been rebuilt.

11:21 *Peter remembered.* Jesus has done something so unusual, so out-of-character that the disciples cannot help but ponder it. What did it mean? Not surprisingly, the next day Peter spots the tree, now withered, and comments on it. Thus, the fact of the coming judgment has made an indelible impression on the minds of the disciples. They will not forget (even in the chaos of the days ahead as Jesus is led to the cross). In cursing the fig tree we see Jesus in his role as master teacher using this acted-out parable to teach the Twelve a vital lesson.

11:22–26 As he has done in the past (see 4:21–34; 9:42–50), Mark adds to the main story a group of similar sayings (this time on the subject of faith and prayer). While the miracle itself is a sign of the judgment to come upon Israel, these verses use it as an example of prayer's effectiveness.

11:23–24 Jesus continues his use of extravagant language. He cannot literally and mechanically mean that whatever is asked will happen. This would turn prayer into magic and God into a cosmic bellhop, attending to the whim of even evil and selfish people. Still, the point is not to be missed: believing prayer is answered. The point is not that Jesus promises his disciples the power to do massive earthmoving feats through prayer, but that seemingly impossible obstacles (such as the resistance of the religious authorities to the message of Jesus) in the way of God's plan can be overcome through faith and prayer.

> *Forgiveness of others does not earn God's forgiveness for oneself, but simply reflects the fact that since one has truly grasped the extent of ones' own sin and need for God's grace, it is inexcusable to withhold forgiveness from others.*

11:23 *this mountain.* This is probably the Mount of Olives overlooking Jerusalem.

the sea. The Dead Sea is visible from the Mount of Olives.

11:25 Forgiveness of others does not earn God's forgiveness for oneself, but simply reflects the fact that since one has truly grasped the extent of ones' own sin and need for God's grace, it is inexcusable to withhold forgiveness from others.

20 Jesus Teaches—Mark 11:27–12:12

THREE-PART AGENDA

ICE-BREAKER	**BIBLE STUDY**	**CARING TIME**
15 Minutes	30 Minutes	15–45 Minutes

> **LEADER: To help you identify people who might form the core of a new small group (or if a new person comes to this meeting), see the listing of ice-breakers on page M7 of the center section.**

TO BEGIN THE BIBLE STUDY TIME
(Choose 1 or 2)

1. As a teenager, with what authority figure did you run into trouble? Why?

2. When have you rented an apartment or house? What was your landlord like?

3. If you were to start your own business, what might it be?

READ SCRIPTURE & DISCUSS
(If you don't have time for all the questions in this section, conclude the Bible Study [30 min.] by answering question #7.)

1. When is a time you faced rejection?

2. Why were the religious leaders in Jerusalem questioning Jesus' authority? How does he cause the leaders' trickery to backfire?

3. In the Parable of the Tenants, who is represented by the vineyard owner? The tenant-farmers? The servants? The son?

4. Who are the "others" (v. 9) that the owner will give the vineyard to?

The Authority of Jesus Questioned

²⁷They arrived again in Jerusalem, and while Jesus was walking in the temple courts, the chief priests, the teachers of the law and the elders came to him. ²⁸"By what authority are you doing these things?" they asked. "And who gave you authority to do this?"

²⁹Jesus replied, "I will ask you one question. Answer me, and I will tell you by what authority I am doing these things. ³⁰John's baptism—was it from heaven, or from men? Tell me!"

³¹They discussed it among themselves and said, "If we say, 'From heaven,' he will ask, 'Then why didn't you believe him?' ³²But if we say, 'From men' . ..." (They feared the people, for everyone held that John really was a prophet.)

³³So they answered Jesus, "We don't know."

Jesus said, "Neither will I tell you by what authority I am doing these things."

The Parable of the Tenants

12 *He then began to speak to them in parables: "A man planted a vineyard. He put a wall around it, dug a pit for the winepress and built a watchtower. Then he rented the vineyard to some farmers and went away on a journey. ²At harvest time he sent a servant to the tenants to collect from them some of the fruit of the vineyard. ³But they seized him, beat him and sent him away empty-handed. ⁴Then he sent another servant to them; they struck this man on the head and treated him shamefully. ⁵He sent still another, and that one they killed. He sent many others; some of them they beat, others they killed.*

⁶"He had one left to send, a son, whom he loved. He sent him last of all, saying, 'They will respect my son.'

⁷"But the tenants said to one another, 'This is the heir. Come, let's kill him, and the inheritance will be ours.' ⁸So they took him and killed him, and threw him out of the vineyard.

⁹"What then will the owner of the vineyard do? He will come and kill those tenants and give the vineyard to others. ¹⁰Haven't you read this scripture:

5. How does this parable answer the question about Jesus' authority?

6. How do you feel about working in God's vineyard? What inheritance are you looking forward to receiving from God?

7. How have you been relating to Jesus' authority over your life lately?

CARING TIME

(Choose 1 or 2 of these questions before closing in prayer. Be sure to pray for the empty chair.)

1. Who would you choose as the leader if this group "gave birth" to a new small group? Who else would you choose to be part of the leadership core for a new group?

2. What is something you're looking forward to this week?

3. How can the group pray for you?

> " 'The stone the builders rejected
>   has become the capstone;
> [11]the Lord has done this,
>   and it is marvelous in our eyes'?"
>
> [12]Then they looked for a way to arrest him because they knew he had spoken the parable against them. But they were afraid of the crowd; so they left him and went away.

Notes—Mark 11:27–12:12

Summary. Mark begins a second cycle of stories in which the various groups of religious leaders confront Jesus one by one. Each of the major groups oppose him—the Sanhedrin, which included the chief priests (11:27–33) and the teachers of the Law (12:28–40); the Pharisees (12:13–17); the Herodians (12:13–17); and the Sadducees (12:18–27). These encounters parallel the first set of conflict stories found in 2:1–3:6.

11:27 the chief priests, the teachers of the law and the elders. The chief priests were the key officers of the temple, just below the high priest in rank. The elders were powerful and (reputedly) wise leaders of Israel. They were generally not priests, but instead were administrators, judges and military leaders of Israel. The teachers of the Law were religious lawyers (see note on 2:6 in Session 3). Taken together, these three groups were the Sanhedrin—the ruling Jewish council—who opposed him as Jesus prophesied they would (see 8:31).

11:28 They go right to the heart of the issue and ask the key question: What right does Jesus have to do what he did in the temple? Where does he get his authority for such an act? While not a subtle question, it was still a trap. If Jesus said he acted on his own authority, they could detain him as a madman suffering from delusions of grandeur. If he said his authority comes from God, then they could accuse him of blasphemy, for which the penalty was death.

11:29 I will ask you one question. Answering a question with a question was common in rabbinic debate. Jesus' question puts them in the same no-win situation they try to put him in (see vv. 31–32). However, this was a real question. Their view of John will determine how they feel about Jesus, since John clearly pointed to him as the Promised One.

11:31–32 They know that no matter how they answer, Jesus' point will be made, not their own. To accept that John's authority comes from God is to admit that John was a true prophet. If this were so, then they would also have had to accept that Jesus comes from God, as John said. Hence, the religious leaders are faced with the choice of either denouncing John the Baptist as a false prophet or explaining why they failed to heed his word. Both positions would put them at odds with the crowds who held John in high esteem.

11:33 Rather than commit themselves, they profess ignorance. Thus Jesus does not have to answer their question, which was not a sincere question anyway.

12:1–12 Rather than withdrawing from the conflict, Jesus keeps up the pressure. He immediately launches into an extended parable, the point of which is that the leaders of Israel have rejected God's messengers and so can expect judgment. That this is an accurate assessment of them is seen in the preceding story, in which they refuse to declare that John is a genuine prophet sent by God.

12:1 parables. The typical parable had a single point. Occasionally, several details add important information to the central point (as, for example, in the Parable of the Sower in Mark 4:1–20). In this case, a number of details have meaning. The Parable of the Tenants is the closest Jesus comes in his teaching to an allegory.

A man planted a vineyard ... dug a pit ... built a watchtower. For the religious leaders, Jesus' use of these phrases would surely call to mind the well-known imagery found in a poem originally delivered by the prophet Isaiah centuries before (Isa. 5:1–7). In Isaiah's song, the symbol of the vineyard was used to describe Israel. Although planted and cultivated by God, Israel was compared to a vineyard that produced only bad fruit. As a result, the landowner destroyed it. With this similarity established in Isaiah's poem, Jesus goes on to make a significant difference: Isaiah identified the unresponsive vineyard as the nation of Israel as a whole, whereas Jesus focuses attention on the fact that Israel's leaders are like evil tenants who refused to acknowledge God's authority over them.

vineyard. Grapes were one of the major crops in Israel. They were eaten fresh, made into raisins, boiled into a syrup, or made into wine. This particular vineyard was carefully built, with a wall around it to keep out animals, a pit in which to crush the grapes to make wine, and a tower where the farmer kept a lookout for robbers and slept during the harvest.

went away. Jesus changes the Isaiah poem here in order to put the spotlight on the religious authorities. While in Isaiah God is the farmer who waits for the fruit which never appears, in this parable God is the landlord who leaves his vineyard in the care of others who are responsible to him. It produces fruit, but the tenants refuse to give him his share of the produce. Absentee landlords were common in Galilee. Such a landlord would get tenant-farmers to work his large estate, requiring part of their harvest in payment for using the land. The tenant-farmers often resented the landlord.

12:2 *servant.* The tenants refuse to listen to the servants, beating and killing them instead. The fate of the servants in this parable (vv. 2–5) matches that which was met by many of God's prophets. Elijah was scorned by King Ahab. Tradition holds that Isaiah was executed by being sawn in two. Jeremiah faced many struggles, including being cast into a cistern to starve, and being taken as a prisoner to Egypt where, tradition teaches, he was killed. John the Baptist, believed by the crowds to

be a prophet, was beheaded by King Herod with no word of protest from the religious leaders.

12:6 *a son, whom he loved.* The crowd didn't know the identity of the son, yet Mark's readers know that it is Jesus. A central theme in Mark 11–16 is the discovery that Jesus is the Son of God. Here is the first hint (though God has declared him to be such, using the very phrase found here—see 1:11 and 9:7).

12:7 *inheritance.* The arrival of the son signaled to the tenants that the owner had died. By law, a piece of ownerless property (which it would be if they killed the son) could be kept by those who first seized it. Since the tenants assumed the land would be ownerless if the son was dead, they plotted to kill him in order to lay claim to the land for themselves.

12:8 *killed him, and threw him out of the vineyard.* Not only did the tenants fail to respect the son, but they killed him and even refused to give him a proper burial. This would have been considered a monstrous indignity to the listeners. Mark's readers, of course, would see the parallels with what happened to Jesus who was crucified and whose body the religious leaders would have been content to leave hanging on the cross, were it not for the intervention of Joseph of Arimathea (15:43).

12:9 *give the vineyard to others.* The appearance of the owner would shatter the illusion that the tenants now owned the land. The owner could enlist the aid of the government to force the evil tenants off his land. The landowner would then rent the vineyard to people who would meet the terms of their contract. The implication in the parable is that God will raise up new leaders to care for his people.

12:10 *capstone.* The reference is to a stone that was rejected in the building of Solomon's temple, which was later found to be the keystone to the porch (a keystone held an arch in place). Rabbis had interpreted the stone in Psalm 118:22–23 (which Jesus quotes) to refer to Abraham, David or the Messiah. Here the stone is Jesus (the Messiah) whom the builders (the leaders) fail to recognize.

12:12 The leaders knew exactly what part they played in Jesus' parable. They were the evil tenants who killed the servants and the heir. From their point of view, such teaching had to be stopped; yet again because of the crowds, they could do nothing.

21 Great Command—Mark 12:13–44

THREE-PART AGENDA

ICE-BREAKER
15 Minutes

BIBLE STUDY
30 Minutes

CARING TIME
15–45 Minutes

> *LEADER: Check page M7 in the center section for a good ice-breaker, particularly if you have a new person at this meeting. Is your group working well together—with everyone "fielding their position" as shown on the team roster on page M5?*

TO BEGIN THE BIBLE STUDY TIME
(Choose 1 or 2)

1. Whose picture appears on a five dollar bill? Ten? Twenty? Fifty? Hundred?

2. What was your first job? How much did you make?

3. In heaven, who or what on earth would you miss most?

READ SCRIPTURE & DISCUSS
(If you don't have time for all the questions in this section, conclude the Bible Study [30 min.] by answering question #7.)

1. In your extended family, do all agree on religion or politics? How do you handle differences?

2. What did Jesus mean when he said, "Give to Caesar what is Caesar's and to God what is God's" (v. 17)?

3. How does the hope of going to heaven affect your everyday life?

4. What is the greatest commandment? How do you show your love for God?

Paying Taxes to Caesar

¹³Later they sent some of the Pharisees and Herodians to Jesus to catch him in his words. ¹⁴They came to him and said, "Teacher, we know you are a man of integrity. You aren't swayed by men, because you pay no attention to who they are; but you teach the way of God in accordance with the truth. Is it right to pay taxes to Caesar or not? ¹⁵Should we pay or shouldn't we?"

But Jesus knew their hypocrisy. "Why are you trying to trap me?" he asked. "Bring me a denarius and let me look at it." ¹⁶They brought the coin, and he asked them, "Whose portrait is this? And whose inscription?"

"Caesar's," they replied.

¹⁷Then Jesus said to them, "Give to Caesar what is Caesar's and to God what is God's."

And they were amazed at him.

Marriage at the Resurrection

¹⁸Then the Sadducees, who say there is no resurrection, came to him with a question. ¹⁹"Teacher," they said, "Moses wrote for us that if a man's brother dies and leaves a wife but no children, the man must marry the widow and have children for his brother. ²⁰Now there were seven brothers. The first one married and died without leaving any children. ²¹The second one married the widow, but he also died, leaving no child. It was the same with the third. ²²In fact, none of the seven left any children. Last of all, the woman died too. ²³At the resurrection whose wife will she be, since the seven were married to her?"

²⁴Jesus replied, "Are you not in error because you do not know the Scriptures or the power of God? ²⁵When the dead rise, they will neither marry nor be given in marriage; they will be like the angels in heaven. ²⁶Now about the dead rising—have you not read in the book of Moses, in the account of the bush, how God said to him, 'I am the God of Abraham, the God of Isaac, and the God of Jacob'? ²⁷He is not the God of the dead, but of the living. You are badly mistaken!"

The Greatest Commandment

²⁸One of the teachers of the law came and heard them debating. Noticing that Jesus had given them a good

5. How do you think the religious leaders who heard Jesus' warning in verses 38–40 felt? What qualities of some religious leaders today do you think deserve a similar warning?

6. What kind of faith did the widow possess in order to give the way she did? How does the way you give financial offerings reflect your faith?

7. What "small" thing of yours could you turn into something great by giving it to God: Money? Time? Talent? Love? Other?

CARING TIME
(Choose 1 or 2 of these questions before closing in prayer. Be sure to pray for the empty chair.)

1. How well is your group working on everyone "fielding their position" as shown on the team roster (page M5)?

2. Rate this past week on a scale of 1 (terrible) to 10 (great). What's the outlook for this week?

3. How can the group help you and pray for you this week?

answer, he asked him, "Of all the commandments, which is the most important?"

²⁹"The most important one," answered Jesus, "is this: 'Hear, O Israel, the Lord our God, the Lord is one. ³⁰Love the Lord your God with all your heart and with all your soul and with all your mind and with all your strength.' ³¹The second is this: 'Love your neighbor as yourself.' There is no commandment greater than these."

³²"Well said, teacher," the man replied. "You are right in saying that God is one and there is no other but him. ³³To love him with all your heart, with all your understanding and with all your strength, and to love your neighbor as yourself is more important than all burnt offerings and sacrifices."

³⁴When Jesus saw that he had answered wisely, he said to him, "You are not far from the kingdom of God." And from then on no one dared ask him any more questions.

Whose Son Is the Christ?

³⁵While Jesus was teaching in the temple courts, he asked, "How is it that the teachers of the law say that the Christ is the son of David? ³⁶David himself, speaking by the Holy Spirit, declared:

" 'The Lord said to my Lord:
"Sit at my right hand
until I put your enemies
under your feet." '

³⁷David himself calls him 'Lord.' How then can he be his son?"

The large crowd listened to him with delight.

³⁸As he taught, Jesus said, "Watch out for the teachers of the law. They like to walk around in flowing robes and be greeted in the marketplaces, ³⁹and have the most important seats in the synagogues and the places of honor at banquets. ⁴⁰They devour widows' houses and for a show make lengthy prayers. Such men will be punished most severely."

The Widow's Offering

⁴¹Jesus sat down opposite the place where the offerings were put and watched the crowd putting their money into the temple treasury. Many rich people threw in large

> amounts. ⁴²But a poor widow came and put in two very small copper coins, worth only a fraction of a penny.
>
> ⁴³Calling his disciples to him, Jesus said, "I tell you the truth, this poor widow has put more into the treasury than all the others. ⁴⁴They all gave out of their wealth; but she, out of her poverty, put in everything—all she had to live on."

Notes—Mark 12:13-44

12:13–17 Beaten badly in their first two confrontations with Jesus, the leaders regroup and consider their strategy. They decide to send representatives from two groups with a trick question they hope will trap Jesus. The question deals with the explosive issue of taxes. If Jesus says that the people should *not* pay taxes to Caesar, then the Roman guard will arrest him for sedition. On the other hand, if Jesus says they *should* pay, then he will lose his popular support. Without the crowd's protection, the leaders would have a better chance of dealing with him.

12:13 *Pharisees and Herodians.* See notes on 2:18 and 3:6 in Session 4. The origin of this unusual alliance is described in 3:1–6.

12:14 *you are a man of integrity.* By these and other flattering words they hope to catch Jesus off guard.

taxes. A poll tax had to be paid to the Romans each year by all adult Jews. The poll tax had been instituted in 6 A.D. when the Romans took over the rule of southern Palestine after the failure of Archelaus, one of Herod's sons, to rule wisely. This tax was deeply resented. At least one anti-tax rebellion had already been crushed. Many Jews felt that since God was the only rightful ruler of Israel, paying taxes would acknowledge the legitimacy of Caesar's rule.

12:15 *hypocrisy.* Jesus knew they were not sincere. This is the essence of hypocrisy: saying one thing while believing another (see note on 7:6 in Session 12).

Bring me a denarius. The stricter Jews would not

even handle these coins. By asking for a coin, Jesus shows that he didn't carry it. A denarius was a small, silver coin (worth about 25 cents today) bearing the picture of Tiberius Caesar and a description of him as "Son of the Divine Augustine"—a man touched with divinity. (This description made the coins doubly offensive to the monotheistic Jews.) The denarius was the only coin that could be used to pay the poll tax.

12:17 Jesus' answer is profound. He grants the legitimacy of governments to collect taxes while at the same time limiting the power of governments. One's final loyalty must be to God and not to the state.

12:18–27 A third group (the Sadducees) attempts to discredit Jesus with another trick question. This time the strategy is one of ridicule.

12:18 *Sadducees.* There is little information available about this group. It seems that they were a small but highly influential party of wealthy, aristocratic priests. The high priest was often a Sadducee. The Sadducees accepted relatively few theological doctrines. For example, they accepted only the first five books of the Old Testament as authoritative. They also rejected the oral tradition (which put them at odds with the Pharisees). This is their first appearance in Mark's narrative, because up to this point, Jesus has been no threat to the Sadducees. However, when he cleared the temple, he invaded their sphere of influence and so became their enemy.

resurrection. The belief that at the end of the age God would bring the dead back to life for judgment.

The Sadducees did not accept this belief since it had no clear basis in the Law of Moses. The question they pose is meant to show the folly of belief in a resurrection. Resurrection life was popularly thought to be essentially a continuation of human life as presently experienced.

12:19–23 The question they pose has to do with so-called "levirate marriage" (see Deut. 25:5–10), which was designed to ensure the continuation of the family name, as well as to keep property within a family.

12:24–27 Jesus takes their question seriously (although it is not a sincere question, since they did not believe in the resurrection) and answers them directly. In so doing, he affirms belief in the resurrection. His own resurrection will take place within a week.

12:25 Jesus indicates that resurrection life will be radically different—more like the experience of angels than the social and physical laws at work now.

12:26 Jesus affirms the fact of the resurrection in a manner which, though strange to modern ears, was convincing to a first-century rabbi. His argument is that if God is still the God of the patriarchs (God says "I *am* the God of Abraham," using the present tense), then the patriarchs must be alive. The implication is that there will be a resurrection. Jesus draws his proof from Exodus 3:6, a portion of the Old Testament which was accepted as authoritative by the Sadducees.

12:28 *teachers of the law.* Jesus has answered successfully the Herodians, the Pharisees and the Sadducees. It is now a scribe's turn to ask a question. (See notes on 2:6 in Session 3 and 11:27 in Session 20 for this group.) His attitude toward Jesus is different from the others. He asks a genuine question.

Noticing that Jesus had given them a good answer. This teacher of the Law is apparently very impressed with the way Jesus answered the questions, so he asks an important question for him personally.

which is the most important? This phrase is, literally, "which is the chief (or first) commandment"; i.e.,

what commandment summarizes all the commandments. Such a question was typical of one of the two tendencies in that day when it came to the Law. The majority group (represented by the Pharisees) sought to expand the Law so as to cover all conceivable situations that might arise. Others, such as this man, sought to reduce the Law to a few foundational principles. For example, the great Rabbi Hillel was asked by a proselyte to tell him the whole Law while standing on one leg. Hillel replied: "What you yourself hate, do not do to your neighbor: This is the whole law, the rest is commentary."

> *Jesus indicates that resurrection life will be radically different—more like the experience of angels than the social and physical laws at work now.*

12:29–31 By his reply, Jesus demonstrates what a great moral teacher he is. First, he combines loving God with loving others, linking what had been seen as two quite different impulses. Second, he makes the commandment positive ("Love your neighbor") rather than negative ("Do not hate your neighbor"), thus calling people to active benevolence rather than merely avoiding conflict. Third, he broadened the definition of "neighbor" from meaning "other Jews" (its meaning in the context of Lev. 19:18) to meaning "all people" (see Luke 10:25–37). Fourth, he made proper self-love (as distinguished from pride) the gauge by which individuals can know if they are loving others (see also 8:34–35; 9:33–35; 10:29–31).

12:29 *Hear, O Israel.* The Shema (a prayer taken from Deut. 6:4), recited by pious Jews each morning and evening. This affirmation captures what was distinctive about Israel's view of God.

12:30 Jesus quotes the Old Testament (Deut. 6:5).

Love. In Greek, this is *agape*. It means an active, benevolent giving to others without expectation of reward. *Agape* is not based on emotion ("I do this because I feel warmly toward you"), friendship ("I do this because you are a friend"), or kinship ("I do this because we are related"). *Agape* is rooted in the experience of God's unconditional love (which frees

108

up a person to love others) and the obedient response to that love ("love your neighbor"; see Matt. 5:43-48).

heart. The inner life; the center of personality; where God reveals himself to a person.

soul. The seat of life itself; the personality or ego.

mind. The organ of knowledge; the intellect.

strength. The power of a living being; the total effort behind heart, soul and mind.

12:31 Jesus now quotes Leviticus 19:18, and in doing so connects loving God with loving people.

12:35–37 The essence of the argument is that if David acknowledges the Messiah's lordship ("David himself calls him 'Lord' "), this means that the Messiah must be something more than simply a descendant. The Messiah is not only David's son, but David's Lord. In saying this, Mark hints once again (see 12:6) that Jesus is more than just the Messiah. They will soon discover that he is also the Son of God. (The Greek word translated "Lord" was used in the Greek Old Testament as a name for God.) Furthermore, the Messiah's kingdom will be more than merely an earthly kingdom. The psalm which Jesus quotes implies that the kingdom will be heavenly—the Messiah will not simply reestablish the Davidic kingdom. He will bring a new kingdom into being—one that will involve all peoples, not just the Jews. See the expanded discussion of Psalm 110:1 (which Jesus quotes) in Acts 2:29–36; 13:23–34 and Hebrews 1:5–13.

12:35 the Christ. This is the Greek word for Messiah: the expected deliverer of Israel.

12:37 How then can he be his son? Jesus' listeners would have been unclear about the answer to this question. But Mark's readers know that Jesus, the Messiah, who died and rose again to sit on the right hand of God, was indeed David's Lord.

12:38–40 At the start of this section, Jesus condemned the priests for their desecration of the temple (11:15–18). Here at the end of the section, he condemns the teachers of the Law for using their position for personal aggrandizement, and not for service.

12:38 flowing robes. Long, white linen garments fringed with tassels that touched the ground. In such a stately garment, a person could not run or work and would be reckoned to be a person of leisure and importance.

greeted. People considered the teachers of the Law to be men of great insight and authority, and so they rose when they passed by and called out titles of respect.

12:39 the most important seats in the synagogue. The choice seat was up front, with its back to the box which contained the sacred Scriptures, and its front facing the congregation so that all would see who sat there.

12:40 They devour widows' houses. Since the teachers of the Law were forbidden to receive pay for their teaching, they lived off others, including poor widows who were little able to support them.

12:41 temple treasury. This was located in the Court of Women (the first of the inner courts of the temple). It consisted of 13 trumpet-shaped receptacles used to collect donations for the temple.

12:42 small copper coins. The smallest coins in circulation, worth 1/400 shekel, or about 1/8 of a cent.

12:43 Jesus redefines greatness by denigrating the scribes (v. 38) and holding up this poor woman as an example to follow.

22 End of the Age—Mark 13:1–37

THREE-PART AGENDA

ICE-BREAKER
15 Minutes

BIBLE STUDY
30 Minutes

CARING TIME
15–45 Minutes

> **LEADER: To help you identify people who might form the core of a new small group (or if a new person comes to this meeting), see the listing of ice-breakers on page M7 of the center section.**

TO BEGIN THE BIBLE STUDY TIME
(Choose 1 or 2)

1. What do you do to make sure your home is looked after when you leave on a vacation?

2. What did your parents warn you about when you learned to drive?

3. If you could take two things with you to heaven, what would they be?

READ SCRIPTURE & DISCUSS
(If you don't have time for all the questions in this section, conclude the Bible Study [30 min.] by answering question #7.)

1. If you knew the world was going to end in six months, how would you live your life differently?

2. How do you think the disciples felt as Jesus was describing the destruction of Jerusalem, signs of the end, and the persecution of Christians? How does this passage make you feel?

3. What questions about this passage would you ask Jesus if you had the opportunity?

Signs of the End of the Age

13 As he was leaving the temple, one of his disciples said to him, *"Look, Teacher! What massive stones! What magnificent buildings!"*

²*"Do you see all these great buildings?" replied Jesus. "Not one stone here will be left on another; every one will be thrown down."*

³*As Jesus was sitting on the Mount of Olives opposite the temple, Peter, James, John and Andrew asked him privately,* ⁴*"Tell us, when will these things happen? And what will be the sign that they are all about to be fulfilled?"*

⁵*Jesus said to them: "Watch out that no one deceives you.* ⁶*Many will come in my name, claiming, 'I am he,' and will deceive many.* ⁷*When you hear of wars and rumors of wars, do not be alarmed. Such things must happen, but the end is still to come.* ⁸*Nation will rise against nation, and kingdom against kingdom. There will be earthquakes in various places, and famines. These are the beginning of birth pains.*

⁹*"You must be on your guard. You will be handed over to the local councils and flogged in the synagogues. On account of me you will stand before governors and kings as witnesses to them.* ¹⁰*And the gospel must first be preached to all nations.* ¹¹*Whenever you are arrested and brought to trial, do not worry beforehand about what to say. Just say whatever is given you at the time, for it is not you speaking, but the Holy Spirit.*

¹²*"Brother will betray brother to death, and a father his child. Children will rebel against their parents and have them put to death.* ¹³*All men will hate you because of me, but he who stands firm to the end will be saved.*

¹⁴*"When you see 'the abomination that causes desolation'ᵃ standing where itᵇ does not belong—let the reader understand—then let those who are in Judea flee to the mountains.* ¹⁵*Let no one on the roof of his house go down or enter the house to take anything out.* ¹⁶*Let no one in the field go back to get his cloak.* ¹⁷*How dreadful it will be in those days for pregnant women and nursing mothers!* ¹⁸*Pray that this will not take place in winter,* ¹⁹*because those will be days of distress unequaled from the beginning, when God created the world, until now—and never to be*

4. Verses 9–11 describe some of the persecution the disciples will face as they spread the Good News. Have you ever faced persecution for your faith? What happened?

5. What comfort do you find in verses 20, 22b and 27?

6. What is most exciting to you about Jesus coming again? What is most distressing?

7. If Jesus comes back this week, will he find you "watching" or "sleeping"? What can you do to wake up your spiritual life and be more alert?

CARING TIME
(Choose 1 or 2 of these questions before closing in prayer. Be sure to pray for the empty chair.)

1. How are you at spending personal time in prayer and Bible study?

2. What is something for which you are particularly thankful?

3. What would you like this group to pray about?

equaled again. ²⁰If the Lord had not cut short those days, no one would survive. But for the sake of the elect, whom he has chosen, he has shortened them. ²¹At that time if anyone says to you, 'Look, here is the Christ^c!' or, 'Look, there he is!' do not believe it. ²²For false Christs and false prophets will appear and perform signs and miracles to deceive the elect—if that were possible. ²³So be on your guard; I have told you everything ahead of time.

²⁴"But in those days, following that distress,

" 'the sun will be darkened,
    and the moon will not give its light;
²⁵ the stars will fall from the sky,
    and the heavenly bodies will be shaken.'^d

²⁶"At that time men will see the Son of Man coming in clouds with great power and glory. ²⁷And he will send his angels and gather his elect from the four winds, from the ends of the earth to the ends of the heavens.

²⁸"Now learn this lesson from the fig tree: As soon as its twigs get tender and its leaves come out, you know that summer is near. ²⁹Even so, when you see these things happening, you know that it is near, right at the door. ³⁰I tell you the truth, this generation^e will certainly not pass away until all these things have happened. ³¹Heaven and earth will pass away, but my words will never pass away.

The Day and Hour Unknown

³²"No one knows about that day or hour, not even the angels in heaven, nor the Son, but only the Father. ³³Be on guard! Be alert^f! You do not know when that time will come. ³⁴It's like a man going away: He leaves his house and puts his servants in charge, each with his assigned task, and tells the one at the door to keep watch.

³⁵"Therefore keep watch because you do not know when the owner of the house will come back—whether in the evening, or at midnight, or when the rooster crows, or at dawn. ³⁶If he comes suddenly, do not let him find you sleeping. ³⁷What I say to you, I say to everyone: 'Watch!' "

^a14 Daniel 9:27; 11:31; 12:11   ^b14 Or he; also in verse 29   ^c21 Or Messiah
^d25 Isaiah 13:10; 34:4   ^e30 Or race   ^f33 Some manuscripts alert and pray

Summary. This section contains the longest unin-terrupted statement by Jesus in Mark's Gospel. It summarizes 11:1–12:44. The temple was the site and sometimes the subject of that section. Here Jesus predicts what will happen to the temple, and points out what lies ahead for his disciples. This is almost a farewell address to them, warning them what to expect after Jesus leaves them. This is a very difficult section of Mark for modern readers to grasp, because it assumes a knowledge of Jewish ideas, aspirations and history. In particular, it draws upon the concept of "The Day of the Lord" found in many Old Testament writings (e.g., Isa. 13:6–16; Joel 2–3; Amos 5:16–20).

13:1–2 Jesus begins his discourse with a prediction that the temple will be destroyed (an event that will take place nearly 40 years later in A.D. 70).

13:1 *What magnificent buildings!* The temple was a wonder to behold. It was built with huge white stones, some measuring 37 feet long by 12 feet high by 18 feet wide. Josephus described the tem-ple: "The outward face ... was covered all over with plates of gold of great weight, and, at the first rising of the sun, reflected back a very fiery splendor. ... The temple appeared to strangers when they were at a distance, like a mountain covered with snow."

13:2 *Not one stone here will be left on another.* Josephus wrote: "Caesar (Titus) ordered the whole city and the temple to be razed to the ground." His orders were, indeed, carried out.

13:3–4 The disciples again come to Jesus, asking him to explain his teaching. To them, an event as cataclysmic as the temple's destruction must indi-cate the new age is coming (see Matt. 24:3).

13:3 *Mount of Olives.* A 2,700 foot mountain east of Jerusalem, it rose 200 feet higher than Mount Zion and afforded a magnificent view of the temple.

13:4 *what will be the sign.* The question assumes that an omen will announce the end of the world.

13:5–37 Jesus answers their question (in vv. 28–31) after he lays a careful foundation. In his reply, he discusses three events: the suffering before the fall of Jerusalem (vv. 5–13), the fall of Jerusalem (vv. 14–23, 28–31) and the Second Coming (vv. 24–27,32–37).

13:5 *Watch out.* This is a key theme in this section (see also vv. 21–23,33–37): vigilance against being deceived by those who claim the end times have begun, or claim they are prophets. Mark urges cau-tion in the midst of the hope of the Second Coming.

13:6–8 Various events will occur prior to the end: false prophets will come (v. 6); there will be wars, earthquakes and famine (vv. 7–8).

13:6 *'I am he.'* A claim by the false prophet to be the Messiah, or to be Jesus come again. Perhaps it will be a claim to deity, since this phrase was used in the Old Testament for the name of God (see note on 6:50 in Session 11).

13:7 *the end is still to come.* The end of the age or the end of the world—that time which precedes the full and open establishment of the kingdom of God. Jesus does not say that the end will come immediately after these events, only that this is the "beginning of birth pains" (v. 8), i.e., they signal that something is coming.

13:9–13 The focus shifts from the woes experi-enced by the whole world to the woes Christians will have to face. Specifically, they will be arrested and brought to trial. As Acts indicates, this happened to the early church (see Acts 4:1–23; 5:17–42; 6:8–7:60; 16:19–40; 22:30–23:10; 24:1–27; 25:1–12). They will be persecuted by both the Jews and the Gentiles (v. 9) and by their own relatives (v. 12). It will seem as if everyone is against them (v. 13). Mark's readers were experiencing this, and so they would take comfort in the fact that such perse-cution was predicted by their Lord.

13:9 *councils / synagogues.* The councils are Jewish courts, where heretics were tried and then beaten publicly in the synagogue.

13:10 Despite the persecution, their mission will be to preach the Gospel to all nations.

13:11 When they stand before their accusers, the Holy Spirit will give them the words of witness.

13:14–23 Having described what will precede the fall of Jerusalem, Jesus next turns to the event itself. When "the abomination that causes desola-tion" takes place, this will signal that the dark days have begun.

13:14 *'the abomination that causes desolation.'* This phrase is taken from the book of Daniel (see 9:27; 11:31; 12:11). It refers to an event so awful that Jews will flee from the temple in horror—such as in 168 B.C. when Antiochus Epiphanes, a Syrian king, captured Jerusalem. He set up an altar to Zeus in the temple and sacrificed a pig there. He also put public brothels in the temple courts. Jesus warns that when such an event occurs again, the fall of Jerusalem is imminent (see 2 Thess. 2:1–4).

let the reader understand. Since Mark wrote after the temple's destruction, this editorial comment may be a hint to his readers that such desecrations might also one day happen within the church, the new temple of God (Hill). "The 'abomination of desolation' has surfaced in history whenever the purposes of God have been violently assaulted by the forces of evil" (Mounce).

let those who are in Judea flee. When the armies of Rome march against the city, Jesus' disciples are to recognize that this is the sign that God's judgment against Israel has come to a head. Instead of flocking to the city in anticipation of a dramatic messianic victory, they must run for their lives. Tradition has it that Christians fled Jerusalem prior to the siege by Titus in A.D. 70.

13:15 *roof of his house.* The flat roof was used for midday prayer. It will be so urgent to flee that there will not even be time to go back into the house to pick up anything to take along.

13:16 *cloak.* The outer garment used as a blanket at night but taken off and left when working in the field during the day.

13:17–18 This will be a hard time, especially for women who are expecting or who have infants—and all others who are in situations that make travel difficult. It will be unfortunate if this takes place in winter when heavy rains swell the streams, making travel a problem.

> *The Second Coming, on the other hand, will bring salvation and blessing to the people of God.*

13:19 *distress.* The destruction of Jerusalem in A.D. 70 was an unparalleled disaster for Israel. When the Jewish revolt broke out, the Roman army moved in quickly to crush all resistance. While Jerusalem was under siege several leaders arose, each claiming that God had sent him to deliver the city. Instead, the city was destroyed and an estimated one million Jews died.

13:20 *the elect.* Whereas judgment has come upon Jerusalem and the temple, mercy is shown to the elect. The implied contrast is between the old order which is being swept away (symbolized by the temple), and the new order which is coming into being (the kingdom of God).

13:21–23 Still it is not yet the end of time, Jesus warns.

13:24–27 Jesus now describes the second coming of the Son of Man in power and glory. The destruction of Jerusalem is the result of human failure and evil. It will bring suffering and hardship. The Second Coming, on the other hand, will bring salvation and blessing to the people of God.

13:24–25 In the Old Testament, such events were seen as a sign of God's judgment (see Ezek. 32:7–8; Joel 2:10–11; Amos 8:9–10).

13:24 *in those days.* No time frame is specified in this phrase. Jesus says that the Second Coming will take place sometime after the fall of Jerusalem.

13:26 *the Son of Man.* Here Jesus clearly reveals the nature of the Son of Man: he is a divine being who will draw history to a close (see note on 2:28 in Session 4).

coming in clouds with great power and glory. In the Old Testament, God is described with phrases like this (e.g. Ex. 19:9; 34:5; Ps. 104:3; Isa. 19:1).

13:27 *gather his elect.* It is God who will do this (see Deut. 30:3–4; Ps. 50:3–5; Isa. 43:5–6). Jesus makes it quite clear who he is: the Son of God (vv. 26–27).

13:28–37 With all this as background (vv. 5–27), Jesus can now respond to the disciples' original question (v. 4). His response is that one event (the fall of Jerusalem) will occur within their lifetimes, but they are not to be deceived. This will not usher in the end time. The final event (the Second Coming) will be at a future, unspecified date known only to God (v. 32). Jesus encourages the disciples to be vigilant, but not to worry about when all this will take place.

13:28–31 Jesus switches back to discuss the disciples' response to the imminent fall of Jerusalem, an event that did occur in their lifetime (v. 30).

13:28 *lesson from the fig tree.* They knew that the fig tree only got its leaves in late spring. When the leaves come it is a sure sign that summer was near. This is a reference to the rather mysterious cursing of the fig tree by Jesus in 11:12–14,20–21 (see notes in Session 19), and has to do with the judgment on Jerusalem, as Jesus' teaching here shows.

13:29 *these things.* The phrase "these things" refers to the things surrounding the fall of Jerusalem (vv. 5–23). They cannot refer to verses 24–27 since those verses describe the end itself and not the events preceding the end.

13:30 Jesus makes quite clear in this verse that he has in mind the near event when he refers to the lesson of the fig tree (the fall of Jerusalem), and not the distant event (the Second Coming).

13:32–37 Now Jesus refers to the Second Coming. Only God knows when this event will occur. The role of the disciples in this case is not to read the signs (as with the fall of Jerusalem), but to be ready (since it can occur at any moment).

> *Jesus makes it quite clear who he is: the Son of God.*

13:32 *that day.* The end of time when God rescues his people and makes manifest his kingdom (see Joel 3:18; Amos 8:3,9,13; 9:11; Mic. 4:6; 5:10; 7:11–12; Zeph. 1:9–10; 3:11,16; Zech. 9:16).

13:34–36 Jesus uses an example. When the master is away, his servants are to attend to their duties. They are not to sleep (in contrast to "watching"). "The work that the servants are to do is of course not primarily scanning the horizon for the master's return and then rushing about in a dither but rather the steady, regular performance of their tasks" (Hurtado).

13:37 It is not just the Twelve who must get on with the mission of God when Jesus is gone. It is everyone.

THREE-PART AGENDA

ICE-BREAKER
15 Minutes

BIBLE STUDY
30 Minutes

CARING TIME
15–45 Minutes

> **LEADER:** *Has your group discussed its plans on what to study after this course is finished? You may want to celebrate the Lord's Supper as a group in place of the usual Caring Time.*

TO BEGIN THE BIBLE STUDY TIME
(Choose 1 or 2)

1. What is one of your favorite places to eat?

2. What is your favorite hymn or praise song?

3. Growing up, what occasion did your family celebrate with a big meal? Whose house was it at? Where did people sit? What was the main course?

READ SCRIPTURE & DISCUSS
(If you don't have time for all the questions in this section, conclude the Bible Study [30 min.] by answering question #7.)

1. What is the most beautiful, touching thing you have ever seen one person do for another? What is the most beautiful, touching thing someone has ever done for you?

2. Why did this woman who anointed Jesus know to prepare him for his burial when the disciples did not?

3. What would you like to do for Jesus that might cause him to make a similar statement as in verse 9?

4. What profound new meaning does Jesus give to the Passover bread (v. 22) and to the Passover cup (vv. 23–24)?

14 Now the Passover and the Feast of Unleavened Bread were only two days away, and the chief priests and the teachers of the law were looking for some sly way to arrest Jesus and kill him. ²"But not during the Feast," they said, "or the people may riot."

³While he was in Bethany, reclining at the table in the home of a man known as Simon the Leper, a woman came with an alabaster jar of very expensive perfume, made of pure nard. She broke the jar and poured the perfume on his head.

⁴Some of those present were saying indignantly to one another, "Why this waste of perfume? ⁵It could have been sold for more than a year's wages^a and the money given to the poor." And they rebuked her harshly.

⁶"Leave her alone," said Jesus. "Why are you bothering her? She has done a beautiful thing to me. ⁷The poor you will always have with you, and you can help them any time you want. But you will not always have me. ⁸She did what she could. She poured perfume on my body beforehand to prepare for my burial. ⁹I tell you the truth, wherever the gospel is preached throughout the world, what she has done will also be told, in memory of her."

¹⁰Then Judas Iscariot, one of the Twelve, went to the chief priests to betray Jesus to them. ¹¹They were delighted to hear this and promised to give him money. So he watched for an opportunity to hand him over.

The Lord's Supper

¹²On the first day of the Feast of Unleavened Bread, when it was customary to sacrifice the Passover lamb, Jesus' disciples asked him, "Where do you want us to go and make preparations for you to eat the Passover?"

¹³So he sent two of his disciples, telling them, "Go into the city, and a man carrying a jar of water will meet you. Follow him. ¹⁴Say to the owner of the house he enters, 'The Teacher asks: Where is my guest room, where I may eat the Passover with my disciples?' ¹⁵He will show you a large upper room, furnished and ready. Make preparations for us there."

¹⁶The disciples left, went into the city and found things

5. Why is it important for Christians to observe Communion? What does the Lord's Supper mean to you?

6. Before you take Communion, the next time, what can you do to make it more spiritually meaningful?

7. Do you think Peter was sincere when he said, "Even if all fall away, I will not" (v. 29)? Have you ever denied Christ when you could have stood up for him? Why can it be difficult to be bold for Christ?

CARING TIME
(Choose 1 or 2 of these questions before closing in prayer. Be sure to pray for the empty chair.)

1. If this group plans to continue, what would you like to study next (see inside the back cover for what's available from Serendipity)?

2. How has God been at work in your life this past week?

3. How can the group help you in prayer this week?

just as Jesus had told them. So they prepared the Passover.

¹⁷When evening came, Jesus arrived with the Twelve. ¹⁸While they were reclining at the table eating, he said, "I tell you the truth, one of you will betray me—one who is eating with me."

¹⁹They were saddened, and one by one they said to him, "Surely not I?"

²⁰"It is one of the Twelve," he replied, "one who dips bread into the bowl with me. ²¹The Son of Man will go just as it is written about him. But woe to that man who betrays the Son of Man! It would be better for him if he had not been born."

²²While they were eating, Jesus took bread, gave thanks and broke it, and gave it to his disciples, saying, "Take it; this is my body."

²³Then he took the cup, gave thanks and offered it to them, and they all drank from it.

²⁴"This is my blood of the[b] covenant, which is poured out for many," he said to them. ²⁵"I tell you the truth, I will not drink again of the fruit of the vine until that day when I drink it anew in the kingdom of God."

²⁶When they had sung a hymn, they went out to the Mount of Olives.

Jesus Predicts Peter's Denial

²⁷"You will all fall away," Jesus told them, "for it is written:

" 'I will strike the shepherd,
    and the sheep will be scattered.'[c]

²⁸But after I have risen, I will go ahead of you into Galilee."

²⁹Peter declared, "Even if all fall away, I will not."

³⁰"I tell you the truth," Jesus answered, "today—yes, tonight—before the rooster crows twice[d] you yourself will disown me three times."

³¹But Peter insisted emphatically, "Even if I have to die with you, I will never disown you." And all the others said the same.

---

[a]5 Greek *than three hundred denarii*   [b]24 Some manuscripts *the new*
[c]27 Zech. 13:7   [d]30 Some early manuscripts do not have *twice*.

Notes—Mark 14:1–31

Summary. Jesus has warned his disciples a number of times about what lies ahead for him: rejection by the religious leaders, suffering, death, and then resurrection. In the final chapters of his Gospel, Mark describes these events as they unfold. They will reveal that Jesus is not just the Messiah; he is also the Son of God.

14:1 *the Passover.* A feast in which the people of Israel celebrated God's deliverance of their nation from Egypt where they had been held as slaves (see Ex. 12). On this particular Passover, God would once again rescue his people, though in a totally unexpected way—namely through the death of his own Son.

the Feast of Unleavened Bread. By the time of the first century, this feast was coupled with the Passover so that there was a week of feasting.

some sly way to arrest Jesus and kill him. The religious leadership had already decided to kill Jesus (see 3:6; 12:12). Now they are seeking a way to do so.

14:2 During Passover, Jerusalem's population rose from 50,000 to several hundred thousand, making the potential for rioting against Rome great, as this huge mob of pilgrims remembered together (in the Passover ritual) past oppression by a foreign power. The Jewish officials could not afford to spark a riot by arresting Jesus, lest they incur harsh Roman repression.

14:3 *Simon the Leper.* Nothing is known of this man, but presumably he was someone Jesus had previously healed.

reclining. Banquets were generally eaten lying on a low couch or pillows.

a woman came. A woman would not be present at a meal like this except to serve. Her entrance would have been scandalous.

perfume. Nard was a much-prized aromatic oil extracted from an Indian root. It was stored in long-necked alabaster flasks to retain its aroma. The neck was broken off when the perfume was used. Possibly this was a family heirloom.

poured perfume on his head. Typically, this perfume was used very sparingly and only for special occasions. This was a lavish gesture indicating the high honor this woman held for Jesus.

14:4 *Some of those present were saying indignantly.* These are the disciples (see Matt. 26:8).

14:5 *the money given to the poor.* The indignation of the disciples is understandable. It was the custom at the Passover to remember the poor with gifts. (Of course, Jesus is himself one of the poor, making the gift to him appropriate.)

14:7 Jesus reminds the disciples that there will always be opportunities to care for the poor (Deut. 15:11). However, there is only limited time left to honor him.

14:8 It is not clear whether this woman knows that Jesus will die shortly. (This fact has repeatedly eluded the disciples, despite Jesus' teaching that he would—see 8:31–33; 9:32; 10:35–38.) This was probably an act of love on the part of one of his followers. Jesus, however, interprets her gift as a preparation for this death.

to prepare for my burial. The bodies of the dead were anointed with oil. However, Jesus would die as a criminal and so would not have been anointed had it not been for this woman.

14:9 As Jesus' words indicate, this is another acted-out parable like the cursing of the fig tree (see note on 11:14 in Session 19).

preached throughout the world. Jesus anticipates the worldwide mission of the church.

what she has done will also be told. Jesus commends the woman's insight into his identity and mission. This is the heart of the good news which will be proclaimed. As she honored him, so her memory will be honored.

14:10–11 In contrast to the single-minded devotion of this woman stands the act of treachery on the part of Judas. Mark gives no reasons for his betrayal. Matthew mentions the money he received (Matt. 26:15), while Luke and John say that he was impelled by Satan (Luke 22:3; John 13:2,27). Judas offers the officials a way to arrest Jesus without the public knowing it. He will tell them when and where Jesus will be alone (see vv. 1–2).

14:12–26 Through this meal, Jesus formally introduced the fact that his death was the means by which a new covenant was to be established between God and his people. It is this meal that declares Jesus' abiding presence with his people and gives meaning to Jesus' death as a sacrifice for sins. Just as at Passover, a lamb was sacrificed as a means of atoning for the sins of the people, so Jesus' death is a sacrifice which leads God to 'pass over' (or forgive) the sin of those who entrust themselves to him.

14:12 *On the first day of the Feast of Unleavened Bread.* The Feast of Unleavened Bread did not officially start until the day after the Passover. However, in the first century, the day on which the lambs were sacrificed was sometimes referred to as the first day of the Feast of Unleavened Bread.

sacrifice the Passover lamb. Each pilgrim sacrificed his own lamb in the temple. A priest caught the blood in a bowl and this was thrown on the altar. After removing certain parts of the lamb for sacrifice, the carcass was returned to the pilgrim to be roasted and eaten for Passover. Josephus estimated that 250,000 lambs were killed at Passover, turning the temple courts into a bloody mess.

make preparations. The disciples have to set out the unleavened bread and the wine (which was mixed with water); collect the bitter herbs (horseradish, chicory, etc.); make the sauce in which the bread was dipped (a stew of dried fruit, spices and wine); and roast the lamb on an open fire.

eat the Passover. The meal began with a blessing and the first (of four) cups of wine. Psalms were then sung and the story of the deliverance read, followed by the second cup of wine and the eating of the bread, herbs, and the sauce (into which Judas and the others dip their bread—see v. 20). Then the meal of roast lamb and bread is eaten. More prayers are said and the third cup is drunk. More psalms are sung; the final cup is drunk, after which a psalm is sung. Two short prayers end the feast.

14:13–16 Instructions for Jesus' arrest had already been issued (see John 11:57). He knew that the officials were looking for him in places away from the crowd. To guard against being arrested at night, he would generally sleep in Bethany, which was outside the jurisdiction of the priests. But the Law required that he eat the Passover meal in Jerusalem itself, hence the need for secret arrangements. The irony is that Jesus knows full well that he will be betrayed from within his own circle of disciples (see vv. 18–21,27–31). Jesus' instructions here parallel those he gave concerning the donkey on which he first rode into the city (see 11:1–6). It is clear that he had been to Jerusalem previously, at which time he made these arrangements. It is also clear that he is arranging the events so that they happen in such a way as to reveal who he is.

14:13 *a man carrying a jar of water.* Such a person would have been easy to spot and follow, since it was highly unusual for a man to carry a jug. Women carried jugs; men carried wineskins.

14:17 *When evening came.* The Passover meal could be eaten only after sunset. It was a night of excited watching in which people asked: "Will this be the night when God comes again to deliver his people from bondage?"

14:18–21 Jesus predicts that one of his disciples will betray him.

14:18 *reclining at the table.* People would eat festive meals by lying on couches or cushions arranged around a low table.

I tell you the truth. Literally, this is "Amen," a word used to announce a solemn declaration.

one who is eating with me. These words "set the pronouncement in the context of Psalm 41:9, where the poor but righteous sufferer laments that his intimate friend whom he has trusted and who ate his bread had 'lifted his heel' against him" (Lane).

14:20 *dips bread into the bowl with me.* To share in a meal was a sign of friendship, accenting the act of betrayal.

14:21 *as it is written about him.* Passages such as Isaiah 53:1–6 point to the suffering of God's chosen servant.

woe to that man. While the suffering of God's Messiah is part of God's plan, the people involved in that act are responsible for their decisions.

14:22 To share in the torn Passover bread, which Jesus reinterprets as his own person, is to share in his life, mission and destiny.

14:22–26 Jesus' celebration of the Last Supper provides the model for how the church came to celebrate Communion (see 1 Cor. 11:23–26). His use of the bread and the cup in a symbolic way was consistent with the way in which the various elements of the Passover meal were used symbolically (e.g., the bowl of salt water was used to remind them of the tears shed in Egypt, and of the Red Sea through which they passed). The symbols in the Passover meal pointed back to the first covenant God made with Israel, while Jesus' words here at the Last Supper pointed forward to his death and the new covenant which would result from it.

14:22 gave thanks. The Greek word is *eucharisto* from which the English word Eucharist is derived.

this is my body. Literally, "This, my body." While the bread used to represent God's provision of food for his people while they wandered in the wilderness, now it is to represent Jesus' body which was broken and torn upon the cross. To share in this bread is to affirm that one finds life in Jesus' sacrifice, is committed to his teaching, and shares in his mission.

14:23 cup. Jesus relates the Passover cup of red wine to the renewal of the covenant of God with his people via his sacrificial death.

14:24 covenant. In general terms, this is a treaty between two parties. Such an agreement was often sealed by the sacrifice of an animal. In specific terms, it refers to the arrangement that God made with Israel (see Ex. 24:1–8) which was dependent on Israel's obedience. Now (as anticipated in Jer. 31:31–33) a new covenant is established, which is made dependent on Jesus' obedience (his sacrificial death). A covenant of law becomes a covenant of love.

poured out. Blood which was poured out symbolized a violent death (see Gen. 4:10–11; Deut. 19:10; Matt. 23:35). This phrase points to the type of death Jesus would have.

for many. This is an idiomatic expression meaning all people (see 10:45). The point is not that each and every individual will experience the benefits of the covenant regardless of their commitments, but that this is a covenant promise for all types of people throughout the world, not only for the Jews.

14:25 I will not drink. This may mean that Jesus chose to abstain from the fourth Passover cup (see note on v. 12) which was passed around at the close of the meal, indicating that this Passover meal will only be consummated when Jesus ushers in God's kingdom in its fullness.

the kingdom of God. The presence of God's reign was often pictured as a great banquet.

14:26 The Hallel (Pss. 113–118) was sung at the Passover; the first part (Pss. 113–114) prior to the meal and the second part, mentioned here, after the meal (Pss. 115–118). The rich promises of Psalm 118 would be on Jesus' lips as he leaves the room to face the Crucifixion only a few hours away.

14:27–31 Jesus predicts that not only will Judas betray him, but so too will the others! Peter protests strongly that he will not betray Jesus, but events show that he (as well as the others) does this very thing (see 14:50, 66–72). This betrayal is the experience that reveals to the disciples the tentativeness and self-interest that characterizes their pre-resurrection faith.

14:28 Not only does he predict their falling away, he also anticipates their rejoining him after his resurrection (see 16:7).

14:31 I will never. This is a very strong negative, meaning "I will by no means." It is inconceivable to Peter that he would desert Jesus.

24 Jesus' Trial Begins—Mark 14:32–72

THREE-PART AGENDA

ICE-BREAKER
15 Minutes

BIBLE STUDY
30 Minutes

CARING TIME
15–45 Minutes

> *LEADER: Has your group discussed its plans on what to study after this course is finished? What about the mission project described on page M6 in the center section?*

TO BEGIN THE BIBLE STUDY TIME
(Choose 1 or 2)

1. When do you have trouble staying awake: Watching the late news? In church? Driving at night? Other?

2. How do you react when someone gives you the "fifth degree"?

3. When have you felt like crawling into a hole, never to return (playing sports, music, etc.)?

READ SCRIPTURE & DISCUSS
(If you don't have time for all the questions in this section, conclude the Bible Study [30 min.] by answering question #7.)

1. How do you cope with sadness? Do you prefer to be alone or with friends?

2. When Jesus came to Gethsemane, why was he so sad? What did he ask God when he prayed?

3. When was your last "Gethsemane"? How did you cope with that situation?

4. Jesus told Peter, "Watch and pray" because "the spirit is willing, but the body is weak" (v. 38). How do these words apply to you?

Gethsemane

32They went to a place called Gethsemane, and Jesus said to his disciples, "Sit here while I pray." 33He took Peter, James and John along with him, and he began to be deeply distressed and troubled. 34"My soul is overwhelmed with sorrow to the point of death," he said to them. "Stay here and keep watch."

35Going a little farther, he fell to the ground and prayed that if possible the hour might pass from him. 36"Abba,ª Father," he said, "everything is possible for you. Take this cup from me. Yet not what I will, but what you will."

37Then he returned to his disciples and found them sleeping. "Simon," he said to Peter, "are you asleep? Could you not keep watch for one hour? 38Watch and pray so that you will not fall into temptation. The spirit is willing, but the body is weak."

39Once more he went away and prayed the same thing. 40When he came back, he again found them sleeping, because their eyes were heavy. They did not know what to say to him.

41Returning the third time, he said to them, "Are you still sleeping and resting? Enough! The hour has come. Look, the Son of Man is betrayed into the hands of sinners. 42Rise! Let us go! Here comes my betrayer!"

Jesus Arrested

43Just as he was speaking, Judas, one of the Twelve, appeared. With him was a crowd armed with swords and clubs, sent from the chief priests, the teachers of the law, and the elders.

44Now the betrayer had arranged a signal with them: "The one I kiss is the man; arrest him and lead him away under guard." 45Going at once to Jesus, Judas said, "Rabbi!" and kissed him. 46The men seized Jesus and arrested him. 47Then one of those standing near drew his sword and struck the servant of the high priest, cutting off his ear.

48"Am I leading a rebellion," said Jesus, "that you have come out with swords and clubs to capture me? 49Every day I was with you, teaching in the temple courts, and you did not arrest me. But the Scriptures must be fulfilled." 50Then everyone deserted him and fled.

5. What perversion of justice do you find in Jesus' trial? What do Jesus' only words before the Sanhedrin mean (v. 62; see Dan. 7:13–14)?

6. How do you think Peter felt when the rooster crowed the third time? Have you ever felt that your failures made it impossible for you to serve Christ again? How did you overcome these feelings?

7. Jesus keeps on loving his disciples, no matter how they disappoint him or misunderstand him. What does this tell you about Jesus' character? What does this tell you about Jesus' persistence in his relationship with you?

CARING TIME

(Choose 1 or 2 of these questions before closing in prayer.)

1. Since this study is almost over, what would you like to share that you haven't until now?

2. Where do you need the God of hope to fill you with joy and peace right now?

3. What prayer requests do you have for this week?

51A young man, wearing nothing but a linen garment, was following Jesus. When they seized him, 52he fled naked, leaving his garment behind.

Before the Sanhedrin

53They took Jesus to the high priest, and all the chief priests, elders and teachers of the law came together. 54Peter followed him at a distance, right into the courtyard of the high priest. There he sat with the guards and warmed himself at the fire.

55The chief priests and the whole Sanhedrin were looking for evidence against Jesus so that they could put him to death, but they did not find any. 56Many testified falsely against him, but their statements did not agree.

57Then some stood up and gave this false testimony against him: 58"We heard him say, 'I will destroy this man-made temple and in three days will build another, not made by man.' " 59Yet even then their testimony did not agree.

60Then the high priest stood up before them and asked Jesus, "Are you not going to answer? What is this testimony that these men are bringing against you?" 61But Jesus remained silent and gave no answer.

Again the high priest asked him, "Are you the Christ,b the Son of the Blessed One?"

62"I am," said Jesus. "And you will see the Son of Man sitting at the right hand of the Mighty One and coming on the clouds of heaven."

63The high priest tore his clothes. "Why do we need any more witnesses?" he asked. 64"You have heard the blasphemy. What do you think?"

They all condemned him as worthy of death. 65Then some began to spit at him; they blindfolded him, struck him with their fists, and said, "Prophesy!" And the guards took him and beat him.

Peter Disowns Jesus

66While Peter was below in the courtyard, one of the servant girls of the high priest came by. 67When she saw Peter warming himself, she looked closely at him.

"You also were with that Nazarene, Jesus," she said.

68But he denied it. "I don't know or understand what you're talking about," he said, and went out into the entry-

way.^c

⁶⁹When the servant girl saw him there, she said again to those standing around, "This fellow is one of them." ⁷⁰Again he denied it.

After a little while, those standing near said to Peter, "Surely you are one of them, for you are a Galilean."

⁷¹He began to call down curses on himself, and he swore to them, "I don't know this man you're talking about."

⁷²Immediately the rooster crowed the second time.^d *Then Peter remembered the word Jesus had spoken to him: "Before the rooster crows twice*^e *you will disown me three times." And he broke down and wept.*

^a36 Aramaic for *Father*   ^b61 or *Messiah*
^c68 Some early manuscripts *entryway and the rooster crowed*
^d72 Some early manuscripts do not have *the second time.*
^e72 Some early manuscripts do not have *twice.*

Notes—Mark 14:32–72

14:32–42 Two themes dominate this section: Jesus' continued obedience to God despite his dread of what was coming, and the disciples' continued failure to grasp what lay ahead for Jesus.

14:32 *Gethsemane.* An olive orchard in an estate at the foot of the Mount of Olives just outside the eastern wall of Jerusalem. The name means literally, "an oil press" (for making olive oil).

14:33 *Peter, James and John.* Once again, these three men accompany Jesus during a time of great significance. Interestingly, neither the rebuke of Peter (8:32) nor the self-centered request of James and John (10:35–40) has damaged their relationship with Jesus. Also note that each of these men has vowed to stay with Jesus through thick or thin (see 10:38–39; 14:29,31). What Jesus asks them to share with him is not glory (which they wanted), but sorrow (which they kept denying would come).

deeply distressed. Literally, filled with "shuddering awe." Jesus is filled with deep sorrow as the impact of submitting to God's will hits him.

14:35 He would have prayed aloud, as was his cus-tom, so the disciples heard (and remembered) his prayer. This is the third time in Mark that Jesus has been shown at prayer (see also 1:35; 6:46).

14:36 *Abba.* This is how a child would address his father: "Daddy." This was not a title that was used in prayer in the first century.

this cup. By this image, Jesus refers to the events of his death that are fast coming on him (see also 10:38–39).

14:37 *sleeping.* It was very late (the Passover could extend up to midnight), and they had drunk at least four cups of wine.

14:38 To "watch" means to "be spiritually alert," lest they fall into the "temptation" to be unfaithful to God (see also 13:37). The "body" or "flesh" (i.e., "inadequate human resources") will fail them despite the willingness of their "spirit" and the available power of God's Spirit. To the very end, even the three disciples most intimately connected with Jesus fail to understand his teaching about what it means to be the Messiah. Had they done so, they would have prepared themselves for the danger that lay ahead.

They would also have helped Jesus as he prepared for the impending crisis. As it is, Jesus is all alone in his sorrow.

temptation. The trial or test that is about to come upon them.

14:41 *into the hands of sinners.* This refers to the religious authorities that Jesus confronted in the previous section (11:1–13:37) who have corrupted the offices they hold. The irony of this assessment is that the term "sinners" was used by these religious leaders to refer to others: to Jews who did not live by the Law, and to all Gentiles. In fact, it is a term they have earned by their actions.

14:43 *a crowd.* The Sanhedrin commanded the services of the temple police (who were Levites) and of an auxiliary police force (servants of the court) who maintained order outside the temple area.

the chief priests, the teachers of the law, and the elders. See note on 8:31 in Session 14.

14:44 *kiss.* This was a normal form of greeting. However, the intensive form of verb used here indicates that Judas' actual kiss was a warm and affectionate greeting and not merely perfunctory.

14:45 *Rabbi!* This title was a form of respect. It meant literally, "My Great One." By his greeting, by his kiss, and by sharing the same bowl (14:20—to eat together was a sign of friendship), Judas conveys the sense of a warm relationship with Jesus.

14:46 *arrested him.* The charge is not given. Perhaps it was blasphemy (2:7), violation of the Sabbath (2:24; 3:2–6), or the practice of magic (3:22).

14:47 *one of those standing near.* According to John's Gospel (18:10), this was Peter.

drew his sword. That Peter should have a sword is not unusual. Travelers carried them as protection against robbers and the disciples have just completed a journey from Jerusalem to Galilee (see Luke 22:36–38).

14:48 What Jesus is saying here is that he is not a bandit nor a guerrilla leading a resistance movement, so why have they come armed to arrest him?

14:49 *the Scriptures.* Jesus is probably referring to Zechariah 13:7 (see also Mark 14:27), but he may also have in mind Isaiah 53:12 and Psalm 41:9.

14:51 *A young man.* It has been suggested that this is Mark himself. He lived in Jerusalem (Acts 12:12), and there is a tradition that the Last Supper was held in the upper room of his mother's house. It is not inconceivable that Mark heard Jesus and the disciples leaving, got out of bed, threw a sheet around himself, and secretly followed after them.

linen garment. Probably a bed sheet. The fact that it is linen means that he came from a wealthy family.

14:53–65 In the trial of Jesus, Mark shows how it is that a criminal could be the Messiah. (This was one of the impediments to belief among the Roman population.) As quickly becomes evident, Jesus was no criminal. No charge was laid against him (much less proved), except that he claimed to be the Messiah, which is exactly who he was. His "trial" was a perversion of justice.

14:53 *the high priest.* The spiritual head of Israel. Caiaphas was the high priest before whom Jesus came (Matt. 26:57).

14:55 *the whole Sanhedrin.* A council consisting of 71 leaders, both priests and laymen, who made up the highest Jewish court. They were given authority by Rome to rule in matters of religious law.

evidence. To convict someone of a capital crime required the unanimous testimony of at least two witnesses. Each witness gave his testimony individually to the judge in the presence of the accused. If two witnesses differed in their accounts (even in the smallest of details), their testimony was thrown out of court (see Deut. 19:15).

14:58 Jesus did, in fact, say something like this (John 2:19), but what he meant is quite different from the way it is understood here. He was referring to his own bodily resurrection after three days (John 2:21). It was a capital offense to desecrate or destroy a place of worship.

14:59 Since the witnesses did not agree, this charge could not be used against Jesus.

14:61–62 These are key verses in the Gospel. The three titles which reveal who Jesus is are combined together here: Messiah, Son of God ("Son of the Blessed One"), and Son of Man. Jesus has referred to himself as the Son of Man, since up to this point had he used the other titles, they would have been misunderstood. Now it becomes clear that the Son of Man is the Messiah, who is the Son of God.

14:61 Since they could not produce evidence, their final recourse was this desperate attempt by Caiaphas to get Jesus to say he was the Messiah. If Jesus admitted to being the Messiah, it would be a clear case of blasphemy, since in their eyes it would be ludicrous that a person such as Jesus could be the Messiah (see 3:22–30).

the Blessed One. Pious Jews would not refer directly to God by name. This phrase was one of a number used as a substitute for his name (see v. 62).

14:62 This is the first time in Mark that Jesus openly and unequivocally declares his messiahship. The time for secrecy is past. The verses Jesus quotes (a combination of Ps. 110:1 and Dan. 7:13–14) simply reiterate, in biblical images, his claim of messiahship (see 8:38; 12:35–37, and 13:26, where these passages are also referred to).

I am. This forthright declaration by Jesus of his identity (despite the consequences) was a powerful example for the Christians at Rome, who were also being called upon at that time to confess their faith before the authorities. This was also an allusion to the name of God (see 6:50).

sitting at the right hand. To sit here was to sit in the place of honor (see 10:40). Jesus too, like the figure in Daniel 7, will be vindicated at the Second Coming, when all his accusers see that his claim was true.

14:63 *tore his clothes.* By tearing his clothes, Caiaphas signaled that he was profoundly disturbed by Jesus' statement (see 2 Kings 19:1).

14:64 *blasphemy.* Dishonoring or slandering another. The penalty for blaspheming God was death by stoning (Lev. 24:10–16). By claiming to be the Messiah, the Sanhedrin understood Jesus to be dishonoring God. In fact, it is they who are guilty of blasphemy by refusing to recognize who Jesus is. God himself has declared Jesus to be his Son (see 1:11; 9:7). Jesus has already been charged with blasphemy several times for being who he is (see 2:7; 3:28).

worthy of death. At that point in history, the Sanhedrin did not have power to carry out a death sentence. Only the Roman procurator could do that.

14:65 In this way the council demonstrated that it was opposed to what Jesus had done. The blows and spitting were traditional ways of expressing abhorrence and repudiation (see Num. 12:14; Deut. 25:9; Job 30:10; Isa. 50:6).

they blindfolded him. Isaiah 11:2–4 had been interpreted to mean that the Messiah could make judgments on the basis of smell alone without the aid of sight.

Prophesy! They are asking him to prove his claim to be the Messiah by naming who it was who had struck him while he was blindfolded.

14:66–72 The account of Peter's betrayal (which began in v. 54) is concluded here. The story of Peter's "trial" is set in contrast to the trial of Jesus. Jesus' forthright declaration of who he is before the high priest (v. 62) is the opposite of Peter's denial of who he is before the servant girl (vv. 66–70a) and the strangers (vv. 70b–71).

14:71 *call down curses on himself.* Peter even goes so far as to call down on himself the wrath of God if he is not telling the truth (which he knows he is not)!

I don't know this man. This, like his previous denial (v. 68), is an outright lie.

this man you're talking about. Peter does not use Jesus' name (see also 8:38).

14:72 *the rooster crowed the second time.* Roosters in Palestine crowed first at about 12:30 a.m., then again at about 1:30 a.m., and for a third time at about 2:30 a.m. As a result of this peculiar habit, the watch kept by soldiers in Palestine from midnight until 3:00 a.m. was called "cock-crow." Peter's denials were therefore spread over an hour.

wept. Peter suddenly realizes what he has done. Despite his vigorous assertion that he would never deny Jesus, this is exactly what he did. To make matters worse, he denied Jesus before rather unintimidating people (a servant girl and anonymous strangers), and did so with a formal oath (vv. 68,71) and by curses (v. 71). The crowing rooster reveals to him his sin, and he weeps tears of repentance.

25 The Crucifixion—Mark 15:1–41

THREE-PART AGENDA

ICE-BREAKER
15 Minutes

BIBLE STUDY
30 Minutes

CARING TIME
15–45 Minutes

> **LEADER: Has your group discussed its plans on what to study after this course is finished? What about the mission project described on page M6 in the center section?**

TO BEGIN THE BIBLE STUDY TIME
(Choose 1 or 2)

1. Were you ever bullied as a child? What happened? How did it feel?

2. When have you been in a *wild* crowd: At a concert? Sporting event? Protest march? Church? Other?

3. Have you ever been with someone who was dying? What was it like?

READ SCRIPTURE & DISCUSS
(If you don't have time for all the questions in this section, conclude the Bible Study [30 min.] by answering question #7.)

1. When have you been accused of something you didn't do?

2. Why did the Jewish leaders bring Jesus before Pilate? Why was Jesus so silent throughout his trial?

3. How does the story of Barabbas illustrate what Jesus did for you?

4. What was the significance of the temple curtain being torn in two (see note on v. 38)?

Jesus Before Pilate

15 *Very early in the morning, the chief priests, with the elders, the teachers of the law and the whole Sanhedrin, reached a decision. They bound Jesus, led him away and handed him over to Pilate.*

²"Are you the king of the Jews?" asked Pilate.

"Yes, it is as you say," Jesus replied.

³The chief priests accused him of many things. ⁴So again Pilate asked him, "Aren't you going to answer? See how many things they are accusing you of."

⁵But Jesus still made no reply, and Pilate was amazed.

⁶Now it was the custom at the Feast to release a prisoner whom the people requested. ⁷A man called Barabbas was in prison with the insurrectionists who had committed murder in the uprising. ⁸The crowd came up and asked Pilate to do for them what he usually did.

⁹"Do you want me to release to you the king of the Jews?" asked Pilate, ¹⁰knowing it was out of envy that the chief priests had handed Jesus over to him. ¹¹But the chief priests stirred up the crowd to have Pilate release Barabbas instead.

¹²"What shall I do, then, with the one you call the king of the Jews?" Pilate asked them.

¹³"Crucify him!" they shouted.

¹⁴"Why? What crime has he committed?" asked Pilate. But they shouted all the louder, "Crucify him!"

¹⁵Wanting to satisfy the crowd, Pilate released Barabbas to them. He had Jesus flogged, and handed him over to be crucified.

The Soldiers Mock Jesus

¹⁶The soldiers led Jesus away into the palace (that is, the Praetorium) and called together the whole company of soldiers. ¹⁷They put a purple robe on him, then twisted together a crown of thorns and set it on him. ¹⁸And they began to call out to him, "Hail, king of the Jews!" ¹⁹Again and again they struck him on the head with a staff and spit on him. Falling on their knees, they paid homage to him. ²⁰And when they had mocked him, they took off the purple robe and put his own clothes on him. Then they led him out to crucify him.

5. On a scale of 1 (wide open) to 10 (closed tight), how would you describe the "curtain" between you and God right now?

6. How do you feel when you think about what Jesus did for you?

7. When did the Crucifixion begin to make a difference in your own life?

CARING TIME

(Answer all the questions below, then close with prayer.)

1. Next week will be the last session in this study. How would you like to celebrate: A dinner? A party?

2. What is the next step for this group: Start a new group? Continue with another study?

3. How can the group pray for you this week?

(If the group plans to continue, see the back inside cover for what's available from Serendipity.)

The Crucifixion

[21]*A certain man from Cyrene, Simon, the father of Alexander and Rufus, was passing by on his way in from the country, and they forced him to carry the cross.* [22]*They brought Jesus to the place called Golgotha (which means The Place of the Skull).* [23]*Then they offered him wine mixed with myrrh, but he did not take it.* [24]*And they crucified him. Dividing up his clothes, they cast lots to see what each would get.*

[25]*It was the third hour when they crucified him.* [26]*The written notice of the charge against him read: THE KING OF THE JEWS.* [27]*They crucified two robbers with him, one on his right and one on his left.*[a] [29]*Those who passed by hurled insults at him, shaking their heads and saying, "So! You who are going to destroy the temple and build it in three days,* [30]*come down from the cross and save yourself!"*

[31]*In the same way the chief priests and the teachers of the law mocked him among themselves. "He saved others," they said, "but he can't save himself!* [32]*Let this Christ,*[b] *this King of Israel, come down now from the cross, that we may see and believe." Those crucified with him also heaped insults on him.*

The Death of Jesus

[33]*At the sixth hour darkness came over the whole land until the ninth hour.* [34]*And at the ninth hour Jesus cried out in a loud voice, "Eloi, Eloi, lama sabachthani?"—which means, "My God, my God, why have you forsaken me?"*[c]

[35]*When some of those standing near heard this, they said, "Listen, he's calling Elijah."*

[36]*One man ran, filled a sponge with wine vinegar, put it on a stick, and offered it to Jesus to drink. "Now leave him alone. Let's see if Elijah comes to take him down," he said.*

[37]*With a loud cry, Jesus breathed his last.*

[38]*The curtain of the temple was torn in two from top to bottom.* [39]*And when the centurion, who stood there in front of Jesus, heard his cry and*[d] *saw how he died, he said, "Surely this man was the Son*[e] *of God!"*

[40]*Some women were watching from a distance. Among them were Mary Magdalene, Mary the mother of James the*

> *younger and of Joses, and Salome.* ⁴¹*In Galilee these women had followed him and cared for his needs. Many other women who had come up with him to Jerusalem were also there.*
>
> ᵃ*27 Some manuscripts left, ²⁸and the scripture was fulfilled which says, "He was counted with the lawless ones" (Isaiah 53:12)* ᵇ*32 Or Messiah* ᶜ*34 Psalm 22:1* ᵈ*39 Some manuscripts do not have heard his cry and* ᵉ*39 Or a son*

Notes—Mark 15:1–41

15:1–20 The Jewish trial is now followed by a Roman trial. The Jewish high court consisted of the 71 members of the Sanhedrin; the Roman court involved only one man. The trial before the Sanhedrin was conducted secretly, out of the eye of the public; the trial before Pilate was held openly in a public forum.

15:1 *Very early.* The court began at daybreak, making it necessary that the Sanhedrin meet in an all-night session. They were anxious to get a quick conviction before the people found out what they had done.

decision. Legally, the Sanhedrin had no authority to order the death of Jesus (see John 18:31). The real reason they defer to the Roman legal system (as Mark makes clear) is their fear of the people (11:32; 12:12; 14:1–2). However, the difficulty they faced is that under Roman law, blasphemy was not a capital offense. Consequently, they needed to present the case to Pilate so as to ensure Jesus' death. Their decision was that when they brought Jesus to Pilate, they would charge him with high treason.

led him away. They probably took him to the palace of Herod, located northwest of the temple, where Pilate stayed when he came to Jerusalem from his home in Caesarea. Pilate was probably in town for the feast.

Pilate. Pontius Pilate was the fifth procurator of Judea. He served from A.D. 26–36. Historians of the time called him an "inflexible, merciless and obstinate" man who disliked the Jews and their customs.

15:2–5 Mark describes Jesus' interrogation by Pilate. The Roman trial consisted of the accusation, followed by an examination of the defendant by the magistrate. Once a ruling had been made, it was carried out immediately.

15:2 *king of the Jews.* This is how the Sanhedrin translated the Jewish title "Messiah" so that Pilate would understand it. Put this way, it made Jesus seem guilty of treason (he would appear to be disputing the kingship of Caesar). There is great irony in this title. Jesus has consistently refused to be the military Messiah pictured in popular culture, and yet now he will be condemned as a guerrilla! This title is used six times in chapter 15, and explains what it means for him to be the Son of God (which is the crucial insight in this section—see v. 39).

Yes, it is as you say. As he accepts the title "the Christ, the Son of the Blessed One" from the Jewish high priest (14:61–62), he also accepts the title "king of the Jews" from the Roman procurator. In both cases, his questioners misunderstood the nature of the title they attribute to Jesus. And in both cases, this misunderstanding led to Jesus' condemnation.

15:3 *accused him of many things.* See Luke 23:2,5 for some of the charges the authorities made against Jesus, all of which would be seen as a direct affront against Rome.

15:7 *Barabbas.* Barabbas was a genuine resistance leader, guilty of murder. His name is Aramaic and means "son of Abba," or "son of the father."

Ironically, in place of this "son of the father," the "Son of the Father" died.

15:8 *The crowd.* It seems ironic that the crowd, who at the beginning of the week hailed Jesus as "he who comes in the name of the Lord" (11:9), could at the end of the week call for his crucifixion. In fact, it was very unlikely that this was the same crowd. There were several hundred thousand people in Jerusalem during the Passover. Jesus was arrested secretly, late at night. Now it is early the next morning. His supporters had little time to hear of his abduction, much less to arrive at the palace for his trial. A different group had gathered that morning. Possibly they were supporters of Barabbas (a hero to many), who wanted him released by means of the Passover amnesty (see v. 6).

15:9–11 Pilate seems satisfied that Jesus is not a true insurrectionist. His desire to release Jesus probably had little to do with justice, and arose more out of a desire to do something that would annoy the Sanhedrin (with whom he had many run-ins).

15:12–14 Pilate seems surprised that the crowd rejects his offer to release Jesus.

15:12 *the king of the Jews?* This is a deliberate jibe at the authorities. He is willing to release the one claiming to be their king for he sees no threat at all in him. This is a way of minimizing their significance as a threat to Rome.

15:13 *Crucify him.* This was not so much a deliberate rejection of Jesus as it was a statement that they would not listen to Pilate's appeal for Jesus instead of Barabbas.

15:14 *Why? What crime has he committed?* By this Mark underscores the point that Jesus was innocent of all charges brought against him (Isa. 53:9).

15:15 *released Barabbas.* The death of Jesus (who is innocent) in the place of Barabbas (who is guilty) is a visual statement of the meaning of substitutionary atonement. It explains what Jesus meant in 10:45 when he said that he came to "give his life as a ransom for many."

flogged. This was a terrible punishment. Soldiers would lash a naked and bound prisoner with a leather thong into which pieces of bone and lead

had been woven. The flesh would be cut to shreds.

crucified. Crucifixion was the most feared of all punishments in the first-century world. It was cruel in the extreme and totally degrading.

15:16–20 The soldiers mock Jesus as the Sanhedrin had done before them (see 14:65). Whereas the Sanhedrin mocked the idea that he was the Messiah, the soldiers mock the idea that he is king.

15:16 *soldiers.* Probably the troops that had accompanied Pilate on his trip from Caesarea.

15:17 *a purple robe.* This was a symbol of royalty.

15:21–39 This is the culmination of Mark's Gospel. It is the death of Jesus that will unlock all the mysteries and open the way into the kingdom of God. This section is rich with allusion to OT prophecy.

15:21 *Simon.* Possibly a Jew, from a Greek city on the north shore of Africa, who had come to Jerusalem for the Passover feast.

Rufus. Romans 16:13 mentions a Rufus. Mark wrote his Gospel for the church at Rome, and if this is the same Rufus, he can verify this detail about their father.

carry the cross. The prisoner carried the heavy cross-beam through the winding streets as an "example" to others. Jesus, however, had already been without sleep for at least 24 hours and been beaten, flogged and beaten again. He was physically unable to bear the weight of the cross-beam. In such a case, the Roman soldiers could press anyone else who happened to be on the way to carry the cross for the prisoner. Simon thus unintentionally becomes a model of a disciple, carrying his cross as he follows Jesus (Mark 8:34).

15:22 *Golgotha.* In Aramaic, "a skull." This was probably a round, bare hillock outside Jerusalem.

15:23 *wine mixed with myrrh.* It was a Jewish custom to offer this pain-deadening narcotic to prisoners about to be crucified (see Ps. 69:21).

15:24 *they crucified him.* Mark has looked to this event throughout his Gospel. When it happens, he records it in the simplest, starkest way. Josephus, the Jewish historian, calls it "the most wretched of all ways of dying." The person to be crucified was first stripped. Then his hands were tied or nailed to the cross-beam. This was lifted to the upright stake, and then the feet were nailed in place.

Dividing up his clothes. The clothes of the condemned person belonged to the four soldiers who carried out the crucifixion (see Ps. 22:18; John 19:23–24).

15:25 the third hour. This would have been about 9:00 a.m.

15:26 The written notice. The crime for which the person was being crucified was specified on a whitened board fastened above the criminal.

the King of the Jews. By posting this sign on the cross, Pilate was simply attempting to further humiliate the Jews. The intent was to communicate that Jesus' fate would be shared by anyone else who tried to assert their authority against Rome.

15:27 robbers. This was a term sometimes used for Zealots, the band of nationalists who were committed to the violent overthrow of Rome. While "robbery" *per se* was not a capital crime, insurrection was. Perhaps they were involved with Barabbas in the incident mentioned in 15:7. In any case, the reference to being crucified alongside criminals is probably an allusion to Isaiah 53:12.

one on his right and one on his left. Earlier on, James and John had asked to sit at Jesus' right and left hand when he came into his kingdom (10:37), a request Jesus denied. That position was left for these two criminals who shared in Jesus' death, the true means by which he would enter into his glory.

15:29–32 These insults and mocking statements fulfill Psalm 22:6–8.

15:31 He saved others ... but he can't save himself. This is just the point! Because he is saving others, his own life is forfeited. Once again Mark uses irony. Something true is said about Jesus by a person who does not understand the accuracy of the statement (see 14:61–62; 15:2).

15:33 At the sixth hour. At noon.

darkness. A supernatural event, showing the cosmic significance of this death. See Amos 8:9. There is darkness from the time Jesus is hung on the cross until he dies.

15:34 It is uncertain what Jesus' cry meant. Certainly he experienced the consequences of being cut off from God because of the sins of many (see Ps. 22:1).

15:35 Elijah. Another irony. Elijah already came in the person of John the Baptist (see note on 9:4 in Session 15).

15:36 Wine vinegar was considered a refreshing drink (see Ruth 2:14). A soldier soaked a sponge in wine vinegar and water and offered it to Jesus.

15:37 a loud cry. This is unusual. Generally the victim is exhausted and unconscious at the point of death. It is almost as if Jesus voluntarily gives up his life. Perhaps what Mark mentions here is the last word in the phrase "It is finished" (see John 19:30).

15:38 curtain of the temple. There were two curtains in the temple. An outer curtain separated the sanctuary from the courtyard. The inner curtain covered the Holy of Holies where only the high priest was admitted. It is not clear which curtain was torn. However, the point is clear: that which stood between the people and God was abolished by Jesus' death.

15:39 This confession concludes the second half of Mark's Gospel. In 1:1, Mark stated that what he was writing was the good news about Jesus the Messiah, the Son of God. The first half of the Gospel ends with the confession of Peter (a Jew) that Jesus is the Messiah (8:29); the second half ends with the confession of the centurion (a Gentile) that Jesus is the Son of God.

centurion. The supervising officer, a pagan soldier who may not have been aware of the significance of what he observed.

15:40 Some women. Mark names three eyewitnesses of the Crucifixion. Mary Magdalene was from the village of Magdala on the west coast of Galilee (see Luke 8:2). The other Mary had well-known sons in the early church. Salome was the wife of Zebedee and the mother of James and John (Matt. 27:56). In contrast, all the disciples have fled.

26 Resurrection—Mark 15:42–16:20

THREE-PART AGENDA

ICE-BREAKER
15 Minutes

BIBLE STUDY
30 Minutes

CARING TIME
15–45 Minutes

> **LEADER: Check page M7 of the center section for a good ice-breaker for this last session.**

TO BEGIN THE BIBLE STUDY TIME
(Choose 1 or 2)

1. How do you feel about attending funerals?

2. Growing up, what was your favorite thing about Easter?

3. What do you like the most about Easter now?

READ SCRIPTURE & DISCUSS
(If you don't have time for all the questions in this section, conclude the Bible Study [30 min.] by answering question #7.)

1. How has this group, or someone in the group, been a blessing to you over the course of this study?

2. Joseph of Arimathea, a member of the Sanhedrin, took great risks by taking care of the body of Jesus. What kind of man do you think Joseph was?

3. How did the women respond to the young man in the white robe who said, "He has risen"? What does it take for you to believe what someone tells you?

4. What do you see as your role in spreading "the good news to all creation" (v. 15)?

5. How would your life be different if Jesus was not risen from the dead?

The Burial of Jesus

42It was Preparation Day (that is, the day before the Sabbath). So as evening approached, 43Joseph of Arimathea, a prominent member of the Council, who was himself waiting for the kingdom of God, went boldly to Pilate and asked for Jesus' body. 44Pilate was surprised to hear that he was already dead. Summoning the centurion, he asked him if Jesus had already died. 45When he learned from the centurion that it was so, he gave the body to Joseph. 46So Joseph bought some linen cloth, took down the body, wrapped it in the linen, and placed it in a tomb cut out of rock. Then he rolled a stone against the entrance of the tomb. 47Mary Magdalene and Mary the mother of Joses saw where he was laid.

The Resurrection

16 *When the Sabbath was over, Mary Magdalene, Mary the mother of James, and Salome bought spices so that they might go to anoint Jesus' body. 2Very early on the first day of the week, just after sunrise, they were on their way to the tomb 3and they asked each other, "Who will roll the stone away from the entrance of the tomb?"*

4But when they looked up, they saw that the stone, which was very large, had been rolled away. 5As they entered the tomb, they saw a young man dressed in a white robe sitting on the right side, and they were alarmed.

6"Don't be alarmed," he said. "You are looking for Jesus the Nazarene, who was crucified. He has risen! He is not here. See the place where they laid him. 7But go, tell his disciples and Peter, 'He is going ahead of you into Galilee. There you will see him, just as he told you.' "

8Trembling and bewildered, the women went out and fled from the tomb. They said nothing to anyone, because they were afraid.

[The earliest manuscripts and some other ancient witnesses do not have Mark 16:9–20.]

9When Jesus rose early on the first day of the week, he appeared first to Mary Magdalene, out of whom he had driven seven demons. 10She went and told those who had been with him and who were mourning and weeping. 11When they heard that Jesus was alive and that she had

6. In this study of Mark, what has been the key thing you learned?

7. On a scale of 1 (baby steps) to 10 (giant leaps), how has your relationship with Christ progressed over the last six months?

CARING TIME
(Answer all the questions below, then close with prayer.)

1. What will you remember most about this group?

2. What has the group decided to do next? What is the next step for you?

3. How would you like the group to continue praying for you?

seen him, they did not believe it.

¹²Afterward Jesus appeared in a different form to two of them while they were walking in the country. ¹³These returned and reported it to the rest; but they did not believe them either.

¹⁴Later Jesus appeared to the Eleven as they were eating; he rebuked them for their lack of faith and their stubborn refusal to believe those who had seen him after he had risen.

¹⁵He said to them, "Go into all the world and preach the good news to all creation. ¹⁶Whoever believes and is baptized will be saved, but whoever does not believe will be condemned. ¹⁷And these signs will accompany those who believe: In my name they will drive out demons; they will speak in new tongues; ¹⁸they will pick up snakes with their hands; and when they drink deadly poison, it will not hurt them at all; they will place their hands on sick people, and they will get well."

¹⁹After the Lord Jesus had spoken to them, he was taken up into heaven and he sat at the right hand of God. ²⁰Then the disciples went out and preached everywhere, and the Lord worked with them and confirmed his word by the signs that accompanied it.

Notes—Mark 15:42–16:20

15:42 *Preparation Day.* Jesus died on Friday at 3:00 p.m. The Sabbath began at 6:00 p.m., after which no work could be done. Great haste was required.

15:43 *Joseph of Arimathea.* Little is known of him, except that he was from a wealthy and prominent family and was a member of the Sanhedrin. (Possibly he was the source of information about Jesus' trial before the Sanhedrin.) To ask for the body was to admit allegiance to the now discredited Jesus and was, therefore, potentially dangerous. Often the Romans just left the bodies hanging on the cross to be eaten by vultures, though they did grant requests by the family to be allowed to bury the person. However, the Romans almost never

allowed those convicted of treason to be buried. The fact that they do so now probably means Pilate knew Jesus was innocent (see the note on 15:9–11 in Session 25).

15:44 *Pilate was surprised.* It often took two or three days for a person to die.

15:45 The centurion confirms that Jesus had died in six hours. As a supervisor of crucifixion, he had expert insight into such matters. Therefore, when Jesus rose several days later, it was resurrection, not resuscitation.

he gave the body to Joseph. The fact that Pilate released the body indicates Pilate's conviction that

Jesus was innocent of the charge of the insurrection (see note on 15:43).

15:46 The body was washed, quickly wrapped, and then placed in a tomb (probably a natural cave or an abandoned quarry). The tomb was then sealed against robbers or animals by means of a large stone. This was all done hurriedly, due to the approach of the Sabbath. Joseph, being wealthy, probably had servants to assist him in this task.

linen. The young man in 14:51 left behind a linen cloth, anticipating how Jesus would be clothed after his death.

15:47 Two of the three women at the Crucifixion saw clearly where Jesus was entombed, so when they returned in two days, they knew where to go.

16:1–8 Mark tells the story of the Resurrection in brief, crisp terms. This account does not describe the Resurrection as such, only the discovery of the empty tomb by the women and the explanation given by the "young man." In fact, none of the Gospels try to describe the Resurrection; only the fact that it had taken place.

16:1 *When the Sabbath was over.* After 6:00 p.m. on Saturday when the shops were open again.

spices. Aromatic oils to anoint the body, not so much to preserve it as to honor it (much like people today would put flowers on a grave). See Mark 14:3–9. Clearly they did not expect Jesus to have risen from the dead, since the perfumes they bought would have been quite expensive.

16:2 *Very early on the first day of the week.* Early Sunday morning.

16:3 *the stone.* It would have been fairly easy to roll the huge, disc-shaped stone down the groove cut for it so that it covered the opening; but once in place, it would have been difficult to push it back up the incline.

tomb. Typically, such tombs had a large antechamber, with a small two-foot high doorway at the back which led into the six- or seven-foot burial chamber proper. This was the tomb of a wealthy family. See Isaiah 53:9, which says the Suffering Servant would be buried with the rich.

16:4 The stone was rolled away, not so that the resurrected Jesus could leave the tomb, but so that his disciples could see that it was empty (see John 20:8).

16:5 *a young man.* An angel (see Matt. 28:2–3). The particular word Mark uses here was used in other contexts to refer to an "angel." Angels were often used as messengers of God's revelation. His words explain why the tomb is empty by revealing to the women the resurrection of Jesus.

a white robe. An indication of his heavenly nature. Jesus was clothed in dazzling white during his transfiguration (9:3).

alarmed. A rare Greek word used in the New Testament only by Mark (see also 9:15; 14:33), indicating great astonishment in the face of the supernatural.

16:6 *He has risen!* In the same way that Mark reports the crucifixion of Jesus in simple, stark terms (15:24), so too he describes his resurrection in a plain, unadorned way. The phrase is, literally, "he has been raised," showing that God is the one who accomplished this great act. His resurrection demonstrates that the cry of the centurion was accurate: "Surely this man was the Son of God!" (see Rom. 1:4).

16:7 *go, tell.* Under Jewish law, women were not considered reliable witnesses. That they were the first to know of the Resurrection was an embarrassment to the early church (see Luke 24:11,22–24), hence guaranteeing the historicity of this detail.

his disciples and Peter. They may have abandoned Jesus, but he has not abandoned them! A special word is given to Peter who, after his abysmal failure, might be tempted to count himself out of further discipleship. Forgiveness is offered. Paul mentions that one of the Lord's post-resurrection appearances was to Peter alone (Luke 24:34; 1 Cor. 15:5).

into Galilee. Jesus said he would meet them again in Galilee (14:28). The ministry of Jesus and the Twelve began in Galilee, and now they are directed back there to meet the risen Lord, thus bringing Mark's account full circle. See Matthew 28:16–20 for the account of that meeting.

16:8 *They said nothing.* Eventually, of course, the women did report what happened (see Matt. 28:8; Luke 24:10).

they were afraid. This was the same sort of fear that the disciples felt on the Sea of Galilee when they discovered that Jesus had power over the elements themselves (4:41). This is how human beings respond in the face of the supernatural. Thus the Gospel of Mark ends on this note of astonishment and fear which was so characteristic of how he described people's reaction to a miracle or supernatural event (2:12; 4:41; 5:15,33,42; 9:6). There is also the hint of mystery and secret, again characteristic of Mark. The ending is abrupt, but fully in keeping with Mark's style of writing.

16:9–20 Scholars generally agree that these verses were composed at a later date by another author. They do not appear in the best ancient manuscripts, and they have a vocabulary and structure quite different from the rest of Mark. (This is seen most readily in the Greek.) This particular ending seems to have been a summation of resurrection stories found in the other Gospels, along with a list of miraculous signs that occurred in the early church. As such, this ending is an early and interesting part of the Christian tradition, but it is not the words of Mark. This ending (16:9–20) is but one of several that have appeared in ancient manuscripts of Mark. This is testimony to the fact that early scribes found Mark 16:8 too abrupt. One of the other endings reads as follows: "But they reported briefly to Peter and those with him all they had been told. And after this Jesus himself sent out by means of them, from east to west, the sacred and imperishable proclamation of eternal salvation." Some scholars feel that the original ending of Mark was lost, though there is no concrete evidence that this is the case.

16:17–18 Although no mention is made of such signs in the other Gospels, such things did happen in the early church (see Acts 2:43; 4:30; 5:12; Heb. 2:4).

16:17 *they will speak in new tongues.* See Acts 2:4; 1 Corinthians 14:18.

16:18 *they will pick up snakes.* See Acts 28:1–6.

drink deadly poison. There is no mention of this elsewhere in the New Testament.

they will place their hands on sick people, and they will get well. See Acts 3:1–10; James 5:14–15.

Acknowledgments

In writing these notes I have made use of the standard research tools in the field of New Testament study. These include *A Greek-English Lexicon of the New Testament* (Bauer, Arndt & Gingrich), *The Interpreter's Dictionary of the Bible, The Macmillian Bible Atlas* (Aharoni & Ave-Yonah), *The NIV Complete Concordance, Synopsis of the Four Gospels* (Kurt Aland), and other standard reference materials. In addition, use has been made of various commentaries. While it is not possible as one would desire, given the scope and aim of this book, to acknowledge in detail the input of each author, the source of direct quotes and special insights is given.

The key commentary used in analyzing Mark is *Commentary on the Gospel of Mark* (The New International Commentary on the New Testament), William L. Lane, Grand Rapids, MI: Eerdmans Publishing Co., 1974. Other commentaries that were of special value include: William Barclay, *The Gospel of Mark* (The Daily Study Bible Series), Philadelphia: The Westminster Press, 1975 (Revised Edition); and Larry W. Hurtado, *Mark* (A Good News Commentary), San Francisco: Harper & Row, 1983.

Reference was also made to the following commentaries: Hugh Anderson, *The Gospel of Mark* (New Century Bible), Greenwood, SC: The Attic Press, Inc., 1976; Robert G. Bratcher and Eugene A. Nida, *A Translator's Handbook on the Gospel of Mark* (Help for Translators, Vol. II) United Bible Societies, 1961; R.A. Cole, *The Gospel According to St. Mark* (Tyndale New Testament Commentaries), London: The Tyndale Press, 1961; Ezra P. Gould, *A Critical and Exegetical Commentary on the Gospel According to St. Mark* (The International Critical Commentary), Edinburgh: T. & T. Clark, 1969; William Hendriksen, *Exposition of the Gospel According to Mark* (New Testament Commentary), Grand Rapids, MI: Baker Book House, 1975; C.S. Mann, *Mark* (The Anchor Bible), Garden City, NY: Doubleday & Co., 1986; C.F.D. Moule, *The Gospel According to Mark* (The Cambridge Bible Commentary on the New English Bible), Cambridge: Cambridge University Press, 1965; D.E. Nineham, *The Gospel of Saint Mark* (The Pelican New Testament Commentaries), Harmondsworth, Middlesex, England: Penguin Books, Ltd., 1963; and Vincent Taylor, *The Gospel According to Mark*, New York: St. Martin's Press, 1966.

Reference was also made to: Craig Blomberg, *The Historical Reliability of the Gospels,* Downers Grove, IL: InterVarsity Press, 1987; F. Ross Kinsler, *Inductive Study of the Book of Mark,* South Pasadena, CA: William Carey Library, 1972; R.H. Lightfoot, *The Gospel Message of St. Mark,* Oxford: Oxford University Press, 1950; Ralph Martin, *Mark: Evangelist and Theologian,* Grand Rapids, MI: Zondervan Publishing House, 1973; and William Telfor (ed.) *The Interpretation of Mark*, Philadelphia: Fortress Press, 1985.

Caring Time Notes

Caring Time Notes

Caring Time Notes

Caring Time Notes

Caring Time Notes